Collis Potter Huntington, Charles Cyrel Post

Driven From Sea to Sea

Collis Potter Huntington, Charles Cyrel Post

Driven From Sea to Sea

ISBN/EAN: 9783744708975

Printed in Europe, USA, Canada, Australia, Japan

Cover: Foto ©Thomas Meinert / pixelio.de

More available books at **www.hansebooks.com**

DRIVEN

FROM SEA TO SEA;

OR

JUST A CAMPIN.'

By C. C. POST.

ELLIOT & BEEZLEY.
PHILADELPHIA AND CHICAGO.
1888.

To THE WORKERS, the men and the women who have given to America her greatness — who have cleared away her forests, bridged her streams, builded her cities, spanned the continent and crossed and recrossed and checkered it with highways of iron — who have planted orchards and vineyards upon every hillside and in every valley between the Atlantic and Pacific Oceans, as they have wandered from sea to sea in search of "that better country, a few hundred or a thousand miles ahead," with tales of which the cunning purloiners of their homes have stifled their thoughts of vengeance and their longings for juster laws, this story of one of their number is respectfully dedicated by

THE AUTHOR.

CONTENTS.

DRIVEN FROM SEA TO SEA.

CHAPTER I.

THE LETTER.

DEAR MARTHA, —I can't come home after you and the babies like I hoped to do, cause I'm broke again; leastwise I hev ben since I wrote you last, and I ain't squarely got onto my feet yet, but I'm goin ter send you some money by next steamer; all I can scrape together, and I want you and the babies to pack up and come out.

I know it looks hard fer you to have to make the trip across the plains alone with the children, but I dont see no way to help it unless we are never to see one another again, and I can't stand that, nor I dont believe you want to either. And there's Rastus ; he must be gettin most a man now, and will help you a heap, and I'll do the square thing by the boy when he gets out here.

Jo Bronson's wife's cousin, Sy Peters, has writ Jo that he is goin to come out this summer with a company, and you can come with him I reckon.

You remember Sy. He's a livin up near Perkinsville now, bein driv off of his land long of the rest of us. Sy will be glad to do you a good turn I know, for when we was both broke up back in New England by goin security at the bank, he and I swopped sympathy with one another, and now that the railroad corporation has gobbled us both, Sy will be willin to do some more swopin of the same kind I reckon, an swopin sympathy means swopin help with poor folks.

I spose you'll want to know what kind of a place I am askin you to come to, and I tell you honest, Marty, when I say that natur done a way up job when she made this country; just about the best she is capable of doin, I reckon, an all I'm askin for now is to have you an the babies, an I'll be satisfied for all the hard work and losses we've had, and they've driv us from sea to sea amost, a gobblin up one home after another after we had made em by hard work.

Seems to me thet ther must be somethin wrong with the law, fer the poor dont stan no chance with the rich, an the more law the less the fellows that works gits.

When I wrote you afore, I was rakin in the dust pretty smart, me an my pard, but some fellows from New York came up there and proposed to form a jint stock company, and offered to put in a lot of machinery for histin out the ore, agin our claim; an bein as we was anxious to get at the dust as fast as possible, so as we could go back to the States fer our families, we agreed to it, but some way it didn't pan out like it ort to a done. The other fellows elected theirselves directors, an pinted one of theirselves bookkeeper, and pard and me never exactly understood how it was, but there was assessments instead of divies, and finally we wus both froze out of the mine entirely after payin back to the company all the dust we had taken out afore we was such fools as to go in with em.

After that I knocked around in the diggins for a spell, an then hearin of this Suscol Ranch I struck out for it, and here I am ; an I tell you, wife, shes just the most glorious bit of country on this side of the big range which nobody doesn't come back from when they hev crost it, and I hev tuck up 160 acres of land, and will hev a cabin up an a good bit of the sile broke afore you git here, and we'll be comfortable in our old age yit, in spite of everything.

This here's the finest valley in the State and would all have been took up long ago only some rich fellows pretended to have a kind of a Spanish claim on to it, and folks were afraid to settle here, most of em, for fear of bein driv off like we have been, but finally some feller took the case up to court and it was decided in favor of the squatters; that is, them as was on the land makin of themselves homes; and now everybody is a-rushin in and pre-emptin quarter sections, and you needn't be afraid of bein lonesome, for we'll have neighbors on every side in less than a year.

Well, this is an awful long letter, but you see I wanted to tell you all about everything, and I hope you wont feel too bad because I cant come for you. You know Id like to if I could, but I cant and I promise you shant ever have to move agin. They cant drive us much further any way, unless they make us take ship fer it; an they cant do that, fer the courts hes decided that no body hes any claim on to this here ranch, ceptin the fellows that pre-empt it.

I think Sy Peters will be down to see you within a week from the time you get this, for I wrote him to go at once so as to give you all the time possible for gettin ready.

Hopin this will find you and the babies as well as it leaves me, I remain

Your lovin husband,

JOHN PARSONS.

The above letter was read by Martha Parsons, first silently, and then aloud to her two little girls, eight and ten years of age, as they stood in front of their mother and listened with breathless attention and wide open eyes as if seeing wonderful things, half glorious, half frightful, but altogether strange and unexplainable.

These were the babies that John Parsons had left six years before, when a corporation representing a railroad laid claim to a large tract of land upon which he and hundreds of others had settled, having bought and paid for it, and holding, as they supposed, incontestible titles thereto.*

When it first became known to them that a corporation

---

* The following is an extract from a letter in the possession of the author, bearing date of Sept. 26th, 1883, written him by Q. A. Wooster, Esq., of Mapleton, Iowa, Secretary of the Settlers Defense Association.

* * "I am thankful for the kind interest which you and others are taking in our behalf. The history of our wrongs is too long to permit me, with my limited time, to write out in full at present. The lands are claimed by the Cedar Rapids & Missouri Railroad Company, under act of Congress of June 2d, 1864. The first suits were commenced in the January, 1877, term of District Court of Monona County, Iowa, against eighty settlers *who held patents at the time.* James F. Wilson, now United States Senator, was the leading attorney. One hundred and twenty-eight suits were afterwards commenced against those who were holding under the homestead act who had not obtained patents, although many of them had proved up and in some cases the patents were in the local land office and were returned to Washington, where they were canceled."

would contest with them the right to their homes and farms, a portion of the settlers threatened vengeance and declared they would give up their own only with their lives, but John loved peace better than contention, and knew by experience the difficulty of fighting bodies that have no souls within them, and he had said to his wife:

"It is no use, Marty. The Philistines are upon us agin, and we have got to git. It's hard, I know; harder fer you ner for me, for you was brought up sort o' tender like and ust to better things, an' you've worked hard and gone without much, and now when we was just gettin' a start agin' after losin' what your father giv us an' all we had added to it, on the spot where you was born, it's mighty tough, but we'll have to stand it.

"They can't put us off the place for a time any way, for some of the fellers are goin' to fight em' with the law, though 'tain't no use, for they'll take everything they want in the end; and they want it all. But while they are a doin' it I'll try an' win enough to make another home for you and the babies. I'll go to California, Marty, and make a fortune, while you stay on the place with the youngsters, and by the time they git ready to turn you out of this, never fear but I'll come back with enough to take you to another home an' a better one. May be it is for the best after all. May be I'll git rich enough to go back east and buy the old place where you was born."

And so John Parsons had got together what money he could by the sale of their few head of cattle and sheep, leaving the family with one cow to supply them with milk, had kissed the babies as they lay asleep in their cradle, had kissed the wife who for long years to come should only know such sleep as comes to those worn with ceaseless labor and study of how to make the income meet the expenses which must be met, and had crossed the plains and mountains that lay between his home and the Pacific ocean, hoping to gather enough gold to repay them for all their past labor and sufferings.

As John had anticipated, some of the homesteaders had contested with the railroad company the right to the land for which they held deeds from the United States government, but only to find by decision of the last court of resort that individuals have no rights which corporations are bound to respect, and in the end to be handed over to the mercies of those whose tenderest mercy is a cunning which led them to move slowly on their prey, exhausting the resources and hopes of the settlers by slow degrees, and letting their first fierce anger burn itself out or give place to hopes born of tales of a yet better country to be found in some distant State or territory where they would be free to again build themselves homes.

While in most cases the delay in evicting the settlers was but robbing them of so many more years of their labor, in the case of John Parsons' little family it was, however little intended, a blessing; for from the land already cleared Mrs. Parsons had been able to make a living for herself and children, aided only by Erastus, an orphan boy whom out of their native goodness of heart John and Martha had taken to their hearthstone and their affections ten years before. He was now a robust lad of fifteen, tanned by the sun, toughened by work, and with a sturdy air of independence, born, in part, of the heavy responsibility which he had been taught rested upon him as "the only man about the place," in part of nature itself and showing itself in his eyes, and through the childish words and actions which had once led John Parsons to remark to his wife that "the little cub weren't exactly lackin' in willingness to claim what was his'n."

When Mrs. Parsons had finished reading aloud the letter from her husband, the little girls stood with hands crossed upon their long gingham aprons silently gazing at their mother, who as silently arose, laid the letter upon the rude mantel over the stone fireplace, and took up her household work where she had left it when a neighbor, in passing, had·brought her the letter.

Her mind was too much occupied with thoughts to which the letter had given birth for her to be fully conscious of what she did, but force of habit, born of the cruel necessity which compels nine out of every ten of the wives of laboring men, and especially of farmers the world over, to be constantly "on the go," always busy, always at work for others, held her to her usual round of duties, even while her mind was busy discussing this and that plan for the' most rapid and profitable disposition of their little remaining accumulations, devising this and that scheme for adding to the comfort of the family upon the long and lonesome journey which she saw rise up before them.

Then, too, her thoughts turned backward over the past; to the scenes of her girlhood; to the time when she wedded the man she loved and whom she was now to join after long years of separation.

She remembered how proud she had been when he first told her of his love and asked her to be his wife, and how hopeful they had been, and how certain of their future happiness when they began life together.

And then came sadder remembrances—the loss of their home through trying to help a neighbor; the death of their first baby that was buried in the little church yard beside her own father and mother, long since gone to their reward—of the other little one, that had come to them only a few months after they landed in the spot from which they were

now being driven, whose tiny grave, she remembered with a
pang keen as the thrust of a dagger, must be left without
any to care for it, without a permanent enclosure even, perhaps to be forgotten, obliterated, trodden upon. But these
thoughts only served to recall her to herself, for with the poor,
to think of the dead is always to recall thought to the living,
the living whose necessities lay claim to every waking
thought, to every effort of the hands and feet.

Her thoughts recalled from the past to the present, from
the dead to the living, without ceasing her work or even
turning around, but intending to address the little girls who
yet stood silent beneath the weight of their childish thoughts
of the wonderful, perhaps dangerous, journey to their father
which they understood was to be taken, Mrs. Parsons asked:

"Where's Erastus?"

Her voice broke the spell which was upon the children,
and snatching their sun-bonnets from the bed upon which
they had thrown them when they followed the neighbor in
with the letter, they whipped out of the house and darted
around the corner in the direction from which came the
sound of the boy's ax.

Across the pasture lot they sped, catching their sun-bonnets from off their heads as they ran and carrying them in
their hands, until out of breath and within talking distance
of the object of their search, the oldest girl broke out with:

"Oh! Ras! what d' spose? Ma's got a letter from pa,
and he ain't comin' home, 'cause he's been froze out again,
but he's going to send money home for us to go to California on, and Mr. Peters is a coming down right away to see
if we can be ready to start next week, and—

"Why, Ras, if you ain't a cuttin' up rails!"

"Wall," replied the boy, his look changing from that of
a very interested listener to one of set determination, "wall,

s'posen I am? Didn't your mother say she wished she had some dry wood to wash with to-morrer? and ain't these rails dry? Guess they are, fur your father split 'em and laid 'em up himself 'fore he went to California. Shud think they ought to get dry in six years if they are ever goin' to."

"But they're rails," protested both the girls at once, their inborn idea of the wrong involved in the destruction of property causing them to forget everything else for the moment. "They're rails, and if you cut 'em up for wood they will be spoilt, and besides the cattle will get into the field."

"'Spose they do, who cares? 'Tain't our field. They stole it. Wish the cattle would get in."

"Bet they don't get many rails with the place," he added, bringing his ax down with all his strength and finishing the destruction of the one he was at work on.

Then he shouldered his ax and the three returned to the house, the girls still swinging their sun-bonnets in their hands and talking excitedly of the coming journey to their father, and the new home which they were to have in the beautiful country to which they were going, while the boy strode on by their side saying less, but with a look and step that proved him not less excited than his companions.

The week that intervened before the coming of Sy Peters, like the weeks that immediately followed it, was occupied by the family in devising means for making the most of their possessions.

They already had a team which Sy thought with good care would stand the trip, but the wagon and harness were not sufficiently strong to risk venturing upon so long a journey, and Mrs. Parsons bent every energy to the task of devising how best to turn this and that and the other article into things it was absolutely necessary that they should have before they could start.

2

A new wagon was bought at the wagon shop in the village, payment being made in the old one backed by two cows. The pigs were sold to get canvas for the wagon cover, the chickens to pay for shoeing the horses all round with new shoes; a better harness was obtained from a neighbor in exchange for the old one and such cheap implements for tilling the soil as they had been using on the farm; calico and muslin for garments for the girls, and cotton jeans for a change for the boy were procured somehow, the few cooking utensils and the beds needed upon the road were packed into the wagon with their remaining provisions; the feeding box was hung to the tail board, a bucket for watering the horses and a pail of grease for greasing the spindles were hung under the hind axle, and one morning in May when the sun came up over the tree tops and looked down into the little clearing, he saw only a deserted and abandoned log house, from whose chimney no wreath of smoke curled upward, upon whose hearthstone no fire was blazing.

The family had again joined the great caravan of toilers that, like the red men, have been driven from sea to sea across a continent, hunting for homes and a resting-place from those who covet all and will be content with nothing less.

CHAPTER II.

THE JOURNEY.

Who shall say that he can truly draw the picture of a six months' journey by wagon train across the continent?

Who has done it?

Who has depicted, or can depict the feeling of loneliness and isolation that takes possession of the hearts of a little band of pilgrims when having, by such tedious methods of travel, placed a thousand miles between themselves and their old home and home associations, they realize that they are yet a thousand miles from the new home which they hope to make in an untried country?

Who can recount the many incidents over which men laugh or women weep, that go to make up the weeks and months of such a journey?

Who can convey to the minds of those who have never seen them, a true picture of the prairies

> That seem bounded,
> Like the waters of the ocean,
> Only by the purple sunset
> And the gray clouds that in patches
> Fleck the sky that hangs low over?

Who shall picture the camp at night upon the open plains —in the rocky pass—by the river side—within some deep defile? Who tell again the stories that were told; who sing the songs that were sung by the camp-fire, or along the weary dusty road?

2

Did those who blazed the way across the continent mark the route for those who followed them?

Those who came after counted the graves by the road-side.

Did these give names to the streams which they crossed?

Others, camping by the streams, drinking of their waters, talked of the memories which those names called to mind.

They who never made the journey can not describe it; those who have, alone could understand it if written; and they—they do not need to read it.

What others saw who crossed the plains in 1850 by wagon train, they saw who made up the little company in which was Martha Parsons, with her two girls and Erastus Hemmingway.

What others suffered of loneliness and hardship, they suffered. They enjoyed all that others enjoyed of the beauties of nature and of the companionship of those with whom they traveled toward the land of golden promise.

They forded the same streams, traveled for days and weeks and months across the same prairies, along the same beaten track, that at times seemed endless; they climbed the same mountains; they greeted with glad cries and thankful hearts the first evidence of the near approach of their journey's end, just as the members of every other company that preceded them had done; just as those of every other company that came after did do; and when they had broken camp for the last time; had made their last day's journey; they received at its end the same hearty, unspeakable welcome from a waiting husband and father that every other husband and father, long separated and anxious for the presence of his loved ones, gave them when their journey was ended and he folded them once more within his arms.

When John Parsons first clasped his wife and little ones to his breast after their long separation, it was in front of the shanty which he had promised should be ready for them upon the quarter section of land which he had pre-empted.

The shanty, however, was not what would be called such in the heavy timbered country of the middle west, but was of redwood boards nailed to a frame of studding, and the cracks battened with narrow strips. The boards being sixteen feet in length and nailed on perpendicularly gave abundant room above for several beds, and for the storage of any article of clothing or of household use not in daily demand.

Instead of being lathed and plastered the walls, both above and below, were covered with heavy muslin neatly and securely tacked on. The ceiling was covered with muslin, but the floors were of boards, and a partition of boards, unplaned but neatly fitted together, divided the lower room into two apartments. It was neither a very grand nor a very costly house, but its builder and owner had taken no small pleasure in thinking that it was better, and more

stylish looking, than the log house his family were leaving
"back in the States."

He had whitewashed the outside carefully, and had built
a porch over the front door, doing everything himself and
lingering long over the nicer jobs ; thinking of how it would
add to the pleasure and comfort of the wife who was under-
going the tedious journey across the plains in order to be
again with him.

" She's worthy of a palace," he had said to himself over
and over again, "an' I'm just goin' to make this here shanty
as comfortable an' as convenient as contrivin' an' fixin' kin do
it." And every evening, after cooking and eating his supper of bacon and beans, with the addition of " slap jacks,"
if he was not too tired or too indifferent to cook them, he
would light his pipe and sit in the front door for hours,
looking out along the track by which he knew they must
come, and wonder where they were at that hour ; if they
were traveling late, as they sometimes must in search of water for their teams ; if all were well ; if they were in danger
from the Indians ; if the horses with which they started were
holding out well, and a thousand other similar things, but
always refusing to believe that evil could come to them now,
when their long separation seemed so near an end, and
firmly clinging to the thought that they would soon all be
together again in the home which he was preparing, and
which he meant never to leave until called over the range to
the better one.

" I wonder now if the little girls will know me," he had
said aloud, as he sat thinking one evening.

" They were such little bits o' tots when I left, that I
really 'spect they have forgotten how their own father looks.
There's Martha, now, she'd recognize me in a minute, I'll
venture ; six years is a long time, though, and I've had some

awful hard knocks durin' that time, wonder now if I am
lookin' much the wus for wear," and he arose a little hur-

riedly and went and hunted up the bit of looking-glass among
his kit of things, and took a long look at himself with a queer
kind of feeling about the heart, that some way reminded
him of the days when he first knew himself to be in love
with Martha Simmonds, and was a little uncertain as to how
his advances would be received.

Every day after that until they came, he had looked in
the glass at least once, and often more than once, and had

kept his hair and beard combed and his clothes looking as well as possible, considering the fact that, to a very great extent, he was forced to rely on strings to do the duty usually performed by buttons.

He had at first thought of meeting his family at Sacramento, and had gone down there in the middle of August with the intention of remaining until they arrived; but as the time of their coming was quite uncertain, and might not be for several weeks yet, and as some things remained to be done to the cottage, he had made arrangements with Jo Bronson, who also had friends in the expected company, to see that they were properly directed after being supplied with anything of which they might be in special need, or to at once notify him in case anything had gone wrong with them, and had returned to the ranch to await them there.

For several days after his return, he busied himself about the cottage; putting in a shelf here; driving up a nail there; going out to look at the garden, the ground for which he had broken early in the spring—almost the first day after he had laid his claim and written his family to come—and which now, thanks to his careful tending and the natural adaptability of the soil and climate, could easily furnish vegetables and melons enough for a larger family than the one whose wants they were intended to supply; and remembering that but a few days or weeks intervened before their coming; that even now they might be in sight from the bluffs at the bend of the creek whose windings the road followed, that they might be coming around the bend at any moment, is it any wonder that he slept but lightly, or that he often raised himself from his blanket, fancying he heard a familiar voice calling to him through the darkness?

Only two days before their arrival a neighboring squatter

called at the ranch, and the two men spoke together earnestly and excitedly, and when the neighbor left, John Parsons hastily mounted his pony and dashed away across the country at break-neck speed, casting anxious glances back over the track in the direction from which he expected any day, any hour, to see the canvas-covered wagon in whose occupants every hope of his life centered.

After an absence of a few hours he returned at the same reckless pace, but only to dash off again, after making certain that no one had been at the cottage during his absence.

He did not follow any beaten track, but struck across country, in a direction nearly opposite to that previously taken, riding at the long swinging gallop for which the native horses of Southern California and Mexico are noted. A ride of two miles brought him to the cottage of another settler, whose wife, surrounded by a flock of little ones, appeared at the door in response to a "halloo" from the rider. To her, Parsons spoke a few words and with a gesture towards her husband who could be seen at work in a distant field and another in a direction slightly different from that from which he himself had come, put spurs to his animal and was off again.

In much the same manner he called at a half dozen shanties, speaking a moment hurriedly with their inmates and always leaving them excited and anxious, his visits in every case being followed by the hasty calling of the husband or father from his work, and his hurried mounting and riding away in the direction pointed out by Parsons.

Just at nightfall he came home, fastened instead of turning loose his pony, and cut for him a bundle of the wild oats that grow so lustily upon the rich soil of the Suscol ranch and surrounding valley.

Then he began to pace back and forth before the porch of the cottage.

He did not cook or eat any supper; he even forgot to light his pipe.

All through that night he paced up and down or stood looking into the sky or out toward the distant hills.

When morning came he cooked and tried to eat his breakfast, but could only swallow with an effort, and when it was over he set the unwashed dishes aside and went and looked in the bit of glass again.

What he saw there seemed to hurt him in some way. The face that was reflected back appeared older and not so good-looking as he had fancied it did when he last saw it; he felt that even Martha would hardly know him; and with the thought, tears, the first he had shed since he kissed wife and babies good-bye away back in the States, almost seven years ago, forced themselves from his closed lids, and he laid down the piece of looking-glass as if ashamed even that the image in it should look upon his emotion.

After awhile he lay down upon his blanket, telling himself that he must not look too care-worn at their coming, but his eyes refused to remain closed. Instead, they persisted in wandering about the rooms; lingering for a moment upon each object in which their possessor had felt a special interest as something that would lighten the labors of his wife; some little thing she would not be likely to expect and which would give her the more pleasure because of it.

All the day through he was up and down, out and in the cottage, unable or unwilling to work, forgetting his dinner until long past the usual hour, and then permitting it to burn to a crisp when he did undertake it; but just as the sun was going down he saw coming around the curve in the road a covered wagon; and although wagons—such wagons

—were far from uncommon sights to him, and although it might well be strangers that approached, yet something told him that it was his own loved ones, and with the thought every look of weariness and care went out of his face, and a moment later the woman in a gingham dress and sun-bonnet had no difficulty in recognizing her husband in the man whose eager arms were thrown about her even before she could descend from the wagon.

CHAPTER III.

THE REUNION.

It was true that the girls who were "such little bits of tots" when he left them did not know how their father looked, and would not have known it was he but for the greeting he gave to their mother and themselves.

It is doubtful, on the other hand, if John Parsons would have known his girls had he met them unexpectedly.

They had grown wonderfully, he thought; so much more than he had imagined.

True, he had counted the years that had flown and had said: "Jennie is almost eleven now, and Lucy past nine," but what did the passage of years signify when memory had all the time pictured them babies, just as he had seen them before the years had come and gone.

Erastus, he thought, had not changed so much. He was quite a lad when he saw him last, and he was not fully a man now. He had grown, of course, and had a manly air and look, but he was not yet sixteen, and then we always expect boys to grow. He had seen boys on the streets of Sacramento and elsewhere of all ages and sizes, and their forms and faces had somehow mingled with the form and face of Erastus and had helped to obliterate the picture of the lad as he saw him last and form a new and much truer one of the real Erastus whose hand he now took and held with a grasp that warmed the boy's heart toward him anew.

"Leave the horses stand a bit and come into the house

with mother and the girls," he said; "we will care for them
by-and-by."

But the boy replied that he would rather care for them
at once and could easily do it without help as he was accustomed to do. They were tired, he said, with the long
drive, as they had all been determined to get through that
night, and had broken camp early and driven hard.

"Yes, John," interrupted Mrs. Parsons, "it has been a
long drive and a hard one; not to-day only, but so many
days; and I'm so glad to think that we are not going to
have to hitch up again in the morning; but that our journey
is ended at last, and that we are all together again."

"I didn't expect so nice a home," she added, coming close
to him and looking up in his face while her eyes filled
with tears. "And oh! I am so glad we have a home of our
own once more. I am sure we shall be very, very happy
here." And she felt hurt when her husband roughly turned
away and began helping Erastus with the animals.

She supposed, however, that he was ashamed to let her
see how deeply he was affected at the thought of their all
being together, and of the happiness which was sure to be
theirs, now that it was so; and she felt very certain that this
was the case when a minute later he came back, and putting his arm around her shoulders, said:

"Come Martha, come babies, let's go in and see the new
home from the inside," and led her up the steps to the porch,
and then into the main room of the cottage.

"How'll she do?" he said, motioning with his hand about
the room.

His wife noticed that his voice was broken as he said it,
but she did not wonder at it, for her own voice was not to
be found at all just then; and sinking into a chair she put

both hands to her face and gave way to the tears that would come in spite of her.

When she could control her voice she said:

"Please don't think me foolish, John; I'm so happy I just can't help crying. Indeed, I didn't expect anything half so comfortable and nice, and now that we are all together again in a home of our own, I can think of nothing else worth asking for."

Going behind her chair her husband took her hands in his own, and, stooping down, kissed her twice, and was silent for a time. Then he said huskily:

"I'm glad we are together again, Martha, and I don't mean we shall ever be parted any more. Now you rest while I go and help 'Rastus with the horses," and turning he left the house.

When he came back in company with the boy he found his wife busy preparing their supper, the material for which Jennie and Lucy were bringing from the wagon.

John brought out his own stores to add to those of the travelers, and soon the family were seated about the table, at the first meal eaten together for so many years; indeed, the first meal that the girls could remember to have ever eaten in company with their father.

Then followed questions and answers regarding the friends in the States, and the journey which was just ended so happily, and at a late hour the family retired to rest upon such beds as could be improvised from the stock in the wagon added to that which the husband and father had been able to provide in view of their coming; and soon all were sleeping the blessed sleep that comes from weariness and a feeling of having passed safely through much of danger;— all but John Parsons, who, despite his last night of waking, slept but little, and arose in the morning with a look that showed his wife at once that there was something upon his mind, a knowledge of which he was striving to keep from the family, and instantly she recalled what had been told her by some friendly squatters near whose cabin they had camped the second night out from Sacramento; of a rumor that some settlers, somewhere further down the valley, were likely to lose their claims through some cause, which those who repeated the tale did not properly understand.

It had not occurred to her at the time that it was possible it could be John's claim that was in danger.

It seemed strange now that it did not. But so full was her mind of thoughts of John himself, of their coming reunion, and of the future when they should all be together in the new home that there was no room for anything else; and so she had scarcely heard the tale at all, or hearing it had dismissed it at once with a single expression of pity for the poor families who were to lose their all—even as she and John had done back in the States—through the greed of those who are not content with what is justly theirs.

But now she understood it.

It was John's claim that was involved and they had come two thousand miles to find a home and resting place, only to be bidden to move on again ere they had shaken the dust of the long journey from their garments.

"Is it the title to the place, John?" she asked; "I know there is something terrible on your mind; something you are afraid to tell me. I ought to have seen it last night, but I didn't. I was so tired and so glad, that I couldn't think of anything. Whatever it is, don't be afraid to tell me. I can bear anything, only so that we remain together." And she put her arms around his neck and laid her head upon his bosom.

Then John Parsons broke down and wept. The children came in and stood wondering and silent. They knew something terrible had happened, or was about to happen, for, young as they were, they knew that men do not weep at the scratch of a briar; and they saw their father weep and saw their mother put up her hand and stroke his beard and face and whisper softly something they could not hear, but which they felt must be words of comfort that were sorely needed.

It was Erastus that broke the spell at last. He had been the first to rise and had gone out immediately to feed and rub down the horses; and returning had entered just in time to hear Mrs. Parsons speak of the title to the claim. Then he, too, remembered the rumor which they had heard, and knew that it was true, and understood all that it meant to those who had been the only real friends he had ever known, and his young blood grew hot and for a moment he felt that he could kill the men who were the cause of so much suffering; and then there came a great wave of affection for the friends who had given him all the love he had ever known, and stepping forward, he said in a tone of voice that gave a weight to his words which his years would have denied him:

"Uncle John, if the land thieves have gobbled this place too, let them have it. There must be land somewhere that they don't claim, and if there is we'll find it, and make a home on it. I'm almost a man now, Uncle John, and I'll help you; so don't give up. It will be all right yet."

"Yes, John, cheer up. We will find a place to start again, somewhere, and all begin together," said his wife. "I know, dear, how badly you feel. You have built the house for us and have thought so much about welcoming us here that it is harder for you than for us, who only saw it for the first time last night."

"I never knew it till just the other day," said John, striving to speak in his natural voice; "they told me when I bought the place that it was all straight, and the courts had decided that nobody had a claim on it that would hold but the settler; but it 'pears that the rich fellows that claim it raised a heap of money and bribed Congris to reverse the thing. The other squatters got wind of it and had a meetin' to see about it. That was while I was at Sacramento arrangin' with Jo fer your comin', and I never knowd anything about it 'til Bill Ritchie, who has the next claim east, came over Thursday mornin' to tell me that another meetin' was to be held that afternoon to hear the report of the committee that had been sent to Frisco to find out if it was true or no. And so I helped Bill to notify the neighbors and we held the meetin' at Bill's house, and the committee was thar an' they said we was done for, sure enough; that Congris had decided that the hul Suscol Ranch belonged to a few fellows that never struck a blow, nor turned a sod, nor put up a shanty; and who never paid nobody fer doin' it, but claimed it because some Spanish king or other once pretended to give it to some of his cronies before there was any United States or anything else on this continent but buffaler, an bars an' Injins.

"I ust to be proud of my country," he continued, "and was fond of sayin' that everybody stood an ekil chance here; but it ain't so. Nobody don't 'stand any chance except he is a raskil and a coward into the bargin; stealin 'thout gettin' in front of the law. There ain't no doubt but that Congris was bribed. Our fellows have even learned where and when the money was raised, and some of the Congrismen and Senators who was bought to vote agin us;* but we can't

* The Suscol Ranch embraces more than 90,000 acres of land lying in the counties of Solano and Napa, in the State of California.
   The claim through which the settlers lost their homes, was said to be a forged Mexican grant. There was no record of it in the archives of the Mexican Government,

prove nothing in court, fer everything works agin the poor
man, who only wants justice, an' in faⱱor of the rich one that
is seekin' to rob him of his earnings; and if it wasn't for the
wimin and children that might be left wus off if their husbands and fathers wus .killed, there would be a fight afore
some of us give up our claims."

This allusion to possible violence frightened Martha Par-

and it was never entered in Jemino's index to land grants in California. When the
land began to be valuable, claimant sold the grant to his son-in-law for $5,000, to be
paid when the money could be made out of it. From the shadow thus cast over the
title, the matter was carried into the courts. After several years' delay, it is claimed
that by the use of $25,000 the court was influenced to give a decision in favor of the
bogus grant. The case was appealed to the Supreme Court of the United States, and
a determined effort was made to induce Judge Jerry S. Black, who was then Attorney
General, to have the appeal dismissed. It is claimed that large amounts of money were
sent to Washington to be used in influencing the Attorney General, but without avail.
Judge Black reported that he had "examined the papers in the case and found that the
title was a base forgery and ought to be utterly rejected." After Lincoln's inaugura-
tion, the same influences were brought to bear upon Attorney General Bates, but with
like results. The case was retained on the docket and the court finally decided that
the pretended title was void, and the lands of the Suscol Ranch were restored to the
public domain. The conspirators at once made an effort to have their title established
by special act of Congress, but for several years they failed in their efforts.

Finally, however, by methods that will never be fully known, a bill was forced
through both houses of Congress, giving the bogus claimants the exclusive right to
enter the land at $1.25 per acre, thus depriving the homesteaders of their rights to
their homes at any price. Two hundred citizens were rendered homeless without com-
pensation by this infamous act of Congress.

Several years afterwards, while George W. Julian, of Indiana, was Chairman of
the Committee on Public Lands, he made a strong effort to have Congress undo the
wrong, but his efforts were unavailing. The following extract from his speech in the
House, delivered July 5, 1866, will show that that body was fully apprised of the
nature of the bogus claim, and were without excuse in perpetuating a wrong perpe-
trated by a previous Congress.

Mr. Julian said:

"Mr. Speaker, I regret very much to occupy the time of the House at this late
hour of the session in the discussion of this bill, and nothing could induce me to do so
but a sense of duty. I believe, and feel very sure in the opinion—without imputing
any improper motives to anybody—that an effort is being made here to overturn the
entire land policy of the United States, respecting the rights of preëmptors and
homestead claimants upon the public lands. I deem it incumbent upon me, therefore,
to discuss with some care the question involved in the amendment submitted by the
committee, affecting the title to this well-known ranch in California, and affecting also
the proper interpretation of the act of Congress of March 3, 1863. The facts of this

sons. What if the squatters should resist and John should be killed? The thought almost took away her breath, and she tried in everyway to calm her husband whom she had never before seen in so violent and bitter a mood.

He did not really meditate resistance, however. Experience and observation had taught him that those who could control both the legislatures and the courts could bring aids to their assistance that made resistance by any force which the squatters could command worse than useless; and after a little while he cooled down and began to talk of what was to be done in the direction of seeking a new home.

"Some of the fellows are talking of goin' up into the foot-hills, above Sacramento, where they say thar ain't no claim of any kind on the land, and where it is most as easy to grow grapes and peaches an' apricots and sich as it is to raise corn an' hogs back in the States. If they would pay for the work I've done on this place, or even enough to get lumber for another house, we could start agin up there, and do purty well maybe, but they won't. Stealin' is their game,

case, which it is necessary to understand, are about these : This Suscol Ranch, in the State of California, is a large tract of about ninety thousand acres, alleged to have been granted by the Mexican or Spanish Government to one General Vallejo. The title was for a long time in dispute and litigation, and the case finally found its way onto the docket of the Supreme Court of the United States ; and that court, after a full hearing of the whole case on the points of law and of fact involved, decided that the alleged title of Vallejo was void. It was not pronounced void on technical ground, as gentlemen may perhaps argue on the other side, for Justice Nelson of the Supreme Court declares, in so many words, that ' in every view we have been able to take of the case, we are satisfied the grant is one which should not be confirmed.'

"This decision was given in December, 1861, and so soon as the judgment of the court was certified to the court below in California, which was in March following, this whole claim of 90,000 acres became a part of the unappropriated public lands of the Government, open from that moment to preëmption and purchase as other public lands. Accordingly, as soon as that decision was thus certified and made known, scores of persons entered upon this Suscol Ranch as preëmption settlers, built their cabins, put up fences, cultivated the land, in some instances planted orchards, and asserted the rights generally of preëmptors under the laws of the United States."

3

and havin' paid Congris to declare stealin' legal, I 'spose they'll go for everything in sight."

Mrs. Parsons professed to be pleased with the idea of raising fruit, which was really the case, for she had already seen evidences since arriving upon the coast of the liberality with which nature dealt with such of her products in this climate, and could she have felt absolutely certain that they could find the right spot and get a claim which would not be wrested from them, she would have felt in no small degree contented with the situation. And now she was ready to encourage any scheme that would help to reconcile her husband to the inevitable.

The result of further conversation between the members of the family was that Mr. Parsons again mounted his pony and rode away in the direction of Ritchie's shanty; and that that evening a dozen squatters, many of them accompanied by their wives, met at the cottage, were introduced to the new comers, and when they departed it had been arranged that John and Bill should make a trip to the locality spoken of and see if it was really suitable for homesteading, while others were to go to San Francisco and ascertain beyond possible question if there was any shadow of a claim hanging over it.

" I don't never mean to settle on another bit of ground that anybody has ever laid claim to 'ceptin God'l-mighty," said one of those present; and all the others echoed the sentiment.

The next morning John Parsons took his wife, and then each of his children in his arms and held them close to his heart for a moment, kissed them and rode away to try to find another resting place.

As he reached the brow of the hill which was to hide the cottage from his view, he checked his pony and turning, looked back, and then away to where he could see other houses dotting the landscape, until a moisture came to his eyes and blurred his sight.

"Only just a campin'," he said: "only just a campin' where they thought to live always; that's what they're a-doin'; that's what I've ben a-doin' all my life."

CHAPTER IV.

EVICTION.

The explorers were gone ten days. Returning just after nightfall on the evening of the tenth day they paused in front of the little grove surrounding Ritchie's shanty to arrange between themselves the route which each should take on the morrow in notifying those interested, of their return and readiness to report.

The Suscol Ranch is not a prairie, but a succession of low ridges or hills. Occasionally a bit of the rock foundation crops out upon some bluffy point, but generally the ridges are tillable clear to their summits, and produce wonderful crops of wheat, an average of fifty and sixty bushels to the acre being considered a no surprising yield even upon fields of several hundred acres. In their natural state they are dotted over with little groves of white and live oak, usually in groups of from a dozen to a hundred trees, and it was in one of these little groves that Ritchie's shanty was situated.

When the two men had agreed upon their separate course for the morrow, and also upon the place at which the squatters were to be asked to meet and decide upon their future action, they separated; Ritchie turning his pony's head toward his shanty, while Parsons loosened the rein upon the neck of his beast already showing signs of uneasiness at being held back when so near home, and started at a brisk pace in the direction in which he knew his family were anxiously awaiting his coming.

He had gone but a few yards, however, when he

heard an exclamation of surprise from Ritchie, who almost instantly rejoined him and crowding his pony close up to that of his companion exclaimed, in a voice shaken with emotion and excitement:

" My God, Parsons, they've torn down my shanty, and heaven only knows what has become of my wife and child."

It was true.

Those to whom the Suscol ranch, comprising thousands of acres of the finest lands, had been given by the purchased votes of corrupt congressmen and senators, had decided to resort to eviction in order to obtain immediate possession, and sent a posse of men with orders to destroy a number of dwellings as a warning to all others, and Bill Ritchie's shanty had been among those selected.

For a moment the two men sat upon their horses like statues, looking at each other through the darkness; and then, with one impulse, they put spurs to their animals and dashed away in the direction of Parsons' house. Neither spoke, but both leaned forward in their saddles, and rode at full speed—rode with bated breath, while alternate hope and fear struggled with fierce anger for possession of their bosoms.

Had they stopped to reason they would have known that there was little probability of bodily injury having been done to the evicted family;* but who would stop to reason of

*At the time this work was written, the author was not in possession of all the details of the horrible outrages committed upon the helpless settlers of the Suscol Ranch, and not believing it possible that personal violence could be offered to women by any one in America who even professed to act under the authority of law, made use of the above expression. But how much he misjudged the extent to which the greed for wealth can brutalize men, may be seen from the following extract from a letter received from one of the victims after the story appeared in serial form. " These large holders, under the Vallejo title, had put up cheap fences around their tracts and gone to work against the preëmpters in the courts, under the common law of possession. Then commenced ejectment suits, and the Sheriff of Solano County, a purchaser under the bogus title, was swift to execute the mandates of the court against the settlers,

the probable amount of injury when he came suddenly upon
the ruins of his home and realized that those whom he loved
better than all else in the world, a defenseless woman with
a babe at the breast, had had the shelter torn from over
their heads, and that they were gone, he knew not where or
how?

Naturally they would seek shelter with their new neighbors, the Parsons, since they were nearer than any other,
and the two men would return together; but suppose the
Parsons cottage was destroyed also? Supposing all the cottages in the neighborhood were destroyed, what then?

And John Parsons? Can the sufferings which he endured during that ride be measured or told? That ride of
a quarter of a mile before coming up over the intervening
rise they saw lights in the window and a camp-fire burning brightly in front of the cottage?

If life were a flame feeding upon the body which it
inhabits, then it would be easy to understand how men sometimes grow old in a day—how the hair may turn white
in a night; for one man may live more, suffer more in an
hour than comes to others in a lifetime.

His deputy, armed with a writ of ejectment, went to the house of Curley while he was
absent and seized his wife, and amid the screams of the children, beat and threw her
out of the house in the most cruel manner, and injured her so seriously that she lay
helpless for several months The Sheriff then went with a posse to eject a Mr Han-
son, and he not being at home, and his wife supposing it to be a mob, made resistance,
when they seized and handcuffed her and beat her in so shocking a manner that in a
few months *she died of her injuries*. He also went to Cornelius Martin's house with
his posse of fifty men—made up of land sharks and their hirelings—and while Mrs.
Martin was sick in bed, they seized and carried her out. Martin begged them to wait
until he could carry out his furniture, and he had scarcely time to do so when the
house was leveled to the ground. This crew of land sharks had all the officials on
their side. Mr. McCullough and another man, in going into their quarter section, had
to cross a temporary fence, and they happened to break a couple of rails, and for so
doing were arrested for malicious trespass, taken before a magistrate and sentenced to
sixty days imprisonment, which they served out in jail. Ashbrook was assassinated at
night, and Cox was murdered in daylight and Rooney seriously wounded—all preëmptors."

The posse sent to evict the homesteaders had gone directly to John Parsons' cottage from Ritchie's ; but they were preceded by Mrs. Ritchie, who, frightened by the threats of men to tear the shanty down over her head if she did not at once leave it, had caught her babe from its cradle and ran directly to the Parsons homestead, where she arrived almost as much dead as alive, and had imparted the dreadful information, believing it to be true, that every dwelling on the ranch was to be torn down, and had urged Mrs. Parsons to take the children and fly with her to some place in the hills where they could hide from those who were bent upon a mission of destruction, and whom her excited imagination had magnified into a small army, ready for any outrage upon the persons as well as the property of those against whom they were sent.

Mrs. Parsons was scarcely less agitated at the recital of the terrible news than was she who brought it; and Erastus who had listened without saying a word to the story of the outrage, made no objection to the proposition, but helped to make into a bundle the scanty wardrobe of the family, and in company with the frightened women and children crossed the creek upon a little foot-bridge made of planks, and placed them all within the shelter of the bluffs on the opposite side, and a little further down, where they would be out of sight of the posse either from the cottage or from any point on the road over which they would pass in continuing their work of destruction.

This done, in spite of the pleadings of the little girls and Mrs. Ritchie, and the almost commands of "Aunt Martha," as he had always called Mrs. Parsons, he returned to the cottage and carefully examined the rifle which he had been allowed to purchase when the journey across the plains began, and also that of "Uncle John," which hung over the

door between the two apartments. Then he closed and barri-
caded as best he could the doors of the cottage and waited.

He had not long to wait, for very soon the posse, composed of a dozen men, halted in front of the dwelling, and
the leader advanced and rapped loudly on the door.

It is probable that the posse had lingered a little, knowing the direction in which Mrs. Ritchie had fled with
her child, and guessing that the family to whom she would
impart the information of the destruction of her own dwelling would be frightened thereby into leaving also, and
thus enable them to avoid the scene which, in justice, it
must be said was no pleasure to them; and evidently they
thought that the ruse had succeeded, for the leader of the
squad remarked as he halted the men:

" Guess we shan't have to frighten anybody to death here
to get them to leave."

He was right. The occupant of the cottage was not
frightened, but in another minute the officer was, for he
heard the click of a rifle lock and knew that there was not
only somebody within, but that that somebody meant business ; and, hastily stepping back off of the porch, he said
to the men : " Nobody at home here ; guess we've done
enough for one day, anyhow ; let's quit and go home." And
in another moment the whole posse was out upon the road
and headed in the direction from which they came.

It is more than possible, it is probable, that the officer
did not intend to destroy the house from which this little
family had fled, and which Erastus Hemmingway had determined to defend at the risk of his life.

It was one of the best cottages in the whole ranch and
was too valuable to be destroyed if the family could be
frightened into leaving without ; hence those nearest it had
been destroyed first, with the expectation that it would result

in its abandonment, if not immediately, at least within a very
short time ; and the purpose of the posse in stopping at all
had been to add to the fright of its occupants by threats and
by their presence ; instead of which their leader received a

fright himself, which induced him to move a little more rapidly than was his wont, and to keep his person well sheltered
behind the wagon in which was deposited the axes and iron
bars, by means of which they had carried on their work of
destruction at other places.

When Erastus was satisfied that the men were really gone, he unbarricaded the door and returned to the anxious group behind the bluff.

At first they could not be persuaded to go back to the house, the little girls crying and begging their mother to "hitch right up and go back to the States," where at least their lives were safe ; but finally venturing far enough out to take a look, they saw approaching a man, whom Mrs. Ritchie recognized as a neighbor, and were reassured.

The neighbor proved to be another of the evicted squatters looking for shelter for his houseless family, and when John Parsons and Bill Ritchie reined up their heated ponies in front of the cottage that night, it was the only one standing within a circle of two miles on every side, and a dozen families with their little stores of household goods were domiciled within, or camping beneath its hospitable shadow.

CHAPTER V.

ON THE MOVE AGAIN.

The report made by Parsons and Ritchie of the advantages and resources of the country which they had visited was quite as favorable as any one had expected.

It was a wild country, of course. There was no land for pre-emption suitable for their purposes without going back from Sacramento some distance, and they must expect a hard life for a number of years ; but it was a beautiful country, and would one day be thickly settled. Already a few families had started fruit ranches, and had obtained the most gratifying results.

Grapes, peaches, pears, apples, apricots, nectarines, pomegranates, and many other fruits were grown of a quality that the men had never seen equalled anywhere "in the States," and that which under the circumstances was of equal importance to these people, was the rapidity with which all fruit-bearing trees and vines began producing.

Grapes at three years from the cutting, and peaches at three years from the pit, would bear no inconsiderable burdens of fruit ; while most other varieties were equally rapid in reaching maturity.

Melons, and indeed all kinds of vines and vegetables, were wonderfully prolific, and Irish potatoes, turnips, carrots, beets, and other root crops, could be raised in abundance, and by the simplest methods of cultivation.

For the present it was probable that the miners in the vicinity would consume, at large prices, any surplus that the squatters might produce ; and if in time this market should fail, a little work would enable them to transport everything they produced to the river, where it could be shipped direct to Sacramento, or down to the coast.

Those whose duty it had been to ascertain regarding the title to the land in the locality under consideration, reported it free from taint of any kind. In point of fact the claim of these men to the land upon which they settled in the foot-hills above Sacramento city, was never disputed.

A motion that they locate upon the lands described was put to a vote and carried unanimously, and preparations for the journey at once began.

The team which had brought John Parsons' family across the plains was again hitched to the canvas-covered wagon, their little store of goods was packed therein, including as much of the products of the garden as could be added without overloading the team, leaving all, even Mrs. Parsons and the children, to walk, and thus they again took up their journey, a dozen families, all told.

Some in the little company were entirely without money. All, not excepting John Parsons, were nearly so. And Martha knew well that worse hardships than walking for a few days, or even weeks, beside the team, awaited her and her children before they could erect a shelter or procure the wherewithal to provide a comfortable home.

True, the men might go back to mining. There would be mines in the vicinity of the claims they expected to locate, but these men had lost all faith in their luck with the pick. They had worked at it, more or less, all of them, but none had ever "struck it rich." Besides they were of that class of men who prefer steady gains, even if slow and small, to the excitement of speculation or searching with a pick and shovel for a fortune which may possibly come at any moment, but in all probability will never come at all.

Mining partakes very much of the character of gambling. It constantly holds out the promise of large gains—of a fortune, to be secured in a day, in an hour perhaps. The next deal, the next shovel-full, the next blow with the pick, may disclose a pocket filled with gold, and convert the finder into a Crœsus ; and so he works on for days and months and years with but one object, one thought—to find that which men have decreed should be of more value than home, or friends or honors ; than the means of sustaining life ; than life itself — nay, more ; that failing to procure this one thing, they shall be denied all others.

But these men were not speculators, not gamblers by nature. They were men who loved best the quiet of home and the peaceful pursuits of agriculture. Farmers and farmers' sons back in the States, a brief experience in mining had satisfied most, and all had tried it until they were satisfied. What they wanted was an opportunity to earn their living and make homes for themselves and families in obedience to nature's laws and their own inclinations, by the cultivation of the soil, and the gathering of its ripened fruits and grains.

They were not unused to hardships. What man or woman was, that had been a miner or miner's wife back of '60 in California ?

And they were not cowards. The cowards went out later, when the wilderness had been, in a measure, subdued; when braver men had proven the immense resources of the country; had bridged its torrents; had opened its mines; had driven out the Indians; had laid the foundation for private fortunes and national wealth—it was then the cowards

came, or were begotten of the spirit of gambling, the greed
for sudden and immense wealth which the ceaseless search
for gold stimulates if it does not create—came and plotted
to rob better men of their hard-earned savings. These men,
I say, journeying from their ravaged homes upon the Suscol
Ranch to the foot-hills to begin again, were not cowards, and
they were inured to hardship, and like all other people
they were too quick to forget wrongs done them under the
cloak of law, and they let their anger die out; refused to
peer too closely or too far into the future, which they could
not control, and laughed as they journeyed, instead of crying; sang scraps of frontier songs, instead of recounting to
each other the story of their sufferings.

And the women? Why, bless you, dear reader, women
learned long ago, some centuries back, I think it was, to
suffer and be still. Not one woman cried out at the hardships she was compelled to undergo during that whole
journey.

CHAPTER VI.

BEGINNING A NEW HOME.

Arriving at their destination each head of a family selected his claim and at once began the work of erecting a shelter.

John Parsons and Bill Ritchie selected claims near to, though not adjoining each other, for the country here is more broken than on the Suscol Ranch, much of it being unfit for farming or even for fruit growing; and very few quarter sections can be found lying wholly in a valley.

Generally, if the squatter could get a claim, one-half of which was in the valley, he was well contented to take the remainder upon the broken lands lying upon the bluffs.

Such a claim was that which John and Martha Parsons, assisted by Erastus, selected.

"The boy has been faithful," said John to his wife. "I don't know what you and the girls would have done but for him, crossin' the plains, an' I mean to do the square thing by him if ever we do get ahead a bit. Besides, the grit which he showed back at the other place ought to entitle him to hev his advice axed, if only for good manners sake; 'specially if it is anything in which he is interested."

And thereafter nothing of importance to the family was ever fully decided upon until Erastus had been given an opportunity to express an opinion of its wisdom or feasibility.

The valley in which most of our pilgrims had sought homes was scarcely more than a quarter of a mile wide; the stream which watered it keeping nearer to the bluffs upon the right

side the greater part of the way, but occasionally curving
outward, near to or past the center of this level strip of
ground between the hills.

Where the stream made one of its curves, leaving between
its channel and the bluff a handsome piece of ground of perhaps twenty-five acres, which was slightly higher than the
rest of the valley, and so not likely to be overflowed by the
water during the winter freshet, and near to the bluff, which
sloped back gradually for some distance, did John Parsons
begin the erection of his humble home.

Material for building was scarce and high. Lumber
could have been obtained had the settlers possessed the
means of paying for it; but, lacking this, they were obliged
to do the best they could with the material furnished by nature upon or near the spot. Some dug into the sides of the
hills, thus securing the walls for three sides of their dwellings, the roof and front being of such bits of lumber as they
had brought with them or could purchase; in some instances
the rude front being of lumber which had once composed
dry-goods boxes and in which the clothing or furniture of
the owners had been brought from the States.

Mr. Parsons and Erastus, in preference to this style of
half dug-out, decided to build of logs, but to obtain these
they were obliged to go several miles further into the hills
and snake down the bodies of small spruce trees. This took
much time and hard work, but willing hands made light of
it, and three weeks from the day of arrival the family moved
into their new house.

There was but one room, and that not large; and the
floor was the earth, smoothed and beaten down. There
were two doors, with a window upon either side: the latter
taken from the cottage in the Suscol Ranch and brought
through in the wagon with the bedding carefully packed

about them. The furniture consisted of some rough shelves in one corner sufficient to hold a few pieces of crockery in daily use, a table, several chairs and two beds, which, with the stove, so filled the single apartment that there was no room for another bed, even if they had possessed it; and for the time Erastus slept in the covered wagon, for which there was little present use, and later on upon a bunk on the dirt floor of the shanty.

It was very far from being as comfortable as the cottage back on the Suscol Ranch, and as for elegance or effort at "respectability" it made none whatever; was, in fact, as much below the log house "back in the States," which the family had left, as the Suscol cottage had been above it in that regard, and this thought kept coming to John Parsons, and causing him twinges of pain all the time they were at work on it, but once fairly domiciled beneath his own roof, poor though he was, with his family about him, and with the cheerful voice of his wife ever bidding him take courage, he soon ceased to dwell upon his disappointment; or at least to make mention of it.

The first thing to be done after the shanty was up and the family safely sheltered, was the securing of provender for the teams; for while domestic animals will live all winter on what they can pick, and in ordinary seasons come through in good condition; yet they cannot do this if required to work, and our friends had sod to break for next season's crop. So they set about gathering the wild grasses which grow with wonderful luxuriance during the rainy months, but turn yellow and brown when the dry season comes on, curing as perfectly where they grow as by the process of hay-making pursued in countries which lack the pure dry atmosphere of the Pacific coast.

The first rains, however, wash the greater portion of the

4

nourishment out of this dried grass, and although the new
shoots spring up at once, it is difficult, for a time, for stock
to get at it through the heavy coating of old and worthless
growth which falls down over it, and is not very nourishing
when obtained.

A portion of the settlers had a cow each, but those in
whom we are most interested were without. Among those
who were so fortunate as to possess one, however, was
Ritchie; and as Mr. Parsons and Erastus were enabled to
give him needed assistance in the erection of his shanty
and the cutting of grass for his team and cow, it was
agreed that the milk should be divided between the two families for the next year, Jenny and Lucy making regular trips
for their share every night and morning.

The shanty up, and a sufficient amount of grass secured,
the settlers next turned their attention to the breaking of the
soil, the planting of trees and vines, and, at the proper time,
of vegetables. For the first year they expected to live
largely upon wild game and the few provisions which they
had brought with them. The second year they would get on
much better.

There is no country where the common domestic fowls,
ducks, chickens and geese, are so easily raised or repay so
well the little attention which they require, as in California;
and our friends were in possession of a sufficient number of
these to enable them to subsist upon eggs and fowls of their
own raising, if need be, by another year; besides which they
would be well supplied with vegetables, so that the prospect
was not so very gloomy after all, especially as all were
blessed with good health; and hope, which usually comes
with a healthful body busily employed in its own service,
gave a coloring as of the sunrise to the future which was
opening up before them.

Fruit trees were already being shipped to the coast by way of the isthmus, and although they were costly and our friends poor, they managed to get a few ; enough, at least, to furnish grafts for future use. Of peach pits and apple and pear seeds the careful housewife who presided over John Parsons' shanty had brought a supply from the States.

Grape-cuttings could be more easily obtained. More than a century before, the Jesuit priests who penetrated up-ward from Mexico, had planted grape-vines brought from Spain, and these, crossed, perhaps, with other varieties brought from the States, and favored by the adaptability of the climate, produced a fruit far excelling anything which the Atlantic States can boast of.

And so when spring came again and the rain ceased, there was quite the appearance of living in the vicinity of the Parsons' shanty. Some twenty acres of the land had been broken, a garden planted, and many of its products were lifting their heads to the sunlight ; a half-hundred fruit trees and a hundred grape-vines had put forth their leaves, and were ready to drink in the sunshine and grow. And they grew. Grew so fast that one could almost fancy he saw them grow and stretch themselves.

It has been said that the only thing which ever distanced a California grape-vine when once it got down to the busi-ness of growing, is the bean-vine of Jack the Giant Killer, known to our childhood days ; the one that Jack undertook to climb to the top of, but which grew faster than he could climb, and so carrying him with it, finally reached clear up to the giant's castle.

And such clusters of fruit as hang dependent upon their stems, and grow and ripen in the long sunny days of September and October, when not a cloud mars the blue

of the sky for weeks and weeks ; clusters that look like
pure globes of clear crystal ; or that turn purple and amber-
colored where they hang among the broad, velvety leaves
that seem as if conscious of the beauty of the picture which
they help to make ; and which turn themselves sideways
upon their long stems, now hiding, now disclosing the fruit
in their midst.

The California grapes shipped by refrigerator cars, and
exposed for sale at the fruit stands in all our eastern cities,
and which attract such universal attention, give but a poor
idea of California grapes when plucked and eaten standing
beneath the vine in California, or sitting at ease at your
own table or that of a friend, with the sea or the mountains
in sight through the open window.

Only the tougher skinned or less luscious of the fruits of
all kinds will bear such long shipping. The finer and
juicier and more luscious varieties of each must be eaten
where they are grown, or be sent to a not distant market.

California plums are wrapped in tissue paper and sent
east boxed up like oranges from Florida or the West
Indies, and sold "a nickel apiece, or three for a dime," to
people who buy them as a curiosity, or a very rare treat.
At home in California the children eat them as children eat
apples in New England, and the housewife drops them into
liquid sugar and takes them out great globes of pearl with
centers of amethyst. Or she cuts them in halves, and,
removing the pit, lets them dry in the sun, and stores them
away in sacks and boxes just as she does figs and grapes ;
only that these latter are packed down hard when but little
more than half dried, and before the rich juices have crys-
talized into sugar ; and which, eaten as freely as bread is
eaten, flushes the veins with the rich blood that crimsons the
cheeks of children and grown people alike in this land of

fruits and flowers; this land of mountain ranges and sea-washed shores; of valleys as rich in the elements of agricultural wealth as its hillsides are with precious ores,—this land that should bear a people as free as the breeze that floats in upon them laden with healing balm from the salt sea waves to find—not freemen, but, delving in mines and upon leagues and leagues of the richest farming lands upon the continent—a million serfs. .

CHAPTER VII.

"A LAND FLOWING WITH MILK AND HONEY."

" I say, mother, it wasn't such a bad thing for us after all, that they driv us off of the Suscol Ranch," said John Parsons to his wife one morning, as he came under the rough porch that had been put up in front of the shanty.

He had just finished helping Erastus get ready to start to market with the usual load of fruit which they were now selling daily.

" I'm sure fruit and poultry raisin' is a heap pleasanter than raisin' wheat; and there's more money into it, too.

" Only think, we've been here less than five years now, and we've got all the fruit growin' that we kin all of us tend to, and the money is just a rollin' in. If the rest of the crop pans out as well as it has so fur, we kin build a new house with a verander all around it next year and have money left to send the girls down to 'Frisco to school."

" Yes, we are getting along very nicely," replied his wife, " and ought to be thankful I'm sure."

" As soon as we git a new house built," continued Mr. Parsons, " we must begin to save up money to buy a ranch som'ers nigh about here for 'Rastus, fer I 'spose we can't in reason expect the boy to stay with us always. Human natur' don't change much I reckon; it's the same on the Pacific as it is on the Atlantic coast, and I hain't forgot that I was mighty anxious to get a place of my own 'fore I was as old as 'Rastus is; 'specially after I got acquainted with a certain girl with checks the color of them there

peaches a hangin' out there in the sun, and eyes that
sort of made me hot and cold by turns, a-wonderin' whether
they was encouragin' me, or takin' note of the size of my
cow-hide boots, whenever they looked my way.

" Not," he continued, "as I've noticed that 'Rastus seemed
particularly took with any of the girls round here—leastwise
them as lives far around here," he added, looking hard at
his wife, as if endeavoring to read her thoughts.

If Mrs. Parsons understood what her husband was thinking of, she made no attempt to reply, and after waiting a
second or two, he began again :

"I don't see as 'Rastus appears to take particular to any
of the neighboring girls, but whether he does or not;
whether he takes a wife from close by or furder off, it's only
fair that we help him to a start. He's been true as steel and
as kind as if he was our own son, and I'm a reckonin' if he
and one of the girls should sometime take a notion to hitch
up and work in double harness, there wouldn't be any objections; eh, mother ? "

" The girls are not old enough to get married, John,"
returned Mrs. Parsons. " Jennie is not sixteen yet and
Lucy is two years younger still. I hope that neither of them
will think of such a thing as marriage for a good while. Erastus
himself is not quite twenty-one, and although many young
men marry as young as that, I do not think that Erastus has
any such intentions. Not that he has ever said anything to
me; but as you say I have not noticed that he appeared partial to any of the neighboring girls, although he is a favorite
with all ; and as for Jennie and Lucy, they probably seem to
him like sisters; indeed, he seems like a son to me, and whoever he may choose for a wife when he does marry will get
an honorable man for a husband and one who will be kind
and loving, I am sure."

"That's so," replied John, "'Rastus ain't a fellow that will ever go to knockin' his wife and babies around, if he ever has any. But I 'spose it ain't no use to try to fix things up for the young folks. We'll have to let 'em take their own head, which 'll be just as the heart directs 'em, I reckon. An' I wouldn't want 'em to do no other way, for unless the heart goes with the hand it ain't no use for to try to pull together. Well, now, here's a youngster that ain't bothering his head about the girls any way, nor won't be for some years yet, will you Johnny? He'll be bossin' the hull ranch, though, if his mother and I don't look out, afore he's big enough to hunt hen's eggs or tie up a grape-vine."

And reaching down he drew upon his knee and gave a great hug to a sun-tanned, tow-headed boy that had just entered; the child of their old age, born the year the shanty had been put up and the first grape-vines planted.

"I is bid 'nough to hunt edds now," retorted the little fellow, squirming to release himself from his father's arms.

"I did found a whole nes'ful out under the roses bush, and you've broke 'em; see."

And he ran his hand into his pocket and withdrawing it covered with the yolk of the eggs stood holding it up, while the liquid dripped down over his clothes.

"You shouldn't have put the eggs in your pocket," said his father, laughing at the spectacle which he presented. "You might have known they would have got broken and spoil your new pants."

"What's 'e use of pantses if 'ou tan't put edds in 'e pottits, I'd lite to know," replied the youngster as he waddled off to his mother to be cleaned up and fitted for some new adventure. "Des I tan put edds in my own potits if I 'ants to," he added by way of a clincher, as his father playfully stooped to chuck him with his finger as he passed out to his work.

"WHAT'S 'E USE OF PANTSES IF 'OU TAN'T PUT EDDS IN 'E POTTITS,

When the season's fruit had all been gathered it was found that the last half of the crop had "panned out all right" as compared with that marketed earlier, and it was decided to send the girls away to school for the winter instead of waiting until spring, when a new house was to be begun, and when their services would be much more needed by their mother. But instead of going to San Francisco they would only go to Sacramento, where there was a very good school under the charge of Professor Cook, and being nearer, they could be the sooner reached in case they should be taken sick.

Letting the girls go from her side was the hardest thing Martha Parsons had been called upon to do since she let John take her arms from around his neck and start on his long journey twelve years before, when they lived in the log house back in the States; but like other mothers she loved her children and was unwilling that her girls should grow up without every advantage possible to give them. Their opportunities for attending school had never been very good, and for a time after they had settled in their present home they were without any instruction except such as she could herself find time to give; and it was she, and not their father, who had suggested sending them away to school.

In fact he had at first opposed it; not because of the expense, but because he thought their mother needed their help, and because he did not like to be separated from them.

His own education was not so good as that of his wife, and he did not look as far into the future in planning for their welfare; or if so, he did not understand as well as she how completely an uneducated woman, married to a man who follows some kind of manual labor for a living, is cut off from all social and intellectual intercourse with her kind, and how barren of all that is beautiful and ennobling her life becomes.

It is bad enough to be tied to an endless round of household duties, even when the mind can take occasional rest and recreation in the perusal of a book or paper; when sufficient taste has been developed to induce the taking of some interest in passing events outside of one's own school district; but when, as is the case with thousands of women, no such taste has been cultivated in girlhood, and the seeming duties of wife and motherhood leave no time to acquire or devote to it at a later period, life becomes no more than an animal existence—becomes a stagnant pool, across whose waters no fresh breezes blow; on whose margin no fair flowers bloom; in whose depths is mirrored no silvery moon, no star of hope; and the spirit which should be prepared at the death of the body to mount to higher planes of thought and action, finds itself bound by chains forged on earth— chains which are not broken by the death of the body, but must still weigh down the soul in its efforts to mount upward into a higher and better and holier atmosphere.

This, Mrs. Parsons not only knew but felt, and she was determined that no sacrifice on her part should be spared, if necessary, that her girls might receive at least sufficient education to enable them to take and retain positions in society with the most intelligent of the men and women with whom they would be likely to come in contact in the humble lives, which she expected and was content that they should lead, as possible wives of the coming men who were to make the valleys and hillsides blossom as a garden, and laugh beneath their burdens of fruits and grains.

CHAPTER VIII. •

A COMFORTABLE HOME.

" Looks sort of showery like," said John Parsons, coming into the shanty the day before the girls were to go to Sacramento, and finding them and their mother with eyes which gave evidence of weeping, packing up their wardrobes preparatory to starting.

" I believe I shall cry myself if you wimin folks don't stop lookin' so sick like about the mouth. You don't want to see an old man like me cry, do you, now?

"Come, mother, cheer up. You know the girls 'll be in good hands, that 'll treat 'em well and let us know if anything happens 'em. 'Tain't fer very long any way ; only a few months, an' I was gone from you all more than six years, and if I hadn't a left you we wouldn't have had this ranch to-day, which will soon be the finest in the whole country ; worth all the hard work and sufferin' we've gone through.

" At least," he added, meditatively, "as well worth it as anything that poor folks gits is worth what it costs 'em.

" And here's Johnny, he's a houseful of himself, ain't you, Johnny ? You won't let mother and me git lonesome, will you ? "

But the youngster had caught the infection 'of tears, and his father's forced attempt at being jocular could not remove the feeling of coming loneliness that was casting its shadow before, and he stood still and looked silently at the preparations for the departure of his sisters with an expression on his face half of sadness and half of baby wisdom, as if he halted between sorrow for the coming loss of the girls and regret that his parents had no better judgment than to permit their going.

The morrow saw them depart. A few months later, a beautiful day in spring saw them return, improved in mind and appearance from the contact with those whose thoughts and deeds had sought, or were seeking, a different channel than that to which their own had been confined.

If John Parsons had been proud of his girls before, he was doubly so now ; for he could not fail to see that association with people of education had given an added grace to the body as well as to the mind. And, unwittingly perhaps, the young people of the neighborhood showed them a trifle more deference than was usually given to those of their own age and condition in life. This deference was in no sense obsequiousness ; it was but the natural expression of that respect which all, even those least ambitious of excellence, feel for others who are known to be striving to make themselves wiser and better.

Mrs. Parsons was not less pleased than her husband. She also noticed the esteem in which her girls were held by young and old ; and that while they aided as willingly and cheerfully in the household work, or in that of the vineyard and orchard, as ever they had done, they saw that the performing of manual labor alone was not all their duty to themselves or to society, but that the mind and the heart were entitled to consideration as well as the body.

As for Erastus, he felt a little shy when he welcomed the girls on their return. True, he kissed both Jennie and her sister, but somehow it was not the hearty kind of a smack with which he had bidden them good-bye, and he held Lucy's hand while he kissed her, instead of giving her a hug as he had done the morning they left.

As for Johnny, he was in ecstacies ; for had not the girls brought him a half-dozen things that he had been wanting and expecting on their return? Besides, he should have some one to help hunt hens' nests and look for ducks' eggs in the water of the creek, where they persisted in laying them if they were not watched and shut up every night.

A few days after the return of Jennie and Lucy the carpenters came and began work on the new house. All the spring and summer they were busy ; and when they left, there stood in front, and a little above the old shanty, which was henceforth to be used for fruit-packing and drying purposes, a two-story frame house with green blinds and a verandah on three sides ; the coolest, most comfortable, most hospitable looking house you would see in a month's travel.

And no more hospitable family ever lived than that which gathered about the table of John and Martha Parsons, and partook of the rich fruits and well cooked meats and vegetables with which it was daily spread.

No straggling miner, weary with travel and wanting rest and food, ever left their gate without at least a silent wish that blessings might descend and rest upon the household.

To ramble about the broad porch and through the open rooms, or to gather around a cheerful fire in the wide grate in the sitting-room, came both the young and the old of the neighborhood.

The occasional traveler through the country on business or pleasure heard of the Parsons' ranch ; its splendidly tilled acres ; its luscious fruits and its hospitable owners, miles before he reached it, and traveled an hour later that he might knock at its gates and obtain permission to spend the night beneath its broad roof.

5

The Parsons' cottage was not the only inviting-looking one in the neighborhood, however. Others who came with them had prospered also, and had built themselves houses, which, if not quite so pretentious looking, or so neat in their surroundings, as that of our particular friends, were at least as good as ordinary farm houses in the States.

Many new neighbors had also settled in the vicinity, some of whom brought little fortunes of two or three thousand dollars, and these had opened ranches and built houses both in the little valley above and in the larger one below, clear down to the river, upon whose banks, a two-hour's ride from our friends' cottage, a town had sprung up, where all needed supplies for the family were obtained, and from which was shipped by steamer the fruit and vegetables and poultry, designed either for the mining towns above or the larger markets of Sacramento and the sea-port.

School-houses had been built ; churches and Sunday schools organized ; the streams bridged, roads over the foot-hills made passable for wheeled vehicles, and altogether the neighborhood had taken on the airs and responsibilities of a community that wished to be regarded as respectable, law-abiding and conservative.

When Jennie and Lucy Parsons returned to school again it was to San Francisco instead of Sacramento, and both father and mother went with them to see that they were safely settled. They were not feeling the stings of poverty now, and could afford a little recreation, John had said, and they would attend the agricultural exhibition, display some of their own products, see the city, and mingle a little with the outside world ; all in addition to getting the girls fixed in a good boarding place.

Mrs. Parsons was not much inclined at first to make the trip. The journey across the plains, she said, was enough to last her her lifetime ; besides, if she went, Johnny would have to go, too, as there would be no one but Erastus remaining at home ; but a little persuasion from the other members of the family, and her natural desire to see how the girls were to be fixed, finally decided her to go, and arrangements were made accordingly.

As there would be no one to cook for Erastus, Mr. and Mrs. Ritchie asked him to make his home with them for the week during which Mr. and Mrs. Parsons were to be absent, but it was finally decided that he should remain at the place and keep "bachelor's hall" rather than leave the house alone.

Mrs. Parsons and the girls, therefore, baked an extra amount of bread and pies, boiled a quantity of beef to be eaten cold, and on Monday morning Erastus drove them all to the little town and saw them take the steamer for San Francisco.

"It seems unfair to leave Erastus all alone," said Mrs. Parsons, as they passed up the gang plank to the little steamer. "He ought to have gone instead of me; there was really no need of my going, and he would have enjoyed spending the week in the city, seeing the sights and attending the fair with the girls, very much."

"Oh, wall, never mind him this time," returned her husband. "He was down and saw the fair all alone last year, and it's your turn now anyway ; beside, he can come down any time almost, when we ain't too busy, and I wanted you to go. It'll do you good to get out a little. You've worked hard all your life, wife ; both of us hes, so fur es that's concerned, and now that we've got enough to be comfortable on, why, let's be comfortable ; that's what I say."

As for Erastus, there was a strange kind of feeling hanging over him as he mounted his seat in the spring wagon, in

5

which they had all ridden down to the steamer, and turned his horses' heads homeward. He had not expected to be lonesome when they were gone. On the contrary, he had anticipated having a pretty good time of it. Not that he did not love those with whom he had always lived, for he did love them all dearly, and, for aught he knew, equally ; and he expected to miss the girls, who were to be absent so long, very greatly indeed. But just for the week during which they were all to be gone, he should not get lonely he had thought. There was something rather enticing in the feeling of absolute personal liberty ; the thought that there was no one, not even the members of his own family, to throw any restraint on his actions or to break in upon his musings for a whole week. Besides, one or two of his particular friends among the young men of the neighborhood had promised to drop in and spend the night once or twice, and the cooking would be but just for a week. He had no doubt but he could do it about as well and as nicely as Aunt Martha or the girls. And why not? Had he not seen it done every day, and three times a day, ever since he could remember?

" It was a pity," he had told them when they had attempted to condole with him over the prospect of having to cook his own meals, " it was a pity if twenty-one years of observation couldn't enable a man to cook a decent meal of victuals," and they had said no more about it.

But now, as he turned his horses' heads away from the town and towards home, there suddenly came into his mind a picture of the house and its surroundings, and this was followed by the queer kind of a feeling of which I have spoken, and which he did not ever remember to have experienced before. He could see the white cottage with the green blinds all closed as an intimation to any passer-by that the family were absent. His old dog, which had come with him all the weary way across the plains, and had met and welcomed him before he reached the gate on his return from short absences, ever since they settled in the valley, would not do so to-day, for he was with him in the wagon.

The dog had become too old and stiff to take pleasure in following the wagon, as a general thing, and preferred remaining at home with the family when Erastus drove the fruit wagon to town, but when he saw preparations taking place for the trip to San Francisco, he had pricked up his ears with evident interest, and when the entire family came out to get into the wagon, old Bose was close at their heels, and neither coaxing nor threats could induce him to remain behind when the wagon started.

Evidently he thought that another journey across the plains was to be undertaken, and though much preferring to lie in the sunshine and keep the chickens out of the front yard, to any more laborious service, he would yet have undergone any torture rather than be separated from the family, and a look of pain and mortified pride came into his honest eyes when told by his master that he must remain and watch the house, and instead of obeying he crept close to their feet and looked piteously up as if begging them not to leave him behind, now that they were going away, never to return. And so they patted him on the head and called him "good fellow" and "brave old dog," and told him he should go if he wanted to. Then his whole demeanor changed. He gave a great bark and showed his teeth in an attempt to laugh, which can not be said to have been an entire failure, and endeavored in every possible way to express his thanks and assure them that he was the proudest and bravest dog on the Pacific coast, and ready and able for any service that might be required of him.

Then he started on ahead of the wagon, looking back
every few rods to make certain that he was leading in the
right direction; but before they were half way to town he
had dropped back to the side of the wagon ; then he fell into
the rear, and finally, looking back and seeing how nearly the
poor old fellow was tired out and how piteously he begged
with his great eyes not to be left behind, the wagon had
been brought to a stop and Erastus had got out and lifted
him in "with the rest of the family," where the girls and Mrs.
Parsons had had some difficulty in inducing him not to show
his gratitude in too demonstrative a manner. When they
descended from the wagon and went on board the steamer
he was so fearful of being left that he kept in front of them
and under their feet until several members of the family
came near falling over him; but when Erastus had said
"good-by " to them all and turning to go called to him to
follow, he went willingly, evidently satisfied that after all he
was mistaken and this was only a holiday excursion.

And now he sat upon the seat with Erastus in perfect
contentment and with a slight air of importance, as if he felt
a consciousness of having proven anew his devotion to those
he served, and had received a recognition of his value.

Ordinarily the presence of the dog might have prevented
any feeling of loneliness in the man had he been disposed
to it; but to-day, although he did feel that the dog was company in a sense, yet his very presence, being unusual, served
to remind him that the house to which they were returning
was desolate, and somehow things took on an unreal look,
and when he turned into the barnyard and saw the chickens
and turkeys scratching in the straw or wallowing in the dust,
he was not quite certain whether they were chickens and
turkeys or just the ghosts of those that were wont to scratch
and strut there before all other signs of life had ceased and

such an unnatural and oppressive stillness had settled down over the place.

After taking the gears from the horses and feeding them he started to the house to get his dinner. The thought of cooking his own meal was not quite so pleasant now as he had thought it might be, and he was half inclined to go without it or take a cold snack and wait until night before cooking anything. Then his appetite began to return, and he concluded to at least fry a couple of eggs and make a cup of coffee.

He entered the house by the back way, and stood for a moment looking about him. The fire was out in the kitchen stove; the chairs stood, stiff-backed and unsociable, against the wall; the room had lost its air of cheerfulness, and his footfall had a lonely kind of a sound as he stepped on the bare kitchen floor.

He threw open the door which opened onto the kitchen porch and let in a flood of sunshine. The old dog had preceded him to the house and taken his accustomed place upon the porch and was resting. When Erastus opened the door, the dog opened one eye sleepily and half raised his head as if to inquire if he was wanted for anything, and then stretched himself to sleep again. Everything seemed asleep or dead, and he cooked and ate his dinner with a feeling as if he was cut off from all human society by a thousand miles of desert.

When he had eaten his own meal he called Bose in and set down a plate with scraps on it for him to eat. Then, not knowing exactly what to do with the remainder of the food which he had cooked, he set that down for the dog also, and took his hat and went out to work.

Several times that afternoon he wondered to himself that he had never before noticed how still it was out there in the orchard, and whether it was always so perfectly quiet on the farm anyhow; and if the geese swimming about in the little pond made for them by means of a low dam across the creek, always moved around without making any more stir in the water; or if their occasional " honk " when one rose up in the water and flapped his wings was always pitched on that particular lonesome key.

As night approached he returned to the house and fed the teams and the pigs and the poultry and then went in and got his own supper. At dinner he had said to himself that he would wash all the dishes after supper, when he should have nothing else to do, but after eating his supper he found that he had no hot water, and decided to defer the job until morning; so he let Bose lick the grease off of them and stacked them up in the sink and went to bed an hour earlier than was his custom, without spending any time poring over his favorite authors, "with nobody to disturb him," as he had fancied himself doing when the idea of leaving him in sole charge of the house for a week had first been broached.

The next morning he arose, built a fire and put on water to heat and then went out to feed the animals. The old dog welcomed him with a wag of the tail, and even followed him to the gate, but went no further. He had not yet recovered from his yesterday's unusual exercise, and when Erastus returned from the barn he found him in his accustomed place on the porch with his head between his paws, from which he did not raise it, although he thumped on the floor of the porch with his tail as an intimation that he was resting well, but was ready for breakfast whenever it was convenient to his master.

On entering the kitchen, Erastus found the fire burned out; but he re-built it and cooked and ate breakfast, after

which he washed the accumulation of dirty dishes, and got
out to work about the middle of the forenoon. He ate a
cold lunch for dinner to save time, and for supper, a friend,
the son of a neighbor, was present, and they piled the dirty
dishes in a sink, where Mrs. Parsons found them, with others,
on her return from the trip to San Francisco.

CHAPTER IX.

A TRIP TO THE CITY.

Some difficulty was experienced by Mr. and Mrs. Parsons in finding a desirable place for their daughters in San Francisco. It had been determined that the girls should do their cooking and care for their rooms themselves, both because it was cheaper and because their parents thought it wiser that they should not forget, but learn still better, how to do that which in all probability they would be required to do all their lives.

Besides this, their health would be less likely to suffer if they took one study less and devoted a little of their time to household duties, such as they were accustomed to at home.

After a day spent in looking, a suite of two very nice rooms was found, at a reasonable rent, in a house occupied by one of the tutors in the school which they were to attend; and as the family appeared to be a pleasant one, the rooms were engaged, and arrangements having been made for the girls to take possession, the whole party proceeded to see the city and the displays of agricultural products and mechanical skill at the exposition.

The first day was largely spent in wandering through the department of fruits and vegetables. It was here that their own products were on exhibition, and they naturally felt more interest in this than in any other. They took no little pride in observing that few, if any, excelled them in the quality of the fruit and vegetables exhibited, although many had displays which embraced a larger variety of products. Next they looked at the poultry, and here Johnny discovered some bantam chickens and then some large white ducks, over which he went into ecstacies, and could with difficulty be induced to leave for the purpose of looking at anything else. When they had succeeded in getting him away and the rest of the family were engaged in examining other things, he slipped his hand out of that of his father and started back to have another look.

He was missed almost directly, of course ; in fact before he had got out of sight in the crowd ; but so eager was he to get another look at the ducks and chickens, and so fast did his short legs stir themselves, that his father was unable to overtake him, and only caught him when he paused before the coops which contained what, to him, was the principal things of value in the exposition.

Having recovered Johnny and impressed upon his mind the danger which he ran of getting lost or being carried off, if he did not keep close to the rest of the family, they spent some further time in looking at the collection of needlework and flowers, and then returned to their boarding place.

The next day, after a glance through the agricultural department to ascertain if their own articles were undisturbed, they went to another part of the building to see the machinery. John Parsons was not a machinist by trade, nor had he any special love for mechanism ; and yet he lingered long and with a kind of fascination over the machinery for mining purposes, and especially over the specimens of hydraulic mining pipe, which were on exhibition.

"I declare, Marty, he said to his wife, " I believe they could wash down Mount Shasta with that thing ; and if they thought there was gold enough there to pay 'em for doin' it, they wouldn't be long in tryin', I'll be bound. I heard yesterday that a company of Englishmen are at work now up in the hills above us some'ers, arranging for hydraulic works."

"Well," returned Mrs. Parsons, "there isn't any gold in our hills, so they won't be wanting to wash them down, anyway."

"No," replied her husband, thoughtfully, "there ain't any gold in the hills close about us, as anybody knows on."

The following day they went again through the fruit and vegetable exhibit, took another look at the fowls, and then Mr. Parsons left them to go alone through the domestic department, while he went again to examine the implements for hydraulic mining.

"Wonder if they will tear down old Shasta," he muttered to himself. "Wonder if they won't wash down all the mountains and fill up all the valleys?"

Returning to his family, they took another short turn about the building, and then returned to their lodgings. Laying off her things, Mrs. Parsons turned to her husband and said, a little reluctantly, for she did not like to seem the first to weary of sight-seeing :

"John, if you have seen enough of the exposition, let us go home. If not, I'll stop with the girls in their rooms until you are ready to go."

"You are not sick, are you, mother?" asked John, anxiously.

"No ; but I am tired, and I want to get back home and rest and see to things. Home is the best place for old folks, after all."

"Why, mother, we are not old folks yet, by a good deal. I feel 'bout as young and spry as I did 'fore I came to the coast ; but if you are tired and want to go home in the morning, I reckon this here youngster 'll be ready to go; eh, Johnny? seen enough of the city and want to get back to the ranch?" inquired the lad's father, drawing him between his knees.

"I'll go if you'll buy me the big white ducks, and the little banta chickens an' a jack-knife with four blades in it," piped the youngster, who thought he saw a chance to make a point in his mother's evident eagerness to go home.

"Tell you what I'll do, Johnny," replied his father, gravely, though with a twinkle in his eye, for he enjoyed the boy's "cuteness," as he called it; "tell you what I'll do. I don't believe mother would like you to have the jack-knife, but I'll split the difference and get you the ducks and the chickens.

Johnny, however, stood out. He wanted the jack-knife, and this looked like the time to strike for it. His father only laughed, and would not promise; but that night as Johnny was being put to bed in the strange house, the thought of home and the cozy cot where he slept at the foot of his parents' bed in the pleasant room that looked out, not upon dusty streets, but upon the vineyard and the orchard, came to him, and he crept up into his father's arms.

"Papa," he said, "I've 'cluded to 'cept your offer of the big white ducks and the little banta chickens, an' go home in the mornin' with you and mamma."

And so it was settled, "settled by a unanimous vote," as his father said, and he kissed his boy good night and went out and bought the ducks and chickens, and arranged to have them put on the steamer in the morning. If the girls had been allowed a voice in determining the going home of their parents the vote might not have been so "unanimous," for they dreaded being left alone in the great city; but knowing they could not detain their parents many days longer anyhow, and that their mother, as she said, was tired and wanted to get home and see to things, they interposed but few objections. ·So the next morning good-byes were said, with many injunctions on the part of the mother, and with kisses, and hugs, and tears, and promises to write often.

The girls did not go down to the wharf to see them off, for they feared the getting back to their rooms; and besides it was better to say good-bye where no stranger's eye could see the tears which they knew would come at the parting; and so chose to part at their lodging where they could have a good cry all to themselves just as soon as their parents and Johnny were out of sight.

Mr. Parsons left them all together at the last moment and went down to say good-bye to the professor in whose house they were, and toward whom he felt kindly, as he was to be in some degree the protector of his daughters during their stay at school. He found him in the sitting-room and shook his hand heartily.

"Good-bye, professor, good-bye," he said. "Take good care of the girls; mother and I think a heap of 'em. You'll find 'em good girls, too, professor, and smart; take after their mother the girls do; both of 'em. Well, good-bye; let us know if anything goes wrong with 'em anyway, and don't be afraid that their bills won't be paid. I'm good for anything I contract for, I reckon.

"Come mother. Good-bye girls. Come Johnny, we must hurry or we'll miss the boat," he called from the foot of the stairs, and a moment later they were gone and Jennie and Lucy were alone and having their cry out all by themselves.

"I don't know how we are to get home from town when we get there," said John Parsons as they neared the landing that afternoon. "Erastus wasn't to come for us until to-morrow night."

"Maybe some of the neighbors will be in," returned Mrs. Parsons. "Most likely they will; if not we will manage some way. It appears to me as if I had been gone an age and I must get home to-night if I have to walk. How do you suppose Erastus is getting along all alone?"

"Oh 'Ras is all right," replied her husband. "Don't you never fear for him. If he ain't capable of takin' care of himself ther ain't no young feller around these diggins as is. Likely he's a little lonesome, but he's gettin' on well enough, never you fear; and home'll seem all the cheerfuler for our havin' been gone. Thet's a pint I kin speak from experience on, fer I kept bach myself fer better'n six years, while you and the babies was back in the States; and I don't never want to do it agin."

As our friends had hoped, a neighbor was in town with his team, and gladly offered them a ride out. He could not carry the ducks and chickens, however, and they were left with other purchases for Mr. Parsons or Erastus to return for on the morrow.

It was nearly dark when, coming over the last rise, they looked down upon their own home, with the orchard and vineyard and the rosebush that clambered over the wide porch, fairly covering it with wreaths of bloom, and gave a sigh of relief at their journey ended.

Johnny was already asleep in his father's lap when the wagon drew up at the front gate, and Erastus, surprised at their unexpected return, came out to meet them.

"I am awfully glad you have got back," he said, as they entered the house; "but I had rather you had delayed another day, or at least until morning. I had promised myself to wash up all the dirty dishes in the house to-night if it

took all night to do it, and now you have come and caught
me with it undone and the house in a terrible fix."

Mrs. Parsons laughed.   "Didn't I tell you, John, that I
ought to come home and see to things," she said.   "A man
don't know anything about keeping house."

"Bet you can't guess what I've got," broke in Johnny,
now fully awakened and conscious of where he was.
"Three big white ducks and two little banty chickens, 'n
I'll bet my banty rooster can whip your big Shanghai!"

"Oh, ho! so you are a sporting man from the city, are
you?" returned Erastus, taking the lad up and hug-
ging him.   "Well, you wait until you get your chickens
home, and if they ain't too awfully fierce looking
I'll put up my old bob-tailed Shanghai against your
bantam rooster, and if the banta licks, you shall have them
both and I'll get you a jack-knife in the bargain, and if the
Shanghai whips I'll have the banta and the white ducks!
What do you say; will you do it?"

This was a poser to Johnny. He had been very certain
that his bantam could whip the big, clumsy Shanghai, whose
cowardice was proverbial among the members of the family,
and who was only kept for the ridiculous appearance which
he cut with his long legs and tailless body, for which latter
old Bose was generally held accountable, but the ready assurance with which Erastus offered to back "old Bob," as they
called the Shanghai, against the bantam, aroused a fear of
the result; and much as he coveted the jack-knife, he feared
to risk losing the bantam and the ducks, and no amount of
bantering could induce him to agree to the wager. He had
a better scheme in his head. He waited until the chickens
were turned loose in the barnyard, and when he had actually
seen the Shanghai in full retreat before the vicious attack

which the bantam made upon him, he claimed the jack-knife and refused to remember that he had not accepted the offered wager.

The vacation between the fall and winter terms of school was so short that Jennie and Lucy did not attempt to spend it at home, but remained in San Francisco, and thus were absent fully six months without seeing any member of their family. They wrote every week, however, and often more frequently, and were so well pleased with their school, and the family in whose house they were was so kind, that those at home had no especial anxiety about them. They were kept supplied with money, and occasional boxes of home-baked pies and cakes, or a jar of fresh sweet butter was sent them by steamer, and every few days Erastus or Mrs. Parsons wrote them, thus keeping them fully advised as to all that was going on upon the ranch or among the young people in the neighborhood.

Their father did not write—he had never been much accustomed to write letters until he left the States and went to the mines; and here his opportunities for sending letters had been so few as to prevent frequent exercise of what little talent he possessed in that direction, so that now he felt no inclination to apply his stiffened fingers to the use of the pen, but was content to hear read the letters received weekly, and with sending messages of love in those of Erastus and his wife; but as the time approached for the return of the girls for the long vacation he was eager for their coming, and was at the landing waiting for them more than an hour before the steamer was due; and when she came, hurried on board the instant the gang-plank was lowered.

" How'd do, Jennie ; how'd do, Lucy; glad you're back again. Give your old father a hug;" and he gathered them in his arms and put his bearded face down to theirs for a kiss, and then turned away and drew the back of his hand across his eyes and led them on shore and helped them into the spring wagon.

"Mother'll be monstrous glad to see you," he said, as they drove homeward; "and so'll Erastus and Johnny. An' the young folks in the neighborhood are arrangin' for a picnic an' a dance in the woods for one day next week, a purpose so you can all see each other agin.

"'Spect the young fellows are mighty anxious to have you back in the neighborhood, bein' there ain't hardly girls enough to go round anyway. I was just a-tellin' mother only yesterday that if you girls hadn't got your heads set on goin' to school another year, I'd a heap ruther you stayed to home and helped her to make the house cheery like, but if you want to go back I ain't a-goin' to 'bject. I reckon 'Rastus will be gittin' married 'fore long. An' maybe he'll bring his wife home; I'm sure there's room enough in the cottage fer all of us, even ef we were all to home, and I s'pose we can't always keep you girls. Even ef you was to leave school for good, some of the young fellows would be coaxin' you away from us."

"Oh, no, pa; I am sure neither Lucy nor I have any thoughts of getting married, have we, Lucy?" laughed her sister.

"You don't mean to say 'Ras is in love with any of the girls though, do you?" she continued. "I wonder who it can be. Funny, isn't it; but I never thought that he could ever get married, had you, Lucy?"

Lucy said she had never thought of it, though of course Erastus would marry some time, she supposed; nearly everybody did.

Then she tried to talk of something else, but Jennie insisted on knowing who it was that Erastus was courting.

"Oh I don't know as anybody in particular," her father replied, "only he's ridin' around with the neighbors' girls some, and it's natural he should marry afore many years. He is a man now, and he knows we are a savin' money to buy him a ranch with after a spell."

"It will be mighty lonesome," he added, "if he should marry and leave mother and me; 'specially if you girls should go too."

The girls both protested that they never meant to marry; had not thought of such a thing.

"You must not talk so, pa," said Lucy, "because we are never going to leave you; but just as soon as we get through school will come home and stay always with you and mother."

Jennie noticed that her sister's voice had a little suspicion of tears in it when she said this, and that she turned her head and looked the other way when she spoke, but forgot it immediately in wondering if it were true that 'Ras really had any one picked out to marry, and if so, whom? She thought over all the girls in the neighborhood, and finally decided that it was Mary Jones. Mary, she knew, had always liked Erastus. She liked Mary herself, and the two had been together a great deal, and if Erastus was going to marry anybody she hoped it would be Mary.

"There's Johnny coming to meet us," said John, Sen., as they came over the hill and struck the little stretch of level ground in front of the cottage.

"You bet he's got a good eye for seein' things. 'Spect he's been watchin' for us for an hour. He thinks a heap of his dad, don't you, Johnny?" he said, as he pulled up the

0

ponies, and reaching down, lifted the youngster into the wagon "where they could get at him," as the girls said; and straightway they began to hug and kiss him, keeping it up until he squirmed away from them, and getting in between his father's knees, insisted on being allowed to drive.

Mrs. Parsons was at the gate waiting to welcome her girls back with a smile and a kiss. The old dog frisked about and barked as if he were still a puppy, fairly knocking Johnny down and upsetting one of the traveling baskets which had been set out preparatory to driving the wagon to the barn. Johnny would have cried, ordinarily, at such rough usage, but now it would have appeared out of place amidst the general rejoicing, and so instead of getting angry or crying, he laughed and tried to mount and ride old Bose as he followed the girls and their mother into the house. Erastus was at work in the fields when the party arrived, but seeing the wagon drive up, he came in immediately. He was, as Mr. Parsons had said, a man now, nearly six feet tall and with a manly air that had just a shade of embarrassment in it as he kissed the girls in turn and asked after their health.

Lucy was a little shy of his caress, and turned her cheek instead of putting up her lips to receive the salute; but Jennie greeted him with the old time smack and even repeated it twice before she released him. Then she broke out with:

"Oh! 'Ras, father says you're thinking of getting married. I don't believe it, though. Say, is it so? Are you going to marry Mary Jones? 'Cause I know Mary always liked you, though she would never own it. Say, 'Ras, is it really true?"

Poor 'Ras! The blood rushed into his cheeks, and gave them a tinge of red beneath the brown tan, and he glanced at

Lucy, and moved away toward the porch, and then he looked a little foolish and finally vexed; and then the idea appeared to strike him as being ludicrous somehow, and he laughed.

"You know better than that, Jen," he said; "I never cared for Mary Jones, or any other of the girls; and, besides, Mary is going to be married to Joe Bronson, week after next, and we are all invited to the wedding."

"Oh, 'Ras, is that so? Why didn't you write us about it?" said Lucy, suddenly turning and coming back. And then both girls began:

"Where are they to be married?"

"At Mrs. Jones', I suppose."

"We'll go, of course."

"Wonder what Mary will be married in?"

"Are they going on a wedding tour?"

"What day next week is it to be?"

"Who is going to marry them?"

"Bet I wouldn't have old Mr. Peters marry me; he is the homeliest man I ever saw. Be just like him to forget their names and marry Mary to somebody else."

"Who's going to stand up with them?"

"Will it be at night or in the morning?"

"Where are they going to live?"

"Has Joe got a ranch of his own?"

"Wonder how Joe managed it, anyway; he used to be awfully bashful."

And a dozen other questions, without waiting for an answer.

"Come, girls; come Erastus, dinner's all ready, and your father's coming in from the barn," called Mrs. Parsons from the kitchen. "Come and let's see how it will seem, to all eat together once more."

As they passed out ahead of him, and all the time as they sat at dinner, Erastus kept thinking how beautiful Lucy had grown. He had never noticed it before, but it seemed to him now that Jennie really looked plain beside her sister.

CHAPTER X.

A SURPRISED ENGLISHMAN.

"Hi say! 'Ello, the 'ouse!

"Would you be kind enough to haccommodate us with a night's hentertainment?"

John Parsons was resting in his arm chair, with Lucy and Johnny near by upon the porch, when his ears were thus saluted. There was something in the tone of voice in which the words were uttered, or in the presence of the speaker as he turned and saw him, which on the instant prompted a thought of denying the request. Perhaps it was that he was not in his usual cheerful mood.

For some time after his return from San Francisco, where he had heard the system of hydraulic mining described, and accidentally learned that arrangements were being made by a company to begin work somewhere in the adjoining county above him, there had been days when he had been gravely silent, if not moody; but as several weeks passed and he heard nothing more regarding it, this feeling had worn off, and he had resumed his usual jovial look and bearing. But only that morning while at the Landing he had learned that the supplies for the mine were being sent up, and that the flume which was to furnish the water was already under way, and at once all his moodiness returned, and all that afternoon he had been silent and thoughtful; not even Johnny, who was his constant companion when about the ranch, being able to draw him into conversation or bring a smile to his face.

The company which owned the mine, so he had been told,

was composed, in part at least, of Englishmen; and although
he had no prejudice against the English, and had once in
his own mining days worked in partnership with an Englishman, and had now no reason to suppose that the owner of
the voice which he heard asking for a night's lodging had
any connection with the company upon whose mining operations he was meditating so gloomily, yet the two facts, that
Englishmen were interested in the enterprise, and that the
party addressing him was an Englishman, somehow formed
a connection in his mind and tempted him to do what he
never yet had done—refuse to extend the hospitalities of his
house to strangers in need of a night's lodging.

As quickly as it came however this thought was dismissed,
and he advanced to meet and welcome the strangers.

"I reckon you kin stay, strangers; an' welcome to such
as we have. Maybe it isn't as good as ye have seen, but
then agin you may see wus if you are goin' fur up into the
mountains. Jest ride yer animals 'round the back way and
they'll be seed to," and he opened the front gate before
which the strangers were sitting upon their horses and led
the way to the gate opening into the barn lot.

"Light down," he said, "an' come in."

There were three men in the party; the one who had
acted as spokesman being, as his speech indicated, an Englishman, and one of the capitalists who were interested in
the hydraulic mining operations of which Mr. Parsons had
recently heard. He had come out from England to see for
himself and his English partners if things were being properly managed, and to get a better knowledge of the actual
value of the claims held by the company.

He had stopped in New York to consult with those who
were furnishing the other half of the capital; and the son of
one of these capitalists had come on with him, not exactly

"'OW DO YOU DO? HI 'OPE HI SEE YOU WELL.

as a representative of any portion of the stockholders there, for they already had one of their number in charge at the mines, but for the purpose of seeing the world and learning something of business. His name was James Annelsey.

The third member of the little party was Silas Ensign, a workman in the employ of the Hydraulic Mining company, who had been sent down to Sacramento to obtain some bit of machinery needed, or to carry an order for supplies, and who had chanced to meet with and was now guiding his companions to the mines.

"Hi say, but this is a 'orrid dusty country," remarked Mr. Jobbers as he alighted from his saddle. "Hensign, you see to the 'orses, an' then you can come in halso," he added as he and Annelsey turned to follow Mr. Parsons who led the way to the pump, where an opportunity was given them to wash, after which they were requested to enter the sitting-room and make themselves at home while their host returned to assist Ensign in caring for the animals, Erastus not being present at the moment.

When Mr. Parsons returned with Ensign, and the two were washing at the pump, Erastus joined them, and together the three entered the room to which Mr. Jobbers and Annelsey had already preceded them.

"This is Mr. Hemmingway, strangers; a member of my family," said Mr. Parsons, introducing Erastus.

"'Ow do you do, Mr. 'Emmingway," said Mr. Jobbers, extending a red and rather fleshy hand, speaking deliberately and with a slight accent upon the first and last word of each sentence, "'ow do you do? Hi 'ope Hi see you well."

Erastus assured him that he was in good health and expressed the hope that their guests were not too greatly worried with the jaunt over the hills.

With Mr. Annelsey he shook hands cordially as he had done with Ensign when meeting him at the well.

In a few moments Mr. Parsons, who had left the room after introducing Erastus, returned and invited the party out to supper.

"This is my wife, and these are my daughters," he said as the gentlemen entered the room where the table was spread.

"'Ow do you do, ladies? Hi ope Hi see you well." And Mr. Jobbers, who appeared to have one formal phrase for the expression of his pleasure at meeting strangers, bowed low in recognition of the introduction.

The younger men bowed, also. Ensign once, with a respectful glance about the circle, Annelsey to each of the ladies in turn and with a slightly affected air and his right hand upon his heart. He was a little surprised, evidently, as was also Mr. Jobbers, at the degree of ease and general air of refinement that characterized the young ladies, and desired to make a good impression.

"Hi, say, you 'ave a huncommonly fine place 'ere," remarked the Englishman, after they were seated at the table, "Hit is wonderful 'ow you Hamericans do things. Great henterprise, that of building a railroad hacross the continent. Hi don't wonder you people hare proud of your country, sir. 'Ow long, may I hask, since you hopened this place, sir?"

"It's eight years last fall since we first camped on this here spot," returned Mr. Parsons, "and mighty rough campin' it was, too. Mother there, 'n' the girls slept in the wagon for nigh onto four weeks, while me and 'Rastus took the ground fer it until the shanty was up and the roof on. We see some purty hard times for the first few years, but, as you say, we hev made a good bit of improvement since then."

"HI DECLARE; HIF THAT DON'T BEAT HANYTHING I'VE SEEN YET. HI DON'T SE 'OW YOU COULD GET
AHEAD WITHOUT CAPITAL TO START HON."

" Hi should say so. And you 'ave done it hall yourselves, without capital?"

" Yes, without any capital 'ceptin' a pair of hosses and a wagon, that brung mother and the girls across the plains."

" Hi declare; hif that don't beat hanything I've seen yet. Hi don't se 'ow you could get ahead without capital to start hon."

"We had the land to commence with, and we had good health ginerly; an' we had willin' hearts," replied the host; "an' I am of the opinion that that is about all the capital a man an' a woman needs to start on. We've opened two places afore this, besides addin' to the one we begun on, and have been driv' off of 'em all; an' I don't see what anybody needs more than an ekil chance with everybody else. I'm sure that's all the men that work for a livin' are askin'."

" Hi say. But there is many a man in Hingland that would be glad of the hopportunity to make 'im a 'ome like this. Hi know several good, honest farmers that could raise money enough to make the trip, and when I go back I shall hadvise 'em to come to Hamerica, and to California."

During the meal the conversation was principally between Mr. Jobbers and Mr. Parsons, with an occasional word from Mrs. Parsons and Erastus.

Ensign made no effort to take part in it, but devoted his attention strictly to the business of satisfying his appetite, unless an occasional glance at the young ladies may be considered an interruption.

Annelsey made several attempts to enter the conversation, addressing his remarks principally in the direction of Lucy, who sat opposite to him, but, although too sensible to be really bashful in the presence of strangers, she was not sufficiently self-confident to engage in a lengthy conversation in the presence of so many gentlemen whom she had

never before met, and so caused Annelsey to fail in his
efforts to be especially entertaining.   But after supper was
over and the girls had removed the dishes, and in company
with their mother joined the gentlemen in the sitting-room,
they found it much more easy to talk together.

Mr. Jobbers had communicated the fact of his having
an interest in the hydraulic mining company to their father,
who was listening very earnestly and attentively to what he
was saying regarding the size of their claim, the length of
the flume and the power which they expected to obtain from
so great a fall. This gave the young people an opportunity
of chatting among themselves in a less formal manner than
they could have done were their elders taking part in the
conversation.

Annelsey, having just arrived on the coast, was full of
the incidents of the journey, which he had made by rail;
and his references thereto naturally called up, on the part of
the others remembrances of their own far more tedious
journey, and soon they felt quite at ease in each other's company.

Then, too, Annelsey had spent a week in San Francisco,
and hearing that the girls were but just returned from there,
found fresh food for conversation in the objects of interest
in that city. At first the custom to which he had been bred,
of looking upon a workman as an inferior had shown itself
in his treatment of Ensign, who was but an employe of the
company in which his father was a large stockholder, but
the perfect equality with which he was received by the
family of intelligent people beneath whose roof they were,
together with the fact that Ensign evidently had himself no
thought that he was not socially the equal of any, soon
forced the young New Yorker to treat him as an equal; and
when the time came for retiring, the young people, with a

single exception, felt that they had passed a pleasant evening.

That one exception was Erastus.

He had noticed that Annelsey appeared especially anxious to make an impression upon Lucy; and without stopping to ask himself the reason for it, was yet conscious that his evening had been spoiled thereby.

" Good-morning, ladies; Hi 'ope I see you well this morning.

It was Mr. Jobbers who had arisen and descended to the dining-room on the morning following the incidents just related.

" Quite well, thank you," replied Mrs. Parsons. " I hope you had a good night's rest."

" Hi never slept better in my life. Riding 'orseback hover the 'ills gives one a happetite for sleep. And I'm sure no one ever 'ad better hopportunities for enjoying it than your 'ospitality furnished us," he added, gallantly.

Seeing that breakfast was not yet ready, he passed out on-to the porch, and plucking a magnificent rose from the bush that climbed over and shaded the whole side of the house, buried his nose several times in its perfumed leaves, and then carelessly throwing it down as he might have done the rind of an orange from which he had sucked the juice, sauntered slowly off the porch, and putting his thumbs in the armholes of his vest, inflated his lungs with the pure, cool air of the morning; meanwhile looking out across the little valley with an air of entire satisfaction with himself and the world.

" Good-morning, Mr. Jobbers," said Mr. Parsons, coming around the house from the rear. " Takin' in a supply of California air, I see. Reckon you don't have such pure air in London."

" 'Ope, I see you well, sir. No, sir, the hatmosphere in London is 'orridly beastly at times, but most of us manage to take a run into the country for a change.and a little 'shooting, once or twice a year; that is, them that can hafford it. Hof course the laboring folks can't hafford it, and what I wonder is that they don't hall leave Hingland and come to Hamerica, where they could get pure hair and 'omes for their families. This is a great country for folks that 'as to labor, sir; great country."

At this point of their conversation they were joined by all three of the young men, who had risen before Mr. Jobbers and gone out to look at the animals and prepare them for the day's journey. Annelsey had at first ordered Ensign to rub down the horses for the party, but had been told in reply that he must take care of his own animal if he expected it done. He was the employe of the company and on the company's business, and not the body servant of those whom he guided to the mines, Ensign had told him. He would rub down Mr. Jobbers' horse as a matter of courtesy to an older man, but as for Annelsey, he was able to care for his own animal, and could do it or leave it undone as he chose. Accordingly the New Yorker had given such care to the animal which he rode as served to smooth his coat, and had fed him from the bin of oats which Erastus had shown them, and then had returned to the house. But seeing no opportunity of speaking to either of the young ladies, they being busy with the morning duties, he had remained for a moment in the sitting-room and then gone out to the vineyard, returning as he saw the others coming toward the house as if in anticipation of breakfast.

Each of the young men respectfully bid the elder ones good morning, to which John Parsons replied with a hearty

"Good morning, boys, good morning."

Mr. Jobbers "'oped he saw them well."

Being summoned to breakfast they entered the house, and gathered about the table.

Ensign and Annelsey, both of whom were feeling a little out of humor over their recent tilt about the care of the horses, had their good nature fully restored in the presence of the young ladies, who greeted them with smiles and pleasant "good mornings."

Had there been no ladies present it is possible that the meal of which they were partaking might have had the same effect. The most delicious coffee; fresh laid eggs with ham; the lightest of bread; the mealiest of potatoes, and such fruit as California alone can produce, went to make up a repast which only required the clear bracing air of the climate to render a feast fit for any occasion and any company.

Mr. Jobbers was profuse in his compliments. He had dined with the Honorable Mr. So-and-so, and been present at the public banquet of the Lord Mayor of London, but he had never eaten a meal "more satisfying to the happetite" than the one before him; and he ended his remarks on that subject, as he frequently did, with the assertion that on his return to England he should advise all the farmers whom he saw to emigrate at once to California.

Breakfast over, Ensign went immediately out and brought around his own horse and that of Mr. Jobbers. Annelsey lingered behind, anxious for a few words with Lucy, and hoping that Ensign would bring his animal with the others. But in this he was disappointed, as Ensign led out two only; and but that Erastus, not willing to appear lacking in courtesy to their guests led out the remaining animal, he would have found himself behind at the starting.

Hitching the horses at the front gate, Ensign returned to the house to thank the family for their hospitality. Annelsey

7

attempted to prevent this by hastening his own departure and that of Mr. Jobbers, but Ensign had too clear a perception of what was due their host to leave without a word of thanks for hospitalities enjoyed, and left his companions—who were ignorant of the direction to be taken—to await him at the gate while he paid his respects to the family.

He did not offer to pay, as Mr. Jobbers and Mr. Annelsey had done, for he knew the customs of the people and that pay was neither expected nor desired; but he thanked Mr. and Mrs. Parsons for their kindness and gave expression to a desire to be of service to the family in return—should opportunity offer.

Then, bidding all good-bye, he rejoined his companions, and together the three resumed their journey.

CHAPTER XI.

THE PICNIC.

The picnic which John Parsons had told the girls was being gotten up for their home coming by the young people of the neighborhood, was held a week later than the events recorded in our last chapter. The place selected for the day's enjoyment was a beautiful grove on the banks of a little lake that lay nestled in the bosom of the hills some seven or eight miles from the Parsons cottage.

Early in the morning the young people started for the rendezvous. Most were on horseback, for among the hills the ladies, almost as much as the men, were accustomed to the saddle. In the spring wagons, with those who chose this mode of conveyance was placed the cakes and roasted fowls, with bread and butter and fruits, which were to furnish the repast.

Among those who elected to go on horseback were Jennie and Lucy Parsons and Erastus Hemmingway.

By a previous understanding a dozen of the young people of both sexes met at the Parsons cottage, from whence they started together. These were joined on the way by others, making a gay and jolly cavalcade that waked the echoes in the foot-hills with their merry laughter and started the quails from their hiding places in the wild oats. Some of the more venturesome ran races across the bits of level ground between the hills. Now and then a couple would drop behind their companions and exchange a look or word of endearment, for it is not to be supposed that in California, more than else-

where, thirty young people—young men and young women
—could come together, and that among them all there should
be none whose hearts had been touched by the boy with the
bow and arrows.

In the main, however, they held their ranks well enough
to be able to exchange merry jokes and witty repartee. Now
they sang a verse of some song in concert; now bantered
each other with accusations of loneliness because of the absence of some lad or maiden who perchance had found
another partner for the day, or been detained at home by
some untoward circumstance.

In all this merriment Jennie and Lucy Parsons took full
part and share. Usually Jennie was more sedate and quiet
than her sister, but to-day was the first time for months that
she had been on horseback among the hills, and the pent-up
gaiety of her nature found outlet, and she rivaled them all
in merry speech and reckless riding.

Arriving at the grove they found a platform erected for
dancing and two musicians ready with their violins. Very
soon others who were to be of the party, but who were later
in starting or had come a greater distance, began to arrive,
and soon a half hundred gaily dressed, light-hearted young
people were on the ground.

Then the violins were tuned up and dancing began.

When tired of dancing they sat in the shade of the live
oaks and laughed and chatted, or wandered away two and
two, and spoke low, and looked love, and maybe planned for
a future to be spent in each other's society. Or they rowed
on the lake, six or eight in one light skiff that had but a
single pair of oars, and sunk so low with their weight that
when some one among their number moved, it dipped almost
to the water's edge, causing screams, half of fright and half
of pure joyousness, to issue from lips as red and ripe as red

raspberries in July, and which were a temptation as hard to be resisted by those young men as are the berries to boys who gaze at them through a crack in the enclosure within which they grow and ripen in the sun.

And if, sometimes, the temptation was too great to be overcome, and some bold youth took advantage of the helplessness of a maiden, who feared, or thought that she feared, to struggle, lest she overturn the boat, and preferred being kissed to getting wet, why, what business is it of mine, or of yours, my dear sirs? There are other lips as red and ripe awaiting to be kissed, and there are other lakes and other boats with single oars, and other sunny days and starry nights to come. Then why should we linger over this picture of a golden day that is past; of red lips and ripened fruit that were not for us; that were gathered by others on this beautiful day in spring, away off in the foot-hills of California?

When the sun became too fierce in its reflection from the calm waters of the lake, they gathered themselves in little knots, all near together, and the provisions were brought from the spring wagons, and spread upon clean linen cloths on the ground, and they ate, and drank lightly of their native wines, and laughed and called back and forth, and twittered just as did the birds that had taken shelter from the sun in the leaves above them; and were as happy and as free from care.

While they were thus engaged there approached two men; strangers they at first appeared to all. Each carried a fishing pole and basket. The younger one was dressed in a very handsome suit, resembling those seen in pictures of English life and supposed to be worn only by very wealthy gentlemen when engaged in hunting or fishing.

The other was a much older man, dressed in the garb of

a citizen of the locality; and might have been either a miner
or a farmer; and was, in fact, an employé of the Hydraulic
Mining Company, for whom Mr. Annelsey—for the young
man in the English hunting suit was none other than he—
had obtained leave of absence that he might accompany
himself as guide and game carrier.

Perhaps young Annelsey had come simply for a day's
fishing in the lake.   Many a man had gone farther with less
sure promise of being rewarded for his labor by the casting
of a hook and line.   Perhaps he had learned from some
casually dropped sentence of Erastus, or one of the girls,
during the evening passed in their father's cottage, that a
picnic was on the tapis, and the day and the spot where it
was to be.   Perhaps he had learned from them only the fact
that one was to be held on a fixed day, and by inquiry had
ascertained where the most pleasant spot for holding such
gatherings was, and had taken the risk and now found himself rewarded by finding those whom he sought.   Perhaps
—but why assign a reason at all for his coming.

He had leisure. He could come and go as it pleased
him, and he had pleased to make a trip to the lake of
which he had heard, and to take with him the fishing tackle
which he had brought from New York. And he had found
on the banks of the lake a company of young people, two
or three of whom he had met before; what more natural
than that he should join them, and if made welcome, spend
the afternoon in their company?

He advanced toward the group of which our friends
formed a part; greeted the young ladies in a gay manner
and shook hands very cordially with Erastus, and was made
welcome and bidden to "eat, drink and be merry, for he was
a long way from home and would regret it if he ever showed
any backwardness in accepting invitations to eat while

among the foot-hills and breathing the appetite-creating atmosphere of California."

When the lunch was eaten he was introduced to others and invited to take part in the dance; for in the country there is less formality than in the city, and in new countries less than in old ones; and here every well appearing stranger was treated as a friend and introduced freely to all, and by all—a confidence less frequently betrayed than might be expected by those who do not know that hearts not altogether hardened are always prompted to exhibit whatever quality of honor or goodness those whom they respect credit them with.

It may be, too, that a knowledge that a betrayal of such confidences generally met a punishment as swift as it was severe, had a restraining influence upon those who were by nature bad.

Be these things as they may, those who are themselves free from guile, ever were, and ever will be slow to suspect evil of others, and consequently ready to receive and treat as friends all who have the outward appearance of respectability and goodness. And what company of young ladies ever failed to look with favor, more or less skillfully concealed, upon the entrance into their circle of a young gentleman whose appearance gave promise that he would at least be an agreeable partner for their festivities. And if the gentlemen were at all disposed to be jealous of one whose wealth or knowledge of the world and the ways of polite society, might give him an advantage over them in the eyes of their lady-loves, they still could not act the part of boors and thus themselves prove his superiority over them.

And so Annelsey's way to mingle freely with all was made easy, and right well he improved it. He danced not only with Lucy and Jennie Parsons, but with a dozen others; but he sought Lucy for a partner oftenest, and when they went for another sail upon the lake he was still at her side, and would have been pleased to have rowed with her alone, but he was unaccustomed to the use of the oars, besides which he feared that she might refuse him, and so contented himself with keeping as near to her as possible in a boat in which were a half-dozen others.

Erastus noticed Annelsey's evident preference for Lucy, and was ill at ease.

Whether it were true or not, he believed that the New Yorker had learned of the picnic and came purposely to renew his acquaintance with her; and although he did not acknowledge to himself that he loved Lucy other than as a sister, he yet did not like this stranger with his stylish clothes, his gold watch and chain, and other evidences of wealth and position, to be crowding in between them; and when he saw, or thought he saw, that Lucy was pleased with the attention shown her by his rival, as he now began to regard him, he became actually jealous, and half wished that the train which had brought Annelsey from the States had plunged down one of the precipices he was so fond of mentioning as among the dangers he had escaped.

Then realizing the awfulness of the thought, he amended it to wishing Annelsey might fall into the water and wet the plush hunting suit which made him so noticeable among his more plainly dressed fellows.

"As if we had never seen any grand scenery," he said, mentally, when Annelsey was describing some of the scenes on the line of the road which he had passed over. And then he tried to make himself believe that Annelsey would not have known that the scenery was grand and wonderful if somebody had not pointed it out to him.

Then again he pictured his rival as shrinking back and covering his eyes lest his head be turned at sight of this magnificent scenery—this almost bottomless abyss, upon the edge of which his train wound, by describing which he fancied the New Yorker was seeking to draw attention to himself. He tried, however, not to show that he objected to Annelsey's presence, or attention to Lucy, by avoiding her and paying court to Julia Ennis, the daughter of a neighbor who had lately come among them.

Neither was Erastus the only one who was inclined to look upon the stranger as an interloper, for Lucy Parsons was a favorite with the young men of the neighborhood. Her fresh young face and lively mien, as well as her kindly nature, attracted to her all with whom she came in contact. And to-day, dressed all in white except a bit of color at her throat, with her clear complexion rendered more beautiful by the few months of comparative close confinement at school, showing yet more plainly in contrast with the other girls, whose cheeks and arms were tanned by exposure to the wind and sun and in the labor of the household, and maybe the vineyard, it is no wonder that she attracted universal homage, and that more than one of the little company wished that Annelsey would return to the city whence he came and leave them to contend among themselves for the favor of the most beautiful maiden in all the circle of their acquaintance.

When the party broke up and the revelers were about to mount their horses for the homeward ride, Erastus noticed Annelsey press close to Lucy and speak to her in a low tone. He also saw Lucy blush, but could only judge from Annelsey's demeanor that Lucy's reply to his words, whatever they were, had not been unpleasant to him.

When they were mounted and on the point of starting, some one remarked to Mr. Annelsey that if he was intending to return to the mining camp that night he would have to ride late ; to which he replied that he should camp on the spot where they were and should spend another day, possibly several of them, in fishing and hunting in the vicinity.

The homeward ride of the merry-makers was made at such paces as suited the fancy of each. A dozen of the young people only, retained each other's company during the entire distance. The others lagged behind, and then dropped off into couples, and so rode homeward over the dusky hills in the twilight—a twilight which was first golden and then purple, gradually changing into darkness not so great as to make traveling dangerous or difficult, but dark enough to set the crickets to chirping ; dark enough to hide the blush of a maiden whose lover was tempted to tell again the story first told in the garden of Eden, and retold by every generation since; too dark to enable them to see the night birds that called to each other from the roadside until frightened into taking wing by the near approach of the riders.

CHAPTER XII.

COURTSHIP.

The second day after the picnic Mr. Annelsey called at the Parsons cottage, and was met at the door by Lucy and invited into the sitting-room. Her demeanor showed clearly that his coming was not unexpected, but whether it caused her more pleasure than embarrassment would not have been so easy to determine.

Mr. Annelsey himself had no doubt about it, however. Had she not told him on parting at the lake that he might call, and was she not blushing and embarrassed now ? What better proof could he desire that she was pleased and flattered by his attentions ?

None, he thought, and he was correspondingly elated and became really entertaining in relating his experience in camping at the lake and at the mine—an experience which to him possessed all the pleasure of novelty.

Lucy had intended to tell her mother and Jennie that Mr. Annelsey had asked permission to call on her, but had not found courage to do so, and not knowing at what time to expect his coming, had deferred speaking of it, hoping some opportunity would arise without herself having to introduce the subject.

But although the family did not know that he had requested permission to call, it is probable that they were not greatly surprised at seeing him. They knew him to be in the neighborhood, and perhaps others besides Erastus sus-

pected that his appearance at the picnic was not purely acci-
dental.

Although the young man had called especially to see
Lucy, Jennie was perhaps more pleased at his coming than
her sister, or than any other member of the family. She
liked him exactly as she liked other young men who were
pleasant company, and hoped he would remain in the vicinity
and take part in their occasional pastimes during the summer ; and she had none of Lucy's feelings of being made
conspicuous by having been selected as an object of especial
attention by him.

As for their mother, she saw nothing objectionable in the
young man. He was gentlemanly, and appeared to her
to be as moral as other young men; and what mother was
ever offended that a young man of wealth and standing in
society saw attractions in her daughter which he did not
see in the daughters of others ?

Mr. Annelsey was given a cordial invitation to remain to
tea ; an invitation which he was not slow in accepting, and
so met Mr. Parsons and Erastus, both of whom treated
him courteously, though the greeting of the younger man
was certainly not excessive in its cordiality; and who, as
soon as the meal was over, made an excuse to leave the
house and did not return until Annelsey had departed.

On the other hand, Mr. Parsons was pleased that he had
called, and showed it. He wanted to see him. He wanted
to learn how the work at the mine was getting on and how
soon they would probably be ready to turn on the water and
begin washing down the hills, and his manner was such as to
still further imbue Annelsey with the idea that he was held in
high favor and that Lucy and her parents felt honored by
his attentions.

In reply to Mr. Parsons' questions he told him that the

work on the flume which was to conduct the water to the reservoir was progressing rapidly—a portion of it over two miles long having been completed; that the remaining mile would be finished by the time the tunnel and the sluice for carrying away the débris and saving the gold would be ready, which would probably be in about three months, and that then they would be ready for active operations.

Not wishing to wear his welcome out, he declined an invitation to remain at the cottage over night and returned to his camp by the lake, where his guide awaited him, and on the following day again took possession of the quarters assigned him at the mining camp, which already aspired to be called a town, a number of clapboard shanties and a lodging house with the usual bar-room attachment having been erected.

It was not long before he was again at the Parsons cottage; and soon it came to be expected that he would make one of any company of young people that assembled for a merry-making in the neighborhood. If he did not always escort Lucy he spent a great portion of the time at all these gatherings in her company, and her companions were constantly reminding her in a laughing way that she had captured the young New Yorker, whom rumor asserted was heir to a million or two.

All this was a source of great annoyance to Erastus, and at times caused him to appear less gracious, both towards Mr. Annelsey and others, than was usual with him. With Lucy his mood was changeable, depending a great deal upon the frequency of his rival's visits.

If a week or more elapsed without a call from Annelsey, Erastus resumed his cheerful appearance and was seldom from home, spending much of his spare time in the house, where he laughed and joked with the girls in the old time way;

but the appearance of Annelsey was the signal for a return of silence on his part, and unless there was a gathering of the young folks from which his absence might provoke comment, he remained as little in the company of the members of the family as possible, making an excuse of a press of work on the ranch, or of an appointment with some of his gentleman friends to spend the evening out. If he did not, on such occasions, visit Julia Ennis at her father's residence, Lucy fancied that he did, and she treated Julia, when they met, with much cordiality and appeared anxious to help on the intimacy which she thought existed between her and Erastus.

Of Mr. Ensign the family saw nothing. Once or twice some member had inquired of Annelsey regarding him, but that gentleman knew, or appeared to know, little about him. Ensign was still in the employ of the company, he thought; perhaps swinging a pick in the tunnel; or maybe at work on the flume. Having nothing to do with the accounts or directing the labors of the workmen, Mr. Annelsey could, he said, tell nothing further about him.

Whether Mrs. Parsons was pleased at the frequency of Mr. Annelsey's visits or not it would have been hard to tell. She treated him courteously, and appeared to throw no obstacles in the way of his attention to her daughter. If she noticed the dislike which Erastus evinced at his presence she held her peace and said nothing.

As for her husband, he looked for his coming with a feverish impatience growing out of the desire he had for news from the mining camp, which now overshadowed every other thought, and caused him to entirely forget that the young man had any purpose in visiting them except to bring the desired information regarding the progress of the work at Gravel Hill, as the cluster of shanties at the mines had been named.

So the summer passed, and again the time approached when the girls were to return to school, and preparations were made for their departure.

"I almost wish we were not going back," said Jennie, as they were packing, "we have had such a pleasant summer. I am sure I never enjoyed myself so much before in all my life, and I awfully hate going back into those dusty fusty little rooms in the city and poring over a lot of books that appear to have been made on purpose to puzzle one's brains without any corresponding benefit to come of it. I'd ever so much rather stay at home and help mother take care of the house and the poultry, and go to a party once in a while.

"I wonder what Mr. Annelsey will do when we are gone?" she went on. "Do you know, Luce, I believe he is dead in love with you? And he is getting further and further in every day he lives. Here twice last week. He couldn't more than have got home from the first visit before he turned right round and came back again. Mrs. Lucy Annelsey, wife of James Annelsey, Esq., millionaire. That sounds well. Believe I'd take him, if I were you, Luce, and then I can spend the winters in New York and catch a millionaire, too, maybe. Did he ever say anything about coming to see you when we get back to San Francisco?

"Say," she rattled on, without waiting for a reply to her first question, "what do you s'pose makes 'Ras hate him so? Do you know that if he were not half in love with Julia Ennis I should think him jealous of you? Why, Lucy, what is the matter? Didn't Mr. Annelsey ask you to correspond with him, or anything?"

"Yes,—he—he—did, and—and I wish he hadn't," sobbed

Lucy, putting both hands to her face and burying it in her lap as she sat on the floor in front of her open trunk.

"I wish I had never seen him," she continued between sobs. "I wish he would go back to New York and never let me see or hear from him again. I never spent so miserable a summer in my whole life, never; and it's all because of him; and I know poor pa is worried to death for fear the mine will wash down upon the ranch and cover us all up, and—and—and I'm just as miserable as I can be, and it's all his fault. We were just as happy as we could be until he came."

Jennie was at a loss to understand this outbreak of Lucy's. She had supposed her not indifferent to Mr. Annelsey's attentions; had thought, in fact, that she was more in love with him than she ever had been with any of her other admirers. She had come to this conclusion because Lucy had avoided talking about him when they were alone; and always before, they had made confidants of each other regarding any of the young men who occasionally escorted them to a dance or picnic when at home, or to a lecture or the theatre when in the city.

No one who knew the sisters or saw them together even for an hour, could doubt their affection for each other; and Jennie, believing that Lucy really loved Mr. Annelsey, had more than once caught herself drawing mental pictures of her as his wife, surrounded with all the luxuries which wealth could purchase; supplementing it with another picture in which she saw herself appearing at one of the grand entertainments which Lucy and her husband would give in their palatial New York home, and being introduced to society as "the sister of Mrs. Annelsey, who had come from California to spend the winter."

It never occurred to her that Lucy could be in love with

anybody else, and now she fancied that some slight misunderstanding had arisen between them, and that Lucy was troubled for fear that Annelsey would not write or would not seek her out when he came to San Francisco. She felt sure he would come to the city soon, for there was nothing to necessitate his staying at the mines, which would not be a very inviting place for a young man of leisure when the rains set in and rendered hunting and fishing impossible for weeks at a time.

"Never mind," she said, making an effort to comfort her sister. "It will come out all right in the end. The course of true love never did run smooth, you know."

This thought seemed to comfort Lucy, and something very like a smile played for a moment about her mouth, and among the dimples in her cheeks.

Jennie did not see the smile, for her sister's face was still buried in her apron; but she noticed that the sobbing ceased and was strengthened in her belief regarding Lucy's feelings for Mr. Annelsey, and wishing to comfort her still further, she continued:

"Father has been driven off of so many pieces of land that I do not wonder he is afraid something will happen him again, though I don't suppose there is any danger that this place will be overflowed by the dèbris from the mines. I don't see how it can be when they are twenty miles away. Mr. Annelsey says there isn't. And if it should happen, of course the company would pay the damages, especially if you and James were married."

Instead of comforting Lucy, this set her crying harder than ever.

Jennie could not understand her sister's mood, and did not know what to do or say to soothe her; and hearing their mother calling them from the kitchen, she stooped and

8

kissed Lucy's hair, where she sat, and went down to assist in
getting the evening meal, telling their mother that Lucy
would be down in a few moments, but saying nothing about
having left her in tears.

When her sister had gone, Lucy gave way to her feelings, and cried and sobbed until her whole form shook with
the violence of her emotions.

Her excitement having worn itself out a little, she raised
her head and wiped her eyes with her apron.

"I believe they are selling me to him," she said, under
her breath; "selling me to him because he is rich and can
help them in case father gets into difficulty with the mining
company; and Erastus is letting them do it."

And again her face went down upon her lap, and the
sobs broke forth afresh.

By and by she lifted her head again, and finally rose and bathed her face and eyes.

" Poor father," she was saying to herself, " I know what the thought of losing this place must mean to him. He has been driven off of so many and he is getting old now, both he and mother. If they were to lose this home they would feel as if there was no place left in the world for them to go to, and if I can save them I ought to be willing to do it; and if Erastus marries Julia Ennis, I shall not care what becomes of me anyway."

Then she began crying once more, but more quietly than before.

When she went down to supper the family noticed that her eyes were red, but thought nothing of it, as the girls always had crying spells for a day or two previous to leaving home for school.

Her father came out of his own gloomy mood at sight of his daughter's sorrow, and made several attempts at joking with the object of raising her spirits again, in which he seemed to succeed admirably, for by the time they arose from the table she was even gayer than usual.

On the morrow, when the parting came, she broke down and cried as if her heart would break; but then Jennie cried a great deal also, as did Mrs. Parsons and Johnny. Even Mr. Parsons felt the tears stealing down his cheeks, and wiped them away with the back of his hand.

Erastus drove them to the landing and parted with them there.

The ride had been an unusually silent one, all of them seeming absorbed in thought. He would kiss them both at parting, Erastus had been saying to himself ; maybe the last kiss he should ever give Lucy. Annelsey, he felt certain, would follow her to the city, and perhaps when she came back she would be engaged to him. She might even be married before she came back, and so save him the pain of being present at her wedding, for he believed she knew of his love for her, and that the knowledge had caused her to feel embarrassed in the presence of his rival and himself.

But now she would not object to his kissing her, as he had always done when she was going to leave them for any great length of time, and he would hold her close to his heart for a moment, if never again. But when they reached the landing the boat was on the point of swinging off, and there was no time even to shake hands, but only to hurry on board and wave their good-bys while the gang-plank was being raised and the boat was swinging round into the current.

Erastus stood upon the shore and watched them until they were lost to sight amidst the hundred other passengers, and then turned away with a feeling at his heart that all of happiness had gone out of his life forever.

As the girls were leaving the office of the steamer, where they had gone immediately to secure their state-rooms, a gentleman among the passengers raised his hat in salutation.

"I wonder," he said, "if I can be of any service that will in part repay your family for the kindness shown in keeping three gentlemen over night one time last spring?"

"Why, Mr. Ensign. Is it you? I supposed you had forgotten all about us long ago, since you never came to see us," said Jennie, feeling that anyone whom they had ever met before was a friend where everybody else was strange. "Have you been at the mines all the time? Mr. Annelsey said he didn't know what had become of you."

"So Mr. Annelsey has improved his chance introduction to the Parsons family," was Ensign's mental comment.

"Well, I can't say I blame him. Maybe I would have done it myself if I had had the leisure he has had."

Then aloud:

"Mr. Annelsey has not felt any especial interest in my whereabouts, I suppose. I have been at Gravel Hill ever since I was at your father's cottage, and if I have not called, it is owing, perhaps, to my not having so much leisure time on my hands as Mr. Annelsey has had.

"Besides," he added, looking straight at Jennie, "I had no reason to hope that I should be made welcome, if I were to come as a friend instead of a weary traveler craving a night's lodging."

Jennie could find no words in which to reply to this, and Lucy had not spoken at all, except barely to show that she recognized Mr. Ensign as one whom she had met before. As they were turning away to seek their state-room Ensign interposed.

"At least," he said, "now that we have met by accident, let us become better acquainted. I am going to San Francisco to run an engine in one of the mills there; you, I suppose, are returning to school. May I not join you when you come upon deck again? Perhaps I can be of some service to you upon our arrival at the city."

"You may help us get our luggage carried up when we get there, if you will," replied Jennie, "and we will be much obliged to you; and we are coming up on deck pretty soon, ain't we Lucy? And you can tell us all about things at the mine."

"They appear to be greatly interested in things at the mine," muttered Ensign, as he turned away; "wonder if that fellow Annelsey has really been making love to one of them—and which one. I believe I should not like it if it should prove to be Jennie he is courting."

After arranging their toilets the young ladies came upon deck. Lucy was tempted to remain in their state-room and would have done so only that she fancied that Jennie was willing to get better acquainted with Mr. Ensign. That gentleman was waiting for their appearance and joined them the moment they came up the gangway, and was so jolly and full of the incidents of his life at the mines that even Lucy, half forgetting her troubles, laughed at his witticisms and finally joined in them.

And so the day which they had thought would be a lonely one was made very pleasant indeed, and when they arrived just before dark at the city docks, Ensign arranged for having their luggage sent up and then walked with them to their rooms, where he bid them good-night after having obtained permission to call at some future time.

"Isn't he a splendid fellow?" said Jennie that night when they were talking over the adventures of the day in their own room.

"I am glad if you like him," replied Lucy.

"Why so?"

"Because I think he is in love with you. I saw it in his eyes when he sat watching you on the boat."

"Nonsense, you little goosey. Most likely he has a sweetheart already."

But Jennie blushed as she said it, and immediately got up and went waltzing about the room, humming a gay air, every few moments pausing to make some remark which showed that she was thinking of Ensign, and that her thoughts were pleasant ones.

CHAPTER XIII.

VISITING THE MINES.

Mr. Annelsey's visits to their father's cottage ceased with the departure of Jennie and Lucy, and John Parsons was thus left without means of obtaining frequent or reliable information of the progress of work at the mines.

He was at the landing every day or two with produce for shipment, and always inquired of such as he met if they had any news from Gravel Hill, but received no information of a positive character such as he had been accustomed to obtain from Mr. Annelsey. He had, in fact, questioned that young gentleman so often and so minutely that he felt as if he knew the mines, and all the details of the work of preparation for working them, as perfectly as if he had located them and superintended the labor of the men himself; but now he only heard rumors, those of to-day being contradicted by those of to-morrow. Of late, too, he had frequently been answered impatiently, almost rudely, by those whom he was in the habit of questioning about the mine. They felt no especial interest in the affairs of the mining company themselves, and could see no reason for his solicitude, and were growing weary of his constant and persistent inquiries.

It was known, of course, that the son of one of the large stockholders had been somewhat intimate with his daughter, and there were found gossips who intimated that "the old man's desire for information from the mines was really a desire for information of a certain young man who made his headquarters there during the time he was not roaming

over the country, flirting with such young girls as were
foolish enough to permit it."

And then the moral vultures, from which even country
neighborhoods are not always free, fluttered their wings and
indulged in another little flight of fancy.

"The pretense of a return to school was only a blind,"
they said. "Lucy's parents had found it necessary to send
her from home for a time, and her elder sister accompanied
her as a nurse and to prevent any suspicion of the true cause
of her going."

No one who knew the family well gave any heed to these
tales, but there were those who did believe them, and who
looked upon the changed appearance of John Parsons as con-
firmation of them; for there was no denying that there was
a change in him. Among his neighbors and at the landing
he had been noted for the hearty manner with which he
greeted everybody, whether boy or man, and for a jovial expression of countenance that gave an instant impression of a
prosperous and contented man, as well as the possessor of a
kindly heart. But now his whole expression and manner
was changed. Often at the landing he passed men whom he
knew, without appearing to see them, and looked at strangers
without speaking, but in a manner which seemed to question
them of their purpose in coming to the locality. All the
jollity had left him, and his greetings, even to his best friends,
had lost their hearty cordiality, and he inquired less frequently
after their health and more and more often if they had any
news from the mines, until even they began to wonder if
there might not be something in the rumors which had
reached their ears, and one day when he had seemed particularly downcast, a neighbor, in reply to his usual inquiries
for news from Gravel Hill, said:

· ' See here, Parsons, I know it isn't any of my business,

but if I were you I believe I would go up to the mines and see Mr. Annelsey. Young men are sometimes a little wild without being really bad at heart, and maybe if you see him yourself and talk to him without showing temper he'll do the square thing."

The "square thing" that John Parsons wanted done was to leave him and his in undisturbed possession of their home, with its vineyards and orchards, its plot of ground where the turkeys and chickens and ducks wandered and nested and raised their young; the rose bush over the cottage porch; the vegetable garden at the side; the fields for pasturage and grain stretching away on every side.

He thought of Mr. Annelsey only in connection with the mine whose washings might flood his ranch and destroy all that Martha and he had labored so hard to accumulate, and leave them in their old age to begin all over again. And what use to begin again if this place, too, should be wrested from them? He would have no heart, no faith to go farther or do more. He should feel that God was out of the universe; that the sun had set in eternal night, if forced again to take his loved ones and flee into the wilderness.

Not the faintest intimation of the meaning of the neighbor's words reached his mind. Had it done so, had he known that the kindly meant words of his friend implied a stain upon the character of his daughter, he would have resented it in a manner to prevent its repetition, at least in his presence; but he saw only a suggestion that he should go personally to the mines, see with his own eyes how great the cause for alarm really was, take advantage of his acquaintance with Mr. Annelsey in the work of securing information, and in case he found the danger imminent, to induce the young man to use his influence to avert it.

The neighbor's allusion to Annelsey as "wild" he did

not notice; or, if he did, supposed that the speaker intended
to convey the thought that the company might not be inclined to give much weight, in matters of business, to the
advice of so young a man; regarding him as inexperienced
and consequently wild in his judgment. But the suggestion
of visiting the mines and seeing for himself the whole situation, struck him as a good one, and he resolved at once
to go.

The next morning at breakfast he announced his intention of going to Gravel Hill. He made no mention of his
purpose in going, and neither his wife nor Erastus had any
need to ask; they understood without asking, and raised no
objections. Possibly they hoped he might learn something
which would relieve his anxiety and bring back his old time
cheerfulness. Martha Parsons felt that the house was terribly gloomy of late. The girls absent, her husband silent
and moody, even Erastus seemed depressed and downcast;
the whole atmosphere of the household was changed, and
but for Johnny, who was too young to feel anxiety about
anything pertaining to the future, the circle which gathered
about their daily board would have been a silent one indeed.

Johnny was, as was but natural, the pet of the family.
Being the baby, and with a goodly number of years between
himself and the next older, he had been allowed his own
way until there had grown up a doubt in his mind as to
who was head of the family, and entitled to have their orders
obeyed.

Of a sunny temperament, he was seldom actually bad,
but was full of life, active but sensitive, and easily hurt by
a harsh word or a refusal on the part of any one to accept
any favor which he might fancy himself to be conferring.
When not asleep or attending to his ducks and chickens he
was constantly with his father, playing in the dirt, while

John, Sen., tied up the grape vines, helping to carry away the limbs when the orchard was trimmed, aiding in bringing in the fruit and vegetables when they were gathered, sitting astride his father's shoulders as he went to and from the barn, or by his side in the spring wagon as he drove about the place or to town.

Sometimes he would hitch Bose to a little wagon his father had made for him, and, climbing into it, would drive him about the place; but, to his sorrow, he had found that the dog was entirely too active for his own comfort; in fact, the last time he had tried to play horse in this way it came so near ending in a serious accident that it put a stop to all such experiments.

The dog had started off on a rapid run, and in making a sudden turn as he passed a little tree that stood in the yard, had caught one of the front wheels upon it in such a way as to violently throw the boy out and badly wreck the wagon. Poor Johnny presented a sorry picture as his little boots were seen higher than his head, while the old dog stood half turned around trying to take in the situation, and looking more troubled, if possible, than the child.

No sooner did his father say he was going to Gravel Hill than Johnny announced his intentions of accompanying him.

"I hardly think he had better go, do you, father?" said Mrs. Parsons to her husband; "it's a long ride over the hills, and you will be forced to stay over night, besides which Johnny will be a bother to you in getting about to see the mines. I guess he had better stay at home with Erastus and me, and help us to take care of the ducks and chickens this time."

But Johnny persisted. He "wanted to see Gravel Hill;" "wanted to see the mines;" "wanted to see 'em throw the water," and finally clinched his argument by asserting that his father would be lonesome without him. And so he had his way and went with his father.

The road over the "hills," which were really mountains, was rocky and often precipitous, but the horses were used to such, and with only Mr. Parsons and Johnny in the spring buck-board, they made pretty good time, arriving at their destination just as the sun was sinking out of sight.

Stopping in front of the largest building in the town, Mr. Parsons gave the lines to Johnny to hold while he went in to inquire if he could obtain lodging for the night. He was promised a bed for himself and boy in a room in which were a half-dozen other beds, and was shown where to get feed for his horses after he had taken them from the buck-board and tied them to a rack in the rear of the boarding-house. No shelter for animals had yet been built, and for the present there was little need of any, the winter rains not having set in.

By the time he had cared for his animals supper was ready, and father and son joined the score of men who gathered about the long table upon which was placed a sub-stantial meal of bacon, potatoes, bread, beans and strong coffee.

The room was lighted by candles, stuck, a portion of them, in tin or sheet-iron candlesticks; others in blocks of wood into which a hole had been bored to receive them.

The men were mostly miners in the employ of one or other of the placer companies having claims in the neigh-borhood, or were working on a small scale for themselves. Nearly all wore red flannel shirts, and most of them had their sleeves rolled up to the elbow, just as they came from their work; or, perhaps, in imitation of those of their number whose garments were lacking sleeves altogether except a few inches at the shoulder.

But if they lacked for wearing apparel, none were lacking in appetite, and the coarsely cooked food disappeared from before them in a way that would have astonished any cook not accustomed to provide provender for a lot of hungry miners.

Of these men John Parsons learned that the work of washing down the mountains had already begun. The water had been brought from a stream three miles distant and many feet above the placers which it was the intention to work, and conducted into an immense reservoir, which had been built on the bluffs above. From this reservoir strong pipes of heavy duck cloth, strengthened by bands of iron, conveyed it to the point below, from which it was directed against the hills which contained the gold.

This piping was six or eight inches in diameter, with bands of iron every few inches, and ended in a nozzle like that of a garden or fire hose, and from the immense pressure of the water above would throw a stream with sufficient force to cut a man or a horse in two instantly, and which ate into the side of the mountain as fire eats into a dry brush heap.

To obtain the gold—which was in fine particles scattered through the whole earth of the hills composing the placers —sluiceways, extending some distance down the gorge, had been built, through which all the earth and stones to be washed down were to be passed.

The bottom of this sluice was of planks, upon which was nailed, or wedged, circular pieces from the ends of logs, alternating with rows of slats also fastened across the bottom of the sluice, into the upper end of which was turned many pounds of quicksilver, which gradually made its way through

the sluice, lodging in little pools between the interstices of
the circular pieces of wood, or on the upper side of the slats,
and served to catch and hold the fine particles of gold as
they sunk to the bottom of the mass of earth passing through
the sluice and being pulverized by the action of the water
and its own grinding motion.

Not one company only, but several, had taken claims and
were prepared for an assault upon the hills with these enormous pipes.   All, however, took their water from the same
reservoir, paying those who had built it by the thousand
feet, for the amount used.

John Parsons slept but little that night, and was up at
the first noise which indicated that any of the other occupants were astir.

Leaving Johnny asleep in the bed he went out and fed
his horses, and then came in and sat down in the bar-room
to wait for breakfast.   When he saw that the meal was nearly
ready, he awakened Johnny, and after eating, started to look
at the mines, which were a good half mile away, taking the
boy with him.

The men who handled the pipes were on the ground as
soon as he.   The day previous they had exploded fifty kegs
of powder in a tunnel which they had dug into the hillside,
and had rent and torn the earth in every direction.   They
now turned the water from long lines of hose upon the loosened mass, and began washing away the earth with a rapidity
which promised to soon reduce the hills to a level with the
valleys.

"Talk about faith movin' mountains," said the man who
handled the pipe, as he watched the dirt crumble and dis-
solve, while great trees and rocks slowly sank into the abyss.
"Talk about faith movin' mountains, and I'm a l-e-e-t-l-e bit

skeptical, I am; but say, faith and a stream of water from one of these here pipes, an' I'll gamble on it every time." *

John Parsons turned from the sight, faint and sick at heart. He had seen enough. They would wash the earth of those hills from their rocky foundations as the dust is washed from the paved streets of a city by a July shower, and the valleys must become its resting place. Farms, and orchards, and vineyards would be covered, at the first great flood, with the worthless earth of the mountain tops which was now pouring through the sluice into the gulch below. Fertile fields would be made barren, their owners impoverished, their homes made desolate; all, all, that a few men already rich might grow richer by possessing themselves of the few penny's worth of gold that lay hidden in each cubic foot of the mountain's top.   •

"'Ow do you do, sir; I 'ope I see you well?"

John Parsons turned squarely around and stood face to face with Mr. Jobbers, who extended his hand with a rather pompous though cordial air.

" 'Ow is Mrs. Parsons and the young ladies; well, I 'ope? Mr. Hannelsey was telling me before 'e left as 'ow 'e 'ad hoften called on you during 'is fishing and 'unting excur-

---

* "A peculiar instance of how thoroughly the placer diggings have been worked is evidenced in Shaw's flat, an exceedingly rich plateau in the County Tuolumne. In 1851 this was a beautiful level park studded with trees, among them many noble cedars. In 1860 the whole plain from four to five miles across was one scene of gaunt desolation. The entire dirt had been washed away ; not a single tree remained. Shaw's flat, once proverbial for the richness of its mines, was silent and solitary. The bed rock was composed of limestone. The headwaters of the river Stanislaus had been brought to bear upon the soil, and had washed away every grain of it through Dragon gulch into the lowlands. Nothing remained but the white bare rocks that looked like tom' stones ; the more so, as they were of all shapes. Some of them flat, others peaked, others needle shaped, and some arched.

With 200 inches of water 250,000 cubic feet of dirt can be washed in a working week."—*From* "SIX MONTHS IN CALIFORNIA," *by J. G. Player—Froud, London, England. Page 96—7.*

9

sions.   Come hup to my quarters and 'ave a glass of wine."

It is not to be supposed that Mr. Jobbers' invitation was caused by his having noticed the look of exhaustion and hopelessness which had settled upon the face of John Parsons.   He was not in the habit of noticing the look of people's faces, unless he suspected them of having designs upon his purse.   He was not a bad man at heart; he was even capable of being generous at times and in a way—or at least he believed he was.

If a beggar appealed to him in a particularly touching manner he gave him a shilling, and had even been known to give a half-crown when feeling especially amiable; but it never occurred to him that a beggar had any feelings except of cold or hunger, and these he supposed only in a modified degree, and not keenly as people in affluent circumstances would do if by accident they were to miss a meal, or be caught out in a storm without sufficient clothing.

Besides, it was intended that some should be rich and some poor; of this he had no doubt whatever; and it was the duty of everyone to be contented in the condition in which God has placed him.   He was contented with his lot, and he felt that he thereby performed pretty nearly his whole duty to society, and he had no sympathy with those who made complaint against their condition in life; but occasionally would give the price of a meal of victuals just to prove to himself and the world that he could be generous as well as strictly just.

Such freaks were not common with him; at least not enough so to excite any fears of his bankrupting himself on the part of his friends; and when it did occur it was invariably after having eaten a hearty dinner.

Then, too, he recognized the claims of hospitality; and having eaten and slept beneath the roof of the man now standing before him, he wished to prove that he could be hospitable in his turn.

John Parsons was not a lover of wine, and seldom drank it, although wine of his own making was always in his house, and often on his table; but now he felt that a glass of it would stiffen him up and maybe clear his ideas, which someway seemed terribly mixed. Then, too, he suddenly remembered that he wanted to talk with Mr. Jobbers.

He had utterly forgotten about Mr. Annelsey, and would have given him no thought had not Mr. Jobbers mentioned him, and now he did not think to inquire why or where the young man had gone. It was sufficient that he was gone, and so could be of no use in influencing the company to cease the work of destroying homes. But Mr. Jobbers was one of the company; he represented that half of the stock which was held in London, and if he could only be made to see how much damage was certain to be done, how many homes ruined if the work went on, he might, voting for those whom he represented, stop the whole thing at once, by stopping work upon his own mine and refusing to sell water to the other companies.

It was a foolish thought, for when have men ever refused to get rich from fear of ruining others?—yet John Parsons said to himself that he would try, and if that failed he would threaten them with the law. No, not the law, for he felt that that was always on the side of the rich. Only the higher law; the right of every human being to all the products of his own toil, and to defend that right regardless of consequences to those who attempted to violate that law, was worthy of being appealed to, he thought; and he called to mind the instances in which men who were being robbed under guise of legal enactments there on the coast, had appealed to this higher law and administered justice with a bold hand.

But now he would go with Mr. Jobbers and would see what could be done to save his own home and those of his neighbors from destruction.

CHAPTER XIV.

DEEPENING SHADOWS.

So that he gathered the red ore and precious stones,
  What has man ever cared for hearts that bled?
What has he recked of altars overthrown;
  Of brave men dead; of hearthstones
Overgrown with weeds?
                    Deeds
Louder speak than words, and deeds
Of man in all the past proclaim
He only cared for gold—gold and a name;
For that his name might live,
He oft has carved it deep in living,
Quivering human flesh;
Just as he mar'd the beauty of the hills,
And bar'd the streams from out their places,
And scar'd the face of nature
With deep seams cut in her face
In his mad search for gold.

A very foolish thought it was—that of John Parsons—
that a rich company which had expended more than one
hundred thousand dollars in erecting water flumes and
sluices for washing down the hills and gathering gold, would
cease operations just because a few thousand acres of vineyard and grain lands would be destroyed, and the homes of
a hundred poor men made desolate.

And yet John Parsons saw nothing foolish in the thought.
On the contrary he felt momentarily certain that when
he should show Mr. Jobbers how the stones and earth
washed down would be carried through the sluice into the

gorge, and from there into the creek, filling up its bed and
causing it to seek new channels; that with the first great
flood the sand and gravel would be carried over the whole
valley, and settling as the water receded, render absolutely
valueless thousands and thousands of acres of fine agricultural lands worth more to future generations than all the
gold in the mountains; land now covered with vineyards and
orchards and the cottages of honest people, who had made
every dollar they possessed by hard work—surely, he thought,
when they know this, these men will not refuse to cease their
work of destruction and leave the settlers in peace. Surely,
these men who are already rich and can provide their families with every luxury, will not deprive others of their homes
in order to pile up heaps of gold that can add nothing to
their own comfort.

"No, no," he said to himself, "it is not possible that
they can be so heartless as that. They have not considered the damage it will do to the ranchmen and their families or they would never have gone on with the work," and
he began to blame himself that he had not sooner called
their attention to the fact, and so have saved these generous
men who were to suffer the loss of so much wealth rather
than wrong others, and to devise means for raising at least a
portion of it among his neighbors, who would thus have
escaped the threatened destruction.

It could be arranged, he thought, and no one suffer very
greatly. He would give five hundred or even a thousand
dollars himself. It was only just that he should, since he
had allowed the company to go to such heavy expenditures
without calling their attention to the damage that would be
done, and doubtless many others would do as much. Yes, it
could all be arranged easily, and his home would be saved
after all.

All this passed through John Parsons' brain in a moment as he turned to follow Mr. Jobbers.

He did not reason it out. It came as an inspiration. In an instant the whole situation, the degree of responsibility of each interested party, and the requirements of justice, stood out as clearly as the clouds, when illumined by the lightnings, stand out against the blackness of earth and sky at midnight.

Yet when he found himself in the office of the company, and had been introduced to the representative of the New York stockholders, he did not feel quite so certain that they would see it in the same light in which he saw it; or that the inspiration which had come to him had reached their minds also. Somehow their look of self-sufficiency and air of assured prosperity, brought back the clouds and made all dark again.

But he would not abandon the idea. He would point out the wrong about to be done, and ask for justice.

And so, slowly and brokenly at first, and then rapidly, and with a native eloquence that his ungrammatical words could not hide, he poured out the story of his hopes and fears, mingled with a bit of his past history; the wrongs he had suffered, he and his, and of his willingness to give largely to help reimburse the company for their expenditures, if they would stop the supply of water and so remove the danger which threatened his home.

When he began speaking, Mr. Jobbers turned towards him with a look of surprise upon his red face that speedily turned to one of incredulity, then anger mingled with the look of incredulity, and both gave place to contempt, and when John Parsons ceased speaking the Englishman turned to his partner.

"Well, Hi never," he said, speaking each word separately and with emphasis. " Hif 'e isn't a-haskin' of us to give up our henterprise and let the gold remain in the 'ills, where it is no use to hanybody, just because the earth that composes 'em may be washed down upon 'is blarsted bit of a ranch."

Mr. Jobbers' partner smiled. At least the muscles of his face drew back from the mouth slightly. He evidently pitied the ignorance of a man who could make such a request, and who now sat with his arm thrown about his boy, Johnny having crept to his side while he had been speaking.

' You evidently fail to comprehend the situation, Mr. Parsons," he said. " What would your ranch be worth if you could not sell its products ?

"Gold," he continued, "is the world's medium of exchange, and gold must be had in order to carry on business. All trade and commerce would cease if the supply of gold did not keep pace with the increased power of the production of the people. You yourself could not exchange your grapes and other fruits for wearing apparel—the comforts and necessities of life—if it were not for the gold which is coined into money.

"We do not know," he went on, "why the gold was placed in such fine particles as to require that the hills be washed down in order to obtain it, but undoubtedly it was for some wise purpose; and in bringing it forth we are doing a great thing for civilization, and for the common people as well as the rich; so you see you are acting very selfishly as well as foolishly in suggesting such a thing as stopping work on the mines."

And to all this John Parsons could answer not a word.

He felt that his opponent's reasoning was fallacious, even blasphemous. That it certainly could not be necessary; that

God could not have intended it to be necessary, that the very means of existence, the soil, which is the origin of all wealth, should be rendered barren and valueless in order to obtain that with which to exchange wealth; and that there was no justice in robbing him and his, that others might possess more of that of which they already had enough for all their needs.

But he was not accustomed to argument. He had just made the longest speech of his life, and these men judged it foolish and him insane. He could say no more, and he arose without a word further, and carrying his boy in his arms, passed out of the building and turned towards the place where he had left his horses.

He had but one thought now—to get back home.

His wife, he dimly felt, would sympathize with him and comfort him: that is, such comfort as she could give, which was all the comfort that he would ever know. He should never be anybody again; never hold up his head again among men. Powerless to protect those he loved, there was but one comfort left him—to hide in the bosom of his family, the members of whom would pity him although they might not be able to have much respect for one who was a man, yet could not protect them from poverty and suffering and hunger. In his over-wrought state of mind it seemed to him that his home was already gone, and he would not have been surprised could he have been suddenly transported to his cottage, to have found it a mass of ruins, with the rose vine dead above the porch, and his vineyard, and orchard, and fields covered with a mass of débris from the mines.

He paid his bill at the boarding house without seeing the party to whom he paid it, watered his horses and hitched them to the buckboard mechanically, and turned their heads homeward with a look of such absolute hopelessness that even Johnny was silent, his young spirits overborne by the weight of his father's woe.

Several times during the first half of the homeward journey the boy tried to arouse his father by pointing to some bird, or flower, by the roadside, but if he heard at all John Parsons replied to the lad only in monosyllables, or at random, and again relapsed into the silence which was so depressing to the child.

When a little more than half way home, as they were winding around a hill upon the edge of a deep gorge, two deer which had been sleeping in a bunch of tall grass by the roadside suddenly sprang up and bounded across, almost under the noses of the horses.

So unexpected was their presence and their movement, that the horses themselves, half asleep and jogging along under a loose rein and with ears dropped forward, took fright and jumped quickly sideways, overturning the buckboard and throwing its occupants out with considerable force.

Clinging to the lines, as he instinctively did, prevented John Parsons from going over the bluff, and after being dragged a few rods he brought the horses to a stop and arose to his feet unharmed, excepting a few scratches and bruises about the face and limbs. But Johnny, having nothing to cling to except the back of the seat, which was wrenched from his grasp in the fall, was thrown violently over the bluff, and rolled half-way down its steep side, being caught at last by a huge boulder which had itself fallen down from above at some previous period.

Mr. Parsons' first thought when he arose was of Johnny, and he looked around, hoping to see him unhurt and scrambling up the bank.

But, no; he was nowhere in sight. His father called once; then again—then he hastily tied the now perfectly quiet

animals to a stunted manzenita tree by the roadside and ran
back to look for the boy.

Not seeing him from the point on the road where the
buckboard was overturned, he rushed over the bluff, nearly
pitching headlong in his haste, and scrambled down its side,
coming upon the body of the boy where it lay, with eyes
closed and one arm bent under in a way in which it could
only be if broken, and with blood issuing from nose and
ears.

For a moment John Parsons stood with a look of awful
horror on his face.

Then his strength left him and he staggered and leaned
upon the rock against which the body lay.

The next instant his strength returned, and with great
beads of perspiration standing out upon his face, he knelt
down and placed his hand over the lad's heart.

There was a faint fluttering there, and raising the body
in his arms he worked his way up to the road, coming out
of the gorge several rods in advance of where the horses
stood, hitched to the manzenita bush.

Still holding the body in his arms he attempted to unsnap
the halter strap with which they were tied, intending to
leave it hanging to the bush ; but the horses were frightened at sight of the limp body and the scent of blood, and
drew back.

He might have untied the strap from the tree without
difficulty, but it was evident that the horses would not permit him with the body in his arms to approach them near
enough to fasten it to any portion of the harness, and if
allowed to drag on the ground it might cause the horses to
stumble and again throw him from the buckboard, which
had righted itself after having thrown its occupants out.

He hesitated an instant, uncertain what to do, then

laid his burden carefully on the ground, untied the strap and
secured it in its place, again lifted his child in his arms, got

upon the buckboard and drove with as much speed as he safely
could down the hill, and then turned to the left into a by-road

which he knew led to a settler's shanty not more than a quarter of a mile away.

By the time he reached it, Johnny was showing signs of returning life, and a hope that he might not be so badly injured as at first appeared was beginning to find lodgment in his father's breast.

As it chanced, the only occupant of the shanty at the moment was a woman, her husband being in the field, and the children at a neighbor's on an errand.

Through the open door she saw a stranger approaching with the limp body of a child in his arms, and understood at once that an accident had happened. Catching the dinner-horn from the nail where it hung, she ran to the back door and blew several loud and sharp blasts, then rushed back, and without stopping to ask any questions, or even for him to reach the door, called to Mr. Parsons to "come right in," at the same time arranging the bed to receive the body.

John Parsons looked his thanks and laid his burden down upon the place prepared for it, the woman assisting him, and placing the poor broken arm in as natural a position as possible. As she did so, the sufferer's eyes opened and closed, then opened again. Then his lips parted and a low moan escaped them.

John Parsons sank down by the bedside and looked at his boy with agony depicted in every lineament of his face more terrible than that of his child's, and when another moan came and the eyes of his boy were turned to him as if pleading for help, he buried his face in the bedclothes and groaned as if his very soul was being wrung from him.

"You had better go for a doctor at once," said Mrs. Jones, for that was the woman's name; "there's none nearer than the Landing, ten miles away, and the sooner he can be got here the better. My husband will be here in a few moments, and we will take the best care of the child we know how until you get back; and after all he may not be so badly hurt as he appears to be; if it is only a broken arm it doesn't really amount to anything very serious except the pain; and the sooner it is set the less that will be."

John Parsons was on his feet and out of the door almost before Mrs. Jones had ceased speaking.

Stripping the gears from one of his horses without even unhitching the tugs from the singletree, he jumped upon the animal's back, dashed down the lane, out upon the main road and across the little valley.

When he reached the hill upon the opposite side he sprang from his seat without more than checking the speed of his horse and ran by his side up the incline, keeping the animal in a trot, but reaching the top with his steed much less exhausted than if he had borne the weight of his rider. Then mounting again he dashed on across the next valley, a race of a mile and a half, with the speed of the wind, again springing to the ground as the steeper portion of the next hill was reached, for he knew that an animal unused to long heats at his best paces will make better time if relieved of the rider's weight for a few moments occasionally in making steep ascents.

And so he reached the little town at the Landing with his animal covered with foam, but still able to keep a sharp run.

The appearance of horse and rider as they passed through the one main street which the town could boast of, drew everybody to their doors, and when they saw him spring to the ground in front of the doctor's office, a dozen persons gathered about to learn the cause of his hasty ride.

As they heard him tell the doctor of the accident to Johnny, and beg that he would hasten with all possible speed, and that he would loan him a fresh horse so he might return with him, making certain that he did not miss the way, there were expressions of sympathy and offers of the loan of horses for both, if the doctor's were not fresh. They also offered to carry the sad news to Mrs. Parsons, that she might hasten to the side of her injured child.

"Ef you would, men, you'd be doin' me a mighty great favor," he said in reply to their kindly offers. "Tell her and 'Rastus to hitch the ponies to the spring wagon and come at once. Tell 'em to follow the Gravel Hill road till they come to the limestone bluffs—'Rastus 'll know where I mean—and then turn to the left, an' it's the first shanty they come to."

Then mounting the animal which had been led out to him, he dashed away, the doctor keeping by his side, his case of instruments in his saddle-bags hanging upon his saddle.

When the party who had volunteered to notify Mrs. Parsons of the accident reached the cottage it was already getting dark, and a lamp was burning in the dining-room, where supper was spread and the family waited the coming of the absent ones, now momentarily expected.

Hearing the clatter of a horse's feet on the hard road, Mrs. Parsons went to the door just as the rider sprang from his saddle, and throwing the bridle rein over the hitching post, advanced up the gravel walk.

In a few words he told his errand.

"An accident had happened; the horses, taking fright, had thrown Johnny and his father out of the buggy. Mr. Parsons had escaped unhurt, but Johnny's arm was broken, and he was lying in a shanty near where the accident occurred, and to which Mr. Parsons had returned with the doctor, while the speaker came to tell Mrs. Parsons, that she might go to her child at once."

Martha Parsons neither screamed nor fainted. She called Erastus and bade him bring the ponies and spring wagon while she hurried to get together linen for bandages, and such other articles as might be most needed.

When Erastus drove up to the gate she called to him to come in and get a couple of feather beds and some covering and put them in the wagon, for she knew that settlers in the mountains were not always supplied with a superabundance of bedding. And, besides, if Johnny was not too badly hurt—and the man who brought the news of the accident had conveyed the impression that a broken arm was the extent of the injury—he could be laid on the bed and brought home in the spring wagon at once.

Driving at night over a hilly road is not the most rapid way of transit, but the ponies were urged forward with as much speed as possible, considering the darkness, and just at midnight were halted at the door of Mr. Jones' shanty.

The inmates had heard them coming and Mr. Parsons was standing at the gate waiting for them.

"I'm mortal glad you're come, mother," he said, as he lifted his wife from the wagon. "Johnny's pretty bad hurt the doctor says, but he's set his arm and the lad's sleepin' a little now.

"The folks here are es kind es kin be, and everything has been done that kin be done to make him comfortable, but the doctor says he can't be moved for several days, an' maybe weeks, and I reckon 'Rastus had better go back an' write to one of the girls to come home at once, for I know you won't leave Johnny, an' there ought to be some one to home to see to things."

Mrs. Parsons was unwilling to have the girls leave school in the middle of the term if it could be avoided, and she suggested that they wait a few days.

It might be that Johnny could be moved sooner than the doctor thought. At any rate they had better wait a little and see; especially as Erastus expressed a willingness to get on as well as he could without a cook and housekeeper for a time, if thought best.

And so he returned home, leaving both Mr. and Mrs. Parsons at the shanty with the injured boy.

The next morning Mr. Parsons went to the Landing, riding the horse which he had left at the shanty the day before when he went for the doctor, and leading the borrowed one, which he returned to its owner. Then taking his own, he rode to his own home. Here he remained but a few hours and was again on his way to the shanty among the hills to resume his watch by the bedside of his child.

The doctor came again the next day, and every day for many days and weeks; for Johnny was not moved from the shanty whose inmates had shown so much hospitality, for three long months; and when at last he was taken home his parents knew that he would never again be the healthy, rollicksome boy he had been, going everywhere about the house and ranch, and carrying sunshine wherever he went, but that he was to be a cripple always; the injury to his back making it impossible that he should ever stand erect or be able to walk again.

When it became evident that weeks, and maybe months, would elapse before Johnny could be moved from the Jones shanty, the girls had been written to as their father at first suggested, and had come immediately home and assumed the care of household affairs.

Occasionally one of them took Mrs. Parsons' place at the bedside of the sufferer, while the mother returned to the cottage to see that everything was going right, or for a rest of a night or two.

10

· John Parsons had also remained at the Jones shanty the greater portion of the time; for Johnny was fretful in his sufferings, and no one could lift or turn him so well as his father, whom quite as much as his mother he wanted constantly near him. And so he had remained, trusting everything on the ranch to Erastus, and going home only when it was necessary to obtain provisions, or a change of clothing for himself or wife, or something for Johnny.

No one could possibly have shown more kindness and sympathy than did Mr. and Mrs. Jones, who were thus called upon to act the part of good Samaritans to those whom they had never before seen. They even consented that their own children should leave them for a time—when the fever had set in, and Johnny was at the worst, that their noise might not disturb him, and they had been taken to the Parsons cottage, where they remained some weeks and were cared for by Erastus and the girls.

When the crippled boy was at last removed to his own home, these kind people beneath whose roof he had been so long, would not consent to make any charge for their trouble or to accept any pay, except such as was forced upon them in the way of presents to Mrs. Jones and the children.

CHAPTER XV.

BUILDING THE DAM.

The events recorded in our last chapter served, for a time, to arouse John Parsons from the unhealthy mental condition into which he was sinking; for so long as the lad's life was in danger, every other thought gave way before the one great fear of losing Johnny, his baby, his only boy. But when the more imminent danger was past, the fear of losing their home came again with redoubled force as he realized that his child must always remain a cripple, dependent upon others for every necessity and enjoyment in life.

It was at thought of this, too, that Mrs. Parsons broke down.

Always heretofore she had been the one to preserve a cheerful countenance, and to encourage her husband with expressions of hope that the danger to their home might not be so great as he feared, or that if so there would come some way out of it.

"The law will compel the company to make good the damages if they occur," she would tell him; "and even if we lose the land we will still have the stock and household goods and a nice little sum of money in the bank, and we are not very old yet and will manage to live comfortable, I am sure; so don't worry, dear, it will all come out right in the end."

But now!

When she got down from the spring wagon, and Johnny was lifted out and carried in and laid upon the cot, from which, unaided, she knew he was never to rise again, an awful feeling of desolation came over her. She was as one bewildered and lost in the woods. The sky, the hills, everything about her, took on the look they have when seen through a piece of smoked or stained glass. The house itself, nay, the very faces of her husband and children, seemed strange and unnatural, and she moved from room to room as if in a dream, and when she spoke she heard her own voice as if it came from afar off, and was the voice of another.

All day she was in this condition; but the second day she aroused herself by an effort of the will and resumed her usual round of duties, except that much of her time was of necessity given to the crippled boy, who lay in a little cot which had been made for him and placed on wheels that he might be moved about the house easily and out into the yard on pleasant days.

Her husband now spent most of his time in the house. The winter rains, which had set in some weeks previously, rendered out-door work impossible for days at a time, and if they had not done so John Parsons had lost all love for work on the ranch. Besides, Johnny claimed his almost undivided attention now.

The little fellow had taken to his father from before the time when he took his first baby steps, and had never been quite so well contented as when in his arms, or perched upon his shoulders, or following him about the place; and now he could not bear to have him out of his sight during his waking moments.

Often, too, in the night he would waken and call in a weak, piping voice, so different from what it had been in health; and his father would arise and sit by his side for hours, moving his poor wasted body this way or that to give him a little more ease, or divert his mind by tales such as children love to hear, until he fell asleep again or forgot his pain.

During the day he wheeled him about the house; or if it was sunny, carried him out in his arms to the poultry yard, that he might drop corn to his chickens and ducks; or to the pasture lot, that he might put out his hand and pet the colt that had been promised should be his when both were grown, upon which promise he had built a thousand castles in the air, of encounters with grizzly bears and Indians, besides taking premiums for speed at all the fairs in the country.

It seemed that the man had but one thought, one object in life now—that of caring for the crippled boy.

Certain it is that he never laughed, except when once in a great while something provoked the child to laughter; then the man always joined in, but at no other time did any member of the family see a smile upon his face; and he never went from home any more, not even to a neighbor's.

One day word came that there was to be a meeting at the school house to devise means to save the settlers from the overflow of the mines, and that his neighbors were anxious for him to be present, for by this time the danger was apparent to all. The floods caused by the rains had overflowed the valley to a much greater extent than usual, although the amount of water which had fallen was no more than common at this season of the year.

The washings from the mines had filled the creek bed, and at places had formed dams that checked the water and caused it to overflow fields never before submerged, and to set back upon little valleys which opened into the larger one through which the creek passed. Much damage to vineyards on the lower lands had already been done or must speedily occur, if the water was not drawn off.

The water was thick with the clay of the hills washed down by the mining companies, and in places where the dams had formed, and for long distances on either side, sand and gravel, brought down by the swift, strong current was being deposited upon the tillable lands in large quantities.

Evidently something must be done, and the messenger who brought notice of the meeting urged strongly that Mr. Parsons be present and advise regarding the action to be taken.

" 'Tain't no use," he said to his wife when the neighbor was gone. " 'Tain't no use, but I'll go ef you want I should. You'd better send Rastus, though, and let me stay home with Johnny."

The man's spirit was sadly broken. He felt that it was useless to contend with the company; that everything was virtually lost already, and had dropped into the habit of leaving everything to his wife and Erastus, doing without questioning whatever they suggested, but appearing unwilling even to advise with them; as if he felt himself unworthy, having failed so utterly, to give advice upon which depended the welfare of others.

" I think you had better go yourself, father," replied Mrs. Parsons to the suggestion of her husband that Erastus should attend the meeting in his stead. " You are the head of the family, and you will have more influence than a younger man. Erastus can go too, if you and he wish. I think everybody ought to go and see if some means cannot be devised to prevent our homes from being destroyed."

The meeting of the settlers was held the following afternoon, and John Parsons went. So did Erastus. So did everybody else in the neighborhood.

Somebody nominated Mr. Parsons for chairman, but he

declined, and Mr. Ritchie was elected to preside, and Erastus Hemmingway was made secretary. Then the meeting was
declared opened and expression of opinion as to the course
to be pursued asked for.

The result was a variety of suggestions and motions.
Some favored applying to the courts for an injunction to stop
the operations at the mines, but others pointed out that such
efforts had been made in similar cases in other parts of the
country and had failed, or been delayed until too late to save
the property of those applying.

Others proposed petitioning the legislature for the passage of a bill forbidding hydraulic mining; but as such a
law could not be obtained for a year, if at all, this proposition was not favorably received, and finally the meeting adjourned without having decided upon anything, but with the
understanding that they were to meet again the next afternoon and consider the matter still further.

When they reassembled the next day the whole question
was again gone over and yet nothing could be agreed upon.

To bring suit in court for damages would be to become
involved in endless litigation; since they would be contending against those whose resources were virtually limitless, and
whose wealth would enable them to protract the suits indefi-
nitely; so that if in the end the settlers should be success-
ful in obtaining judgment against the companies it would be
quite as disastrous as to quietly submit to the outrage.

If they sued at all, they must make every company, the
débris from whose mines emptied into the gulch above them,
parties to the complaint, and would thus find arrayed against
them men worth millions of dollars, organized in the form of
a corporation, proverbially soulless, and certainly without
mercy, or sense of justice, or honor, to prevent them from
taking advantage of every quibble of the law, made, too, in

many instances, expressly to delay justice, and administered by officers who owed their election to the men who controlled the corporate capital of the state.

Threats of personal violence were not lacking.

There were those who recalled the fact that more than once in the history of the state, thieves, blacklegs and ballot-box stuffers, even those who assumed to have been elected to high offices, had been hung upon hastily-erected gallows by men whose only authority for doing so was their natural right to protect themselves and families from being robbed and insulted by organized bands of plunderers. A large majority, however, favored only legal means for the protection of their homes, and it was finally agreed to build a dam across the gorge through which the débris from the mines flowed, at a point above the agricultural settlements, and by cutting through the hill, turn the mass of slickings into another gorge, which would cause them to enter the river at a point below, and where no damage would be done to occupied lands.

During the discussions at these meetings John Parsons had said little, and that little only when appealed to for his opinion; but when the building of the dam and the cutting of a new way for the overflowing débris had been decided upon, he called Erastus aside, and after conferring with him a moment, returned and subscribed five hundred dollars towards the work to be done.

The announcement of his subscription was greeted with cheers by the little body of men there assembled.

"It ain't all my own subscription, men," he said, when the cheering had ceased. "I don't know if any of it rightfully is mine. It's part of the money we was a savin' up fer to buy a ranch fer Erastus with, and it honestly belongs to him. He's earned every cent of it, an' more, too; but you

see if the work goes on an' our homes is saved, there's got
to be lots of money comin' from somewhere, an' doctors'
bills and sich has tuck 'bout everything we made last year,
an' bein' as Rastus is willin', we'll plank up the five hundred
es soon es the committee that is to have charge of the work
is ready to begin."

Others now came forward and subscribed, a few putting
down five hundred each, and many others, smaller sums;
the understanding being that such as could not pay money
should be allowed to work out their subscriptions at the
price paid to other workmen. Committees were appointed
to solicit assistance from those living further up the valley
who might in time be injured if the proposed work was not
done, and to have charge of the work, which it was decided
should be commenced immediately.

And now John Parsons took fresh hope. It was possible
after all that his home might be saved, and with the possibility something of his old cheery manner came back to him.

The work of cutting through the hill into the neighboring gorge was begun at once. A large number of workmen
were employed, and everybody who was directly interested
turned out and worked with a will, rain or shine. A tunnel
was driven into the side of the hill, and whole kegs of powder exploded therein, rending the earth and aiding greatly
in the work of excavation, and at last the work was so far
completed that a portion of the water and floating débris was
turned aside into the new channel.

The rains, too, had now ceased, and as the waters sub-
sided the extent of the damage done could be positively determined.

In places, banks of sand and gravel many feet deep extended across fields regarded by their owners as the most
valuable in their possession. In other places the channel of

the little stream had been entirely choked up, and a new one cut by the waters through pastures and grain lands, and in yet others, where little of the coarser débris had been deposited, the long standing of the water had greatly injured vineyards and orchards, the vines and tree trunks being thickly coated with the fine clay which the water had held in solution.

On the whole the damage was less than many had feared, and with the expectation of preventing any further injury by the erection of the dam, hope revived in the breasts of all, and they began repairing as fast as possible the injury already done, and the cultivation of their vineyards and fields for the coming crop.

The Parsons ranch had suffered with the rest, but not more than many others. A hundred grape vines standing upon ground near the creek, were killed or badly injured. Several banks of gravel, mingled with larger stones, extended across some of the most fertile fields, the total injury amounting to a thousand dollars or more, in prospective, but not seriously affecting the immediate income of the family occupying the white cottage under the bluff, around whose open porch still clambered rose bushes heavy with their weight of yellow, and red, and crimson blooms.

As soon as possible after Johnny had been brought home from the shanty in the hills where he lay so many weeks, Jennie and Lucy had returned to school in San Francisco, Mrs. Parsons being now more than ever determined that they should not fail to obtain an education.

"If we leave them nothing else, John, let us at least give them an education," she had said to her husband, and he had made no objections, though the house seemed doubly lonely without them.

To help Mrs. Parsons with the lighter work they secured

the assistance of a young girl whose parents had moved into the neighborhood but the year before, and who, having but little to begin on, were not unwilling that their daughter should find a home where she would be kindly treated and paid for washing the dishes and such other chores as her age and experience fitted her for.

As they had missed a portion of one term the girls did not go home for the short spring vacation, but remained in the city and studied, in order to keep up with their classes; and when they did return in midsummer Lucy was engaged to be married to James Annelsey.

"The wedding was not to take place for at least a year yet," she told her mother in announcing the engagement.

Mr. Annelsey had desired an immediate union, but to this she had interposed a decided negative, and he had at last consented that she should remain at school a year longer, when they were to be married and he would take her to New York to reside.

This was not wholly unexpected by the family. They knew that Mr. Annelsey had followed the young ladies to San Francisco, and that he had been a frequent caller upon them while there. Jennie had even intimated in one of her letters to her mother that she thought Lucy and he would be married some day.

She said less of Ensign, who was almost as frequent a visitor as Annelsey.

In fact the two young men had made up their slight differences and frequently called upon the girls in company, or together arranged with them for attending upon places of amusement; and if Jennie had chosen she could have informed her mother of probabilities of another marriage, almost as certain of taking place as was that of Lucy to Mr. Annelsey.

Jennie, however, was not formally engaged to Mr. Ensign.

He had his own way to make in the world, and had passed the age when men are apt to act hastily in such affairs. He meant Jennie to understand that he preferred her to all others, yet he did not think it well to bind her by formal engagement until he had something more ahead upon which they could begin life together.

Times for laboring men, and especially for skilled mechanics like Ensign, were good just then, but the standard of living for all classes was also high, and the art of saving large fortunes out of salaries of thirty dollars or forty dollars a week in private life is even yet not well understood except by a few railroad officials and presidents of savings banks.

Mr. Annelsey, infatuated with Lucy, and having no necessity for delay on account of pecuniary matters, had proposed the moment he found his courage sufficient for the ordeal; and she, although knowing in her heart that she loved Erastus better, yet thinking that he cared nothing for her, and that her parents desired her union with Mr. Annelsey, accepted him. But when he urged an immediate marriage, her heart failed her, and she begged for time, giving as her reason a desire to remain at school another year, and so fit herself the better to fill the position which she should occupy as the wife of one who had the entrance of polite society in the first city of the country.

In this Lucy was partially sincere. She did not greatly love the man to whom she had engaged herself. As an escort to places of amusement, or a companion upon days of merry-making, she would perhaps have chosen him in preference to any gentleman of her acquaintance, and was not very sorry that she had promised to be his wife. She cried a little when she was first alone after having done so, and even told herself that she was doing it to save her father and the rest of the family from poverty, and because her heart was broken at Erastus's desertion of her for Julia Ennis; but when she had cried her cry out, she did not worry greatly about it, but began picturing to herself the life she would lead when she was the wife of one who could supply every want, without having to stop to consider whether something else would not do as well, and be more economical.

She honestly wished to fit herself as far as possible to appear well in the society into which her husband would take her, and intended to study harder than ever, hoping thereby to accomplish it.

And so it had been agreed between them that Annelsey should go at once to New York, where his presence was desired by his parents, and that Lucy should remain in school another year, when he was to return, and their marriage be consummated.

CHAPTER XV.

THE DISAPPOINTED LOVER.

Of course, Erastus was told of Lucy's engagement to Mr. Annelsey. In fact, he learned it from Jennie in advance of any other member of the family.

As they were driving home from the landing on their return from San Francisco and chatting of those things which are of more interest to young people, namely, other young people, Jennie suddenly broke out with:

"Say, Luce, I'm going to tell Ras," and without waiting for a reply or giving any heed to the blushes which flooded her sister's face and neck, she rattled on with all the speed which her tongue could command, "How'd you like t' have Mr. Annelsey for a brother-in-law, Ras? I know you didn't used to like him very well, but you'll have to now, for Lucy and he are engaged, and are going to be married when he comes back from New York in about a year. There now, Luce, it's out, and you won't have to be carrying the awful load of having to tell it any longer."

"I think you are just as mean as you can be," retorted Lucy, half angry and uncertain whether to laugh or cry. "I hadn't said a word about Mr. Ensign, who has been almost as constant as your shadow ever since we met him on the boat. You would be engaged to him, too—you know you would—if it wasn't that he has got nothing to go to housekeeping with. So, there now, Ras, you know all about us girls, and can confess that you are going to marry Julia Ennis if you want to without blushing."

But Erastus made no such confession, and instead of blushing, his face became very white, and he looked straight ahead and did not speak for some seconds, and then said in a voice which sounded hoarse and unnatural:

"I am not going to marry Julia Ennis or anybody else."

After that little more was said for some time.

Once or twice Jennie, who felt that she was the innocent cause of the sudden silence which had fallen upon them, attempted to start the conversation again by asking questions about neighbors or affairs on the ranch, but Erastus only replied in the fewest words possible, and still looked straight in front of him.

Jennie was half inclined to be offended at this. She thought him angry because Lucy had engaged herself to a man whom he did not like. Could she have seen his face she would have known that some feeling deeper than mere dislike for Annelsey was at work within his breast.

As for Lucy, the assertion of Erastus, that he was not going to marry Julia Ennis or anybody else, gave her a sudden start and a momentary insight into his true feelings.

Was it possible after all that he loved her?

The thought sent all the blood rushing back upon her heart, and for a moment she felt that she should suffocate. Then came another thought. Perhaps Erastus had proposed to Julia and been rejected. This she felt could not be unless Julia had suddenly become enamored of some new admirer, for certainly she had always shown a preference for Erastus over the other young men of the neighborhood.

Still the thought clung to Lucy that such might be the case, and that instead of feeling bad because of her own engagement to another, his silence was caused by pain at being reminded of his refusal by Julia, and her whole mood

11

changed, and she became as cold and hard as he himself appeared.

As they neared home she began talking glibly of anything and everything she could think of—the presents they had brought for each member of the family—toys for Johnny, a dress for mother, a neck-tie for Erastus himself, and a silver tobacco-box for father—all bought with money saved out of that sent them for their own use; going on from this to tell of their school, and of a couple of girls who came on the boat with them as far as Sacramento, where their parents lived; and how these girls were related to one of their own neighbors, and how in answer to their inquiries, Jennie and she had told them all about this neighbor ; how near they were to their own home; how their ranch looked, and how it had been injured by the washings from the mines.

Here she came to a sudden stop.

She had unintentionally run upon that which they were all trying to avoid the mention of, and there came to her not only a knowledge of her blunder, but an entirely new feeling —a feeling that she was somehow responsible for the losses and sufferings of this family and of every other family in the valley whose homes were endangered by the operations of the hydraulic mining companies at Gravel Hill.

At least she had arrayed herself on the side of the companies; was engaged to be married to one who was interested in the continuance of the work which was certain to bring more loss and suffering to these people.

She was no longer of them or with them; for from the moment she became the wife of James Annelsey her interests would be opposed to those of everyone she had known since they settled in the valley.

Even her father and mother, and Erastus, must feel that she had deliberately chosen to desert them in the hour of their greatest loss, and had gone over to their enemies in order to save herself from sharing in the hardships which might be coming upon them.

All this passed through her mind in an instant, and she sank down in her seat with a feeling of shame, and a hatred of herself which made it impossible to say a word more.

"No wonder Erastus is silent," she thought. "He cannot bear even to speak to one who seems so utterly selfish. Oh! why did I never think of it in that light before? It is that which has made him so cold to me ever since Mr. Annelsey first came. He has thought all the time that I was trying to save myself from any suffering that may come upon the rest of them. Oh, if I could only die!"

By this time, however, Erastus had partially recovered from the blow which had fallen so suddenly, if not unexpectedly, and was able to take up the thread of conversation where Lucy had dropped it; and Jennie, anxious not to reach home in such a frozen silence as to attract the notice of their mother, also chimed in, thus giving her sister time to rally again; and when they stopped in front of the cottage and Mr. and Mrs. Parsons, the former carrying Johnny in his arms, came out to welcome them, they thought they had never seen their daughters in a gayer mood, and attributed it to joy at being home again after such a long absence.

When Mrs. Parsons told her husband of Lucy's engagement he remained silent for a time, and then said:

"I s'pose it's natural, Marty, an' what's natural is ginerally right, but someway I'm afeard Lucy will be sorry fer it some day.

"I ain't got nothin' in particular agin the young man, but I'd a heap ruther she'd a married Rastus, an' I feel certain he'd a asked her ef Mr. Annelsey hadn't got in his way and he seen that Lucy kind o' took to him; though I never

11

could make out that she loved him so very much while he
. was a comin' here to see her.

"Maybe it's all right as it is," he continued, after a moment's pause. "At least she won't want fer somethin' to eat
or to wear. An' maybe it don't make any odds how it's got,
only so you get it.

"I used ter think," he went on, "that nobody couldn't go
to heaven that took what they hadn't earned, but I d'know.
Maybe there ain't no heaven, 'er no hell; an' no right and no
wrong,—that we're just put here like the wild beasts to fight
fer what we git, and that them that can git the most is the
best fellers.

"If a man or a child is hungry and takes a loaf of bread,
they send him to jail, because that's a vi'lation of the law;
but ef he has money to start on an' bribes congris to pass a
law so he kin rob a lot of poor folks of everything they have,
as fast as they can get anything together, why, they're makin'
money because they've got more talents than other fellers
have; and everybody is entitled to all they can make in this
country!

"I don't believe Christ ever taught any sich doctrine es
that, but there is them as pertends to be His followers and
to speak for Him as is always cuddlin' to the rich, a knowin'
too, that no man can get a million of dollars without gettin' .
some that belongs to other folks.

"Wall, Annelsey's rich, an' Lucy'll be his wife an' dress
in silks an' satin, and I hope she'll be happy. Maybe when
we're dead an' gone he'll let her take care of Johnny, ef the
boy outlives us. There ought to be some good come out of
so much sufferin', an' maybe that'll be the way it'll come.

"I wouldn't take a cent of it myself ef I was a-dyin' of
hunger, but ef some time Johnny should need their help it
won't be a gift exactly, for the company that's a puttin' dol-

.ars into Annelsey's pocket is a takin' 'em out of ourn, an' though they ain't the same dollars exactly, it amounts to the same thing—it's a robbin' of us to get rich themselves."

A few days after this Erastus informed Mr. Parsons, and, later in the day, the other members of the family, that when the hurry of the season was over he intended to leave them and strike out for himself.

He hoped they would not feel that he was deserting them, for he would never do that; but he was now two years past his majority, and ought to begin for himself, and a number of young men of his acquaintance were going down to the Mussle Slough country to take up land, and he had decided to go with them.

This decision of Erastus was the cause of much regret on the part of John and Martha Parsons. They loved him as their own son, and had hoped and planned that when he should start for himself it should be in the immediate neighborhood of their own home, if, indeed, he did not marry one of the girls and remain always with them.

They readily conceded his right to go, however, and as there was now little prospect that they would soon be able to buy him a place they did not wonder that he wished to leave them and start a home of his own.

Perhaps they divined something of his feelings for Lucy; at least they realized that they could offer no objections to his going which would not appear purely selfish.

At first they insisted that he take the few hundred dollars remaining in bank, and a pair of horses and a wagon.

The money he positively refused to touch, except a few dollars necessary to enable him to make the journey to the Slough, although both the girls joined their parents in begging him to do so, and declared they would remain home from school, or even teach school, rather than permit him who had done so much tó aid in accumulating what they possessed, to leave without anything.

Finally it was agreed that he should take a pair of three-year-old colts and one of the wagons, together with provisions and money sufficient to last him until he could reach his destination, look about him a little and decide just what he would do.

During the time intervening before the day set for his departure he worked even harder than usual, that he might leave the fall work in good shape, and so relieve Mr. Parsons as much as possible. The colts, too, were harnessed every day and made to do some light work that they might be hardened a little before starting upon the journey, which, although not such a very long one, would yet be a hard one on animals of their age.

It was a very sad household, that of John and Martha Parsons, during these few weeks of work and preparation; perhaps the saddest that had ever gathered about their board.

When Johnny was brought home crippled for life, and when it was thought that their home was to be destroyed by the overflow, very dark indeed had seemed the days, especially to the parents ; but always a hope that the home might be saved, and the thought that even if worst came to worst the family could be kept together, had enabled the mother to keep up a cheerful appearance. And young hearts are ever buoyant ; so long as they have no very grave sorrows of their own, the sorrows of others, even those they love best, cannot prevent the occasional overflow of youthful spirits in merry laughter, and the young folks of the Parsons household had always expected that in some way the clouds that overshadowed them for a time would be lifted, and that the warm sun of love and prosperity would be found to have a permanent abiding place in their firmament.

But now all knew to a certainty that the family circle was to be broken, and broken somewhat rudely.

To Lucy there constantly came the thought that Erastus was going because of his love for her, although he made no sign and she could only surmise.

She realized, too, more and more, how dearly she loved him, and that a union with Mr. Annelsey, separating her as it would do from all she held most dear, would not bring her happiness. She saw now that her lover had no influence which could be used to aid the settlers in obtaining justice from the mining company, and that, even if he should be generous enough to give direct personal assistance to her own family, which somehow she doubted, her father was far too proud to accept it.

Then the thought which had come to her during the ride home from the Landing, when the announcement of her engagement had been made, that her family must think her selfishly seeking an alliance with one who was connected with the cause of their misfortunes, returned to her again and again, producing a feeling that she was excluded from their innermost thoughts and affections, which could not but affect her actions, however much she might struggle against it, and which, re-acting upon the others, very nearly produced the feeling she deplored.

Mrs. Parsons felt that her flock of younglings were about to take wing; that the children for whom she had labored and planned and lived, were to go from her, in all probability never to be reunited again on earth. Not only Erastus, but Lucy, and then Jennie, would soon seek homes for themselves, and that, too, far away from their parents, who were to be left alone and lonely in their old age.

No, not quite alone. Johnny would never leave them; no matter what else might happen, the bird with the broken wing would not leave the home nest.

But what if the nest should be destroyed, and the crippled bird be left to suffer from lack of food and shelter?

She and John were getting old now. She had never recognized this as a fact before, but now she felt that it was true. Supposing that the ranch should be destroyed, and they in their old age, and with a helpless child, be turned out to begin again?

Suppose—but no, she would not think of it. The Lord would provide. They had been through many trials and their sufferings had not been more than they could bear, and she must not permit herself to be gloomy and so add to the sufferings of the others.

She went about her work with a cheerful air; putting Erastus's clothing in the best possible repair; made him new shirts and under-clothes, and did many little things besides, which she thought might add to his comfort when he should be far from her, with none to do these little favors for him.

As for John Parsons, he was simply passive.

The gleam of sunshine which had come to him when hope revived with the beginning of the work on the dam had died out, and he saw nothing bright in the gloom which enveloped him.

He went around in a quiet kind of way, saying little, but striving to add what he could to the physical comfort of each member of his family, but neither suggesting nor opposing anything.

And now the morning of the day on which Erastus was to leave them had arrived.

The wagon which he was to take had been loaded the day before. There was a bed and bedding, his trunk containing his personal effects, and a box into which Mrs. Parsons and the girls had managed, unknown to him, to put several little articles of comfort or luxury as a pleasant surprise and reminder of them when he should unpack it at the end of his journey.

There was also a plow and a few other agricultural and mechanical implements, several sacks of grain for the colts, and provisions sufficient to last a little time after he should reach his destination.

Silently he took the hand of the man who had been the only father he had ever known. With all his might he strove to say good-bye, but could not master his voice, and he dropped the hand, kissed each of the women in turn, and without a word sprang upon the wagon and drove away out of their sight.

As the family turned to enter the house, old Bose, who had appeared not exactly to understand the cause of all he had seen, looked inquiringly up into their faces and then away in the direction in which the wagon had disappeared, as if to ask if this was anything more than the usual daily trip to town.

Apparently convinced by the sorrowful looks of all, that something grave had occurred, he lifted his nose in the air and gave a long, low, mournful howl, and lay down with his head upon his outstretched paws, and continued to look down the road.

He never returned to his old place upon the kitchen porch, but always, until he died, was to be found near the same spot in the front yard, with his head turned in one direction, and if not sleeping, with his old eyes fixed upon the point in the road where a wagon coming over the hill would **first be** visible.   Occasionally if hungry, he would **go** to the kitchen for food, but usually it was carried to him, **and** one morning when they went to feed him, they found him dead, his head upon his outstretched paws, as if still looking down **the** road.

CHAPTER XVII.

DESOLATION.

Erastus was six days in making the journey to Mussle Slough, and a desolate looking country he found it.

For miles and miles, at this season of the year, not a green thing appeared upon which to fasten the smallest hope of ever changing the waste into fertile fields of grass and grain.

The settlers already there seemed upon the verge of starvation. But three or four inches of rain fell during the entire year, and for months at a time the soil was unmoistened even by dew. Those who possessed a little money when they came, had expended it in futile efforts to produce a crop, and all were now dependent for the means of subsistence upon small patches of ground near the lake, distant in many instances from four to seven miles from their claims.

Even these patches had to be constantly guarded from droves of ravenous and half wild cattle belonging to the herdsmen who gave them little attention, and who were illy disposed toward any attempts at inclosing or cultivating the land which, although seemingly little better than a desert, at certain periods of the year produced a thin growth of wild alfalfa upon which their stock fed, being in the main driven to better pastures as the dry season advanced.

These patches of ground were made fertile by their nearness to Lake Tulare, and by being but little above the level of its waters.

Veritable oases in the desert these spots seemed, and upon them the settlers raised the few bushels of corn and beans and vegetables which formed their sole means of subsistence while prosecuting the work of redeeming their claims by the herculean task of digging an irrigating ditch upwards of twenty miles long, by means of which they were to obtain water from the river above them, and convert the desert into a garden.

But if these oases furnished garden spots for the settlers they were also desired by the herdsmen, for a few of whose cattle they supplied pasturage the year round, and being without the means of fencing them in, the protection of their little crops meant a constant watch upon the cattle, and one which consumed the entire time of some member of each family.

Owing to the lack of feed, but few were able to keep teams, and that they continued the unequal contest for their homes can only be understood when it is known that of all the rich farming lands of the State, not an acre remained for pre-emption or purchase except at second-hand, and as a rule, in large bodies, being held by corporations or individuals who claimed it under pretended grants from Spain or Mexico, given before California was ceded to the United States, or by act of Congress since that time. So that this barren, sandy plain offered the only hope for poor men in California of obtaining a portion of the inheritance of the race.

Besides, they had confidence that, once irrigated, it would produce abundantly, and well repay all their labors by future yields of fruit and grain.

All efforts to induce men with capital to invest in the enterprise of cutting the ditch, and depending upon the sale of water privileges for reimbursements, had failed,—the idea that any amount of water could render the sand of the plains fertile being scouted as visionary, the land being judged not worth paying taxes upon,—and the settlers had undertaken the task themselves, all unaided, and had been two years at work on the main ditch when Erastus Hemmingway arrived in the community.

So dreary and forbidding was the outlook that he felt tempted to leave again immediately, but knowing that no land remained open for pre-emption elsewhere in the State, at last decided to stay and cast his lot with those who were so manfully struggling to overcome the difficulties by which they were surrounded.

Guided in part by the advice of such acquaintances as he had made since his arrival, he located a claim of one hundred and sixty acres, and made arrangements to live for a time in the family of a settler who was on a claim adjoining his own, agreeing to pay a small sum weekly for such food and accommodations as they could offer.

Of the half dozen men who accompanied Erastus to the Slough, not one had the hardihood to remain. All were too much discouraged by the outlook, and either returned to the old neighborhood or sought places for rent in other portions of the country.

When he had staked out his claim, Erastus hitched up and drove across the country until he found pasturage, and a rancher who was willing to let the colts run with his own stock until such time as the light rains, which might be expected to fall a few months later, should revive the seemingly dead grass of the Mussle Slough country. He then returned to the Slough on foot, and went to work with his fellow settlers upon the ditch, which was their only hope.

For weeks and months he worked in company with these men, many of whom had worked through all the weeks and

months of the two **previous** years; ill-fed—often without
bread of any kind for **long** periods at a time, **sleeping** upon
the ground almost **as frequently as in a bed,** working at night
as well as by day, their families camping **in wretched** little
huts at the **lake** watching the patches of **vegetables** and
corn upon which their very existence **depended.**

When the rain came and vegetation **started** up, the colts
were **brought down** from their pasture and made to do a
portion of **labor on the ditch;** their young master taking the
best **care of** them possible under the circumstances.

He had written home soon after positively deciding to
locate at the Slough, but had refrained from giving **a very**
accurate description of the country **or of his prospects, not**
wishing to excite any anxiety **in the minds of his friends**
regarding his welfare.   **In reply he had received letters from**
the **family telling him of affairs in the old neighborhood.**
Then for some weeks he was silent, not feeling that he had
anything cheerful to communicate, **and dreading, yet long-**
ing, to hear further regarding the engagement **between Lucy**
and Mr. Annelsey.

Meantime the dam which was to save the Parsons settle-
ment from the overflow had been completed, but scarcely was
the work accomplished before it became evident that it would
not long stay the mass of slickings which was coming down
in such immense quantities from the mines above as to have
filled the gulch itself a hundred feet deep for ten miles below
Gravel Hill, and in spite **of the fact that** large quantities **of**
it were turned aside into the new channel cut for it above the
dam, **it was** slowly but surely filling the whole gorge and
would soon rise above that structure, even if **it** did not sweep
it away.

Another meeting **of** the settlers was called, at which it
was resolved to apply to the courts for a perpetual injunction

restraining the companies from emptying their slickings into the gorge.

The services of a prominent attorney of San Francisco were secured and application for the injunction made.

But there were delays.

The attorneys for the mining companies asked for time in which to produce evidence to show why the injunction should not issue, and although the settlers pleaded the absolute necessity to them of immediate action, the time asked was given and even twice extended.

Then some technicality in the law or the papers in the case was discovered, and still further time consumed.

By this time the fall rains had commenced, and a few days later the gorge above the dam was full, not of water alone, but of earth and stones, which, pressing against that hastily built structure, swept it away and went pouring over the valley and farm lands below.

The bed of the creek was at once filled with sand and gravel. Brush and timbers from the broken dam, together with whole trees washed down by the operations at the mines, were swept along with the current and finding lodgment, formed a barrier which in turn banked up the water and earth behind it, until over whole farms the worthless soil from the mountains rose to a depth of ten and twelve feet, burying orchards and vineyards, and even some small buildings beneath the accumulated mass *

---

* "At Rose's Bar, where I am told Judge Field at one time practiced law, and where there was once a considerable town, its site is now sixty feet under the mining tailings." * * * * * "In the Gold Run case the defendant proved by a Mr. Fairchild that the breaking of a dam at the head of Pilot Creek, in El Dorado County, one of the tributaries of the South Fork, washed out of Pilot Creek in a jiffy, and into the south fork of the American River, 2,639,000 yards of earth and rock, including the great trees which the wave of water tore up by the roots in its downward course." * * * * "The extent to which the débris comes down is illustrated by the fact

Such was the fate of the Parsons ranch.

Powerless to stay its course, John and Martha Parsons saw the flood of death rise about them. Saw first their lower fields flooded and made valueless. Then saw the flood rise about the grape-vines until they were buried from sight, and the mass of earth and water, rising more slowly now, reached the orchard and the higher ground upon which stood the cottage with its outlying farm buildings.

Day by day they watched the horrible mass close in about them.

Now the topmost limbs of the peach trees alone appeared in sight, and then disappeared entirely.

At night the garden fence had been reached; in the morning it was a foot deep within the enclosure, and was rapidly approaching the door yard from three sides.

Now it reaches the front gate, creeps through the latticed fence and up the gravel walk. One by one the flower-beds disappear, swallowed up by the horrible anaconda that is winding its folds about the doomed cottage, whose inmates watch its approach in helpless agony, knowing that no human power can prevent the total destruction of all that years of toil and economy has enabled them to accumulate.

What is to be done?

Already a dozen of the neighbors have been driven from their houses and are domiciled in those more remote from the scene of the overflow, or are camping out upon the hills overlooking their desolate homes.

A few more days and the ocean of mud and water will enter their own cottage; where shall they seek for refuge?

that the Parks Dam across the Yuba, 12,460 feet long and over six feet in height, was filled full during three days and nights of the freshet of 1881."

Address of Geo. Cadwalader in the case of Edwards Woodruff vs. the North Bloomfield Gravel Mining Co., et al., tried in the Circuit Court of the United States, District of California, Dec. 22, 1882.

There is no one in the cottage now but John and Martha Parsons and the crippled boy; the young girl who was with them for a time having returned to her own home, and Jennie and Lucy being still in San Francisco.

Evidently the girls could not long remain at school now, for their parents had no longer any means of paying their expenses. Every dollar of the income of the past year had been expended in paying for work upon the dam and in the effort to obtain the injunction, and but fifty dollars remained in bank of that once laid aside to aid Erastus, now upon his own claim at the Slough.

"The girls must come home," Mrs. Parsons had said when word came that the dam had broken and all was lost.

"We must send for them, father. If we are to lose everything we cannot pay their expenses in the city any longer, and if you will take it to the office I will write a letter at once, telling them to come by the first boat."

But her husband pointed to the lake of mud and water, already six or eight feet deep, over the road across the creek bottom.

"We can't git to the Landing," he said. "A horse would mire in that stuff 'fore he got half way to the bridge."

"Then we must go to the landing above. Can't you get some of the neighbors to go for you? Mr. Ritchie's Henry will go, I think. You know they are not in as much danger yet as we are.'

"I kin git some one to go I s'pect, Marty," replied her husband; "I kin git some one to go, I reckon, but there ain't no home fer the girls to come to; er ther won't be by the time they 'ud git the letter and git here."

"Oh, John! John! is it possible that we have lost everything!" sobbed Mrs. Parsons, dropping into a chair and burying her face in her apron.

12

John Parsons made no reply, and after a few moments his wife checked her sobs and raising her head asked:

"Is there no way? Cannot the dam be rebuilt and made strong enough and high enough to stop this awful destruction of the homes of honest people?"

"I reckon we've did everything that kin be done," he returned, "except it is to push for the injunction on the companies, and that ain't any use now that the damage is done; and as fer the dam, why the hull gulch is chock full o' slickens and stuff, and there ain't no possible chance of doin' anything.

"No, wife," he added in a hopeless tone of voice, "there can't nothin' be done. We're driv out agin by them as cares nothin' for others, or who think that nothin' is wrong that the law can't punish 'em for,* and we have got to work hard in our old age and maybe die in a poor-house at the end. If it wasn't for you and Johnny I should wish I were dead a'ready, and I don't see as there is any use in my livin' any longer anyway, for I can't seem to pertect them as is dependent on me, though the Lord knows I've tried to do it."

Mrs. Parsons arose and came and put her arms around his neck and laid her head upon his shoulder.

"You have done all you could, John, and all anybody could have done," she said, "and you must not feel so, dear. It is better for us a thousand times to lose the place and everything on it than to lose you." And then feeling her

---

* It may seem incredible that mining corporations should be allowed to thus destroy homes that had been made long before they took up their claims and began their work. But until within the last year (1883) the courts afforded no relief. A recent decision has granted a perpetual injunction against the mining companies, and unless the influence of the heavy capitalists who are interested can procure a reversal of the decision it is now hoped that a stop has been put to such scenes as that described in this chapter. But only the future can determine the influence that money can exert upon the courts. We shall see.

voice choking, she paused a momeut and then resumed: "We have each other yet, and the children, and will manage some way. The girls will probably marry soon, so that they will not suffer greatly by the loss of the ranch, and we shall then have only ourselves and Johnny to provide for, and if we live to be too old to work I am sure the children will be glad to have us live with them."

"Maybe, maybe," returned her husband. "I hope so, for your sake and Johnny's, but I want to die before I become a burden on any one. Ef Lucy and Erastus, now, had a' married and could have had the place all right, I shouldn't ever have thought of bein' a burden on them, 'cause they're both our own children like; but now we have no place for ourselves, let alone givin' it to them, and Lucy has took a notion to marry one of the chaps as is responsible fer our ruin, and I'm thinkin' he wouldn't be overly proud of the old folks ef they was to ask for a place by his fireside in the big house they's agoin' to hev in New York. At any rate I'll never ask it. I'd rather starve.

"The young folks had best git married, though, ef they're goin' to; both of 'em. I've no fear fer Jennie an' Ensign. They'll git on all right, as far as they let folks git on that works for a livin', and if Lucy loves Mr. Annelsey I s'pose that's all right too, and she had better write fer him to come and get her at once ef he don't want her to get tanned up with campin' out in the foot-hills."

Mrs. Parsons thought the whole situation over and over, again and again.

All night she lay awake thinking of their changed circumstances and of her husband's words, and in the morning she did substantially what he had suggested—she wrote her daughters, telling them the ranch was flooded and destroyed, that the cottage itself would be untenable before many days,

12

but forbidding them to return home until they heard further
from their parents.

"Your father and I do not yet know what we shall do,"
she wrote. "There seems no place for us to go to. Some
of the neighbors, whose houses are on higher ground than
ours, have offered to let us stay with them until we can find
a place to rent, but we cannot long be a tax on the hospitality of those who have themselves lost everything except the
shelter over their heads, and who must, like us, soon seek
other homes.

"We are talking of going down into the great valley and
renting a place of some of the big landlords, but it is very
hard to think of working all the rest of our lives without
hope of ever having a place of our own again, and if we can
find a little place anywhere that is for sale, if it is only a few
acres with nothing but a shanty on it, we had both rather
buy it than to rent, even if we go in debt for it; but we do
not know of any such that is safe from the overflow of these
terrible mines.

"You must not worry about it too much, dears; and you
must not come home until you hear from us again, which will
not be long, for we must do something, and that quickly.

"You could not help much if you were here until we know
what we are to do, and would probably be more expense
here than there, and we will write you again just as soon as
we determine where we shall go."

Then she added in a postscript:

"You know how much your father and I love you, and how
anxious we are to have you always with us; but this we know
cannot be, and if the men whom you are to marry urge you
to a speedy union you have our consent, and it may be
best so."

This letter John Parsons mailed at Phippsburg, a little

town on the river ten miles above the Landing where they usually did their trading.

When Johnny saw his father preparing to start he began to cry piteously, and begged him not to leave them to be swallowed up by the terrible flood.

The poor child was not only nervous, but actually fright-ened. He had sat propped up in his little wheeled cot at the low window and watched the slowly rising flood until it had grown to seem a thing of life, a frightful monster, such as he had read about in fairy stories, only a thousand times more horrible, ready to swallow them all alive; and his pale face grew paler still, and his eyes, large with suffering, grew larger yet with fear, and he would not consent that either parent should remain long out of the room, and at night went to sleep holding to his father's hand only to awaken when all was still with screams of fright at the things which he saw in his dreams.

Then John Parsons would arise and sit by his side and talk to him, and tell him stories, and soothe him until his sobs ceased and gradually he dropped off to sleep again, only to see once more the horrid shapes that peopled his sleeping fancy, and awake in an agony of fear and trembling.

And now he begged and cried until his parents feared he would go into convulsions at his father's leaving, but there seemed no other way, for they knew that the neighbors were either busy trying to save something from the general wreck, or absent looking for some place to move to. People who are so foolish as to build their houses where wealthy corpo-rations may wish to empty the garbage from their back yards cannot humor the fancies of their crippled children. They are like the birds that build their nests upon the ground where the farmer desires to sow his grain—whose nests are turned under by the plowshare with never a thought of the

loss to the little **bunch of brown feathers that cries so pite-**
ously and flutters about the spot where its little **ones lie buried**
beneath the **sod.**

It was early in the morning when John Parsons started
with the letter. He knew that he would be forced to follow
a somewhat devious route in order to avoid the overflowed
district, but he was on horseback and expected to make the
canter of ten miles and back by noon at **farthest, and so told**
his wife **and** Johnny.

But noon came and no father. Then one o'clock, and
still he had not come.

Mrs. Parsons kept the dinner warm **and waited.** She had
spent the morning in packing, as best she could, their household goods in **shape** for moving, at the same time amusing
Johnny **with talks of the new place to which they** would go.

She did not know where it would be, yet tried, for the
lad's sake, to picture it as pleasant as possible, and so half
made herself believe that they might not **fail** in getting another home and being happy once more, and now while she
waited she continued the preparations for moving; but as the
hours passed and her husband was still absent, she **became**
uneasy and fancied all kinds of evils that might have befallen
him.

Had he attempted to cross some place in the **road** that
was covered by the overflow, and miring down been unable
to extricate himself?

The thought was horrible, and her brain reeled beneath it.

Then she told herself that it could not be; that instead
he had been forced to go further around than he had anticipated, and so more time was consumed.

Then again, she feared that his horse had taken fright
and thrown him, and she pictured him lying by the roadside

dead, or with broken limbs, calling in vain for help, or carried to a friendly shanty by some chance passer by, as he had carried Johnny when the accident which made him a cripple occurred.

"They say it never rains but it pours," she said to herself, as she stood gazing intently and anxiously into the rapidly gathering twilight. "Can it be possible that to all our other troubles is to be added an injury to John?"

She could not bear to think of it, and put the thought from her, and tried to keep from dwelling on it by talking to Johnny as he lay in his cot watching her pack the boxes and trunks with clothing and the various knick-knacks about the house.

Then a more hopeful thought came.

"Maybe father had heard of a place that he can get, and has gone to look at it," she said to Johnny, and the thought gave her fresh courage.

But as the day passed and night settled down upon the scene and still he did not come, hope turned to fear and she grew sick at heart.

She attended to the out-door chores when she saw it getting late; fed the pigs and the chickens and milked the cows, and then went in the gathering darkness and noted the rise in the slow creeping flood, and estimated that in two days more it would enter the cottage.

Then she returned to the house, lighted a lamp, and sat down by the cot of her crippled child, too utterly exhausted and broken in spirit to talk.

The boy seemed to understand, for he said nothing; did not cry nor moan, but lay with his large eyes fixed upon his mother's face with a look of wondering helpless resignation, as if he saw the approach of the horrid monster of his dreams, but felt that now no cries for help could avail anything, until, unable longer to control herself,

Martha Parsons sank upon her knees and buried her face in her handkerchief and sobbed aloud :

"My God, my God, why hast thou forsaken me ?"

CHAPTER XVIII.

DRIVEN TO THE MOUNTAINS.

For a half hour Martha Parsons remained kneeling by the side of her crippled child.

When she arose she was calm again, but neither the boy nor herself spoke, and finally sleep came and closed the lad's eyelids, and he lay quietly resting while his mother sat by his side as silent and motionless as he.

Her thoughts had gone back to the days of her childhood, and one by one she recalled all the incidents of her past life. She remembered the old church where she had been christened and near where she was born. In imagination she sat again in the straight-backed pew in company with the homely, old-fashioned congregation, and listened to the preaching of the venerable, gray-haired minister whose words she had been taught were those of one commissioned to speak for God and Christ.

Again she heard the sermon in which all men were commanded to accept their lot, whatever it might be, as from the hand of the Most High, who gave to each of His creatures as to Him seemed best, of the goods of this world; heard, mingled with much of sympathy for the impoverished and the outcast and the sinful, the poor bidden to be content with the condition in life to which it had pleased God in His wisdom to call them; and was dumbly conscious of feeling surprised at herself, and, maybe, a trifle frightened at daring to wonder for the first time in her life if God ever authorized anybody to say such things in His name; if, indeed, it were not blasphemy to tell the poor, who were made poor by being robbed, and the rich, who were made rich by the robbery, that such was God's will, and bidding them to be content in the condition in which they were thus placed.

She recalled the talks which she and John had during the days of their courtship and after their marriage. What plans they had laid ; how hopeful they had been of the future; how prosperous they had meant to be; and how much pleasure they had taken in thinking of the good they would do, and of the quiet old age they were to spend together after the hurry of life was over and their children settled comfortably near them, receiving and entitled to the respect and esteem of their neighbors.

They had worked hard; they had been honest; they had reared their children to be worthy members of society; they had done all they knew how to do to make the world better for their having lived in it; and now, their home lost, their children scattered, she sat by the bedside of her crippled child at midnight, waiting for the return of her husband, with a great fear at her heart that he, too, had been swallowed up by the terrible flood.

The moan which involuntarily escaped her lips as her mind returned to the present, awoke Johnny; but seeing his mother sitting by his side he did not cry or speak, but lay quietly gazing into her face for a time and then his quick hearing caught a sound which had escaped the duller ear of his mother, and a look, half of inquiry, half of fear, passed over his face, but still he did not speak.

Again the sound, and now his mother hears it too—the neighing of a horse upon the winding bluff road back of the house; then an answering neigh from the hill pasture, and both know that the husband and father has returned.

Hurrying to the door, Mrs. Parsons heard the pasture

bars let down; heard the short whinny of recognition and welcome which the horses exchanged as the home-comer entered the field, then heard the barn door open as the rider went to hang up his saddle; then the footsteps turned towards the house, and a moment later John Parsons, weary and covered with mud, but sound of limb, entered, and bending down kissed wife and child.

"I s'pose you an' Johnny hev been worried most to death about me, Marty," he said, "but I couldn't very well help it; leastwise I thought it best to do as I done."

"Yes, dear, we have been fearful that something had happened you. Did you meet with an accident, or what was the matter? I know you must be tired and hungry, whatever it was, and I'll have a cup of tea for you just as soon as the kettle boils again. It won't take but a moment; it was boiling only a little bit ago."

"Wall, you see when I got to town I concluded to ask around an' see if I could hear of a place for rent or to sell on time, an' after inquirin' a spell I heard of a claim, mostly wo'thless, but with enough good land to make a livin' on, that was for sale or trade, fifteen miles further back in the mountains; an' as, ef I come home first I'd hev to go right back agin to-morrow, if I took a look at the place at all, I concluded to go right on an' see it, hopin' to get home, though, afore it was so late. But when I got back to town it was almost dark already, an' neither me nor the horse had et a bite since mornin', an' I was jest obleeged to stop an' let the animal rest a couple of hours. That gave me a dark ride home, an' the roads is purty bad over the hills since the rains come. What time o' night is it? Nigh on to midnight, I reckon."

"The clock struck twelve some time since," replied Mrs. Parsons. "But what about the place? Is there any house on it, or an orchard, or anything? And what does the man ask for it?"

"There's a bit of a shanty on it," returned her husband, "an' a few scatterin' grape vines, an'. a dozen or two peach and pear trees. The place is well up on the mountain an' is off of the main road, an' sort o' lonesome like; leastwise, I'm afeared 'twould seem so to you an' the lad. But there's a chance to make a livin' there even if it ain't a very good one, an' I s'pect maybe grapes will do purty well on part o' the claim. It's mighty rough an' broken, though, an' won't be so pleasant cultivatin' as this place used to be.

"There ain't no bottom land onto it, ner within ten miles of it fer that matter. An' there ain't many neighbors, an' such as there is, is poor folks, that couldn't git claims no-wher's else. I talked with one of 'em, an' he said he was satisfied they could raise as good fruit of most kinds as grew anywhere in the state; an' anyway there ain't any danger of their floodin' it from any mines; it's too far up on the moun-tains fer that, an' maybe the best thing we kin do is to take it, 'specially as the owner, who lives in town, is willin' to take a pair of horses an' purty near anything else we have to turn out to him, I guess."

"Then we had better take it," replied his wife. "I had rather have a place of our own, however poor, than to be de-pendent upon somebody else and obliged to move every year perhaps, and never feel that anything is our own, as we would do on a rented place. But are you sure about the title, John? Don't for pity's sake let us buy a ranch to which there is not a good title."

"That's just what I told Mr. Blake, the man that owns it. I told him that if there was anything at all wrong with the title I wouldn't touch it with a ten-foot pole, but he says it's all right, an' he is to get an abstract of it from the recorder's office. The place has never had but two or three owners, an' it's clear outside of the land grant, so if there's no mortgages onto it I don't see how there can be any danger, an' of course the abstract will show."

"I almost wish you had told him we would take it. I'm afraid somebody else will step in and get it first, there are so many looking for places now. When did you tell him you would give him an answer?"

"He is to come over to-morrow and look at the things we have to trade. If we kin agree, then he is to get the abstract, an' if that is all right, it's a trade. I wish you could see the place, mother, before we decide about it, but I don't see how you kin, unless we take Johnny over to Ritchie's and leave him while you go an' take a look at it.

"What do you say, Johnny? Will you stay at Mr. Ritchie's while mother goes with me to see the new place?"

"Won't the water and mud rise clear over us and bury us?" asked the boy, in his weak little voice.

"Oh, no," replied his father, "Mr. Ritchie's house is higher up than ours, you know. There is not a bit of danger."

"Then I'll stay."

But Mrs. Parsons did not wish to go to see the place.

"It would be a hard day's ride," she said, "fifty miles there and back, and we would have to go on horseback, I suppose, for it must be awful slow getting along with a wagon, now; and besides it would make no difference any way. If you think we can make a living on it, we had best take it, for we can't stay here many days longer. We have no other place to go to, and it will not be easy to find places that we can trade for."

And so they talked on while the tea was made and drank.

Then they lay down, but it was almost day before sleep came to either of them.

About noon the next day Mr. Blake came as he had promised.

He was a man of medium size and pretty well built. He had a red face and a large mouth, and appeared about fifty years of age.

Certainly not a handsome man, he was yet not noticeably homely. In fact, there was nothing especially noticeable about him in any way. To all appearances he was an ordinary kind of man, who had doubtless mined some; been a farmer back in the states, perhaps, and at some period in his life had probably kept a hotel in a country town, or engaged in some other occupation which had given him a little more the air of a man of business, and a little less that of a day laborer.

At dinner, of which he was invited to partake, he asked a blessing. As they ate he commended the cooking; spoke of the great loss which his host had sustained from the destruction of his ranch by the overflow, and condemned in strong terms the outrage upon the rights of so good citizens as those at whose table he sat.

Then he passed on to a description of his own ranch, which he wished to sell.

It was well up in the hills, he said, but it was a fine place for fruit, and was out of danger from the overflow, and all it needed to make it a valuable property was the cultivation and care which Mr. Parsons knew so well how to give it.

He offered it for sale cheap because he was going back east, and wanted to clear everything up before he went, and get what he had together.

He would prefer to sell for cash, but if he could not do that, he would take a pair of horses and any other stock they might have to turn out. And if he could not dispose of them readily in the neighborhood, would drive them to Sacramento, on his way to New York, and sell them there.

After dinner he went out, in company with Mr. Parsons, and looked at the different animals and things which the now nearly impoverished family had to offer. He readily agreed to take one pair of the horses and a wagon and the top carriage, also three cows. But this still left a difference which he proposed should be made up by a note to be signed by Mr. Parsons and a couple of his neighbors.

To this Mr. Parsons would not consent. He doubted if any one would sign a note with him now, and he could not bear to think of asking and being refused, and preferred giving a mortgage on the place which he was to get of Mr. Blake.

Finally it was agreed to pay him the fifty dollars remaining in bank, and in addition to the other articles named, to turn him out the six head of fat hogs in the pen and certain articles of household furniture, the most valuable in their possession, but for which there would not be room in the shanty to which they were going, and so the bargain was made.

The Parsons were to retain possession of all the property until they had moved on to the new place; then to put the goods and animals at the disposal of Mr. Blake and receive the deed.

When this was all settled between them, and a memorandum of the whole matter made and carefully deposited in the pocket-book of Mr. Blake, that gentleman returned the pocket-book to his pocket, buttoned up his coat, and mounting his horse, rode back to town.

When he was gone Mrs. Parsons gave a sigh of relief. "Well, I am glad it is all fixed up," she said, "and I

shall feel better still when the deed is made and we are in
possession. All the time he was here I was afraid that the
trade would fall through some way, and I cannot begin to
tell how anxious I am to get away from here, or how I
dreaded having to rent a place. I'd rather live in a hut and
have it my own, than in a palace that belonged to another,
and I am like Johnny; I begin to feel as if this awful mass
that is about us might raise suddenly and swallow us all in
a moment."

"Yes," replied her husband, "it is better that we go, though
it's mortal hard to leave this place, which was the purtiest
and best in the valley. But it don't make much odds, I
s'pose, where one is, so they have enough to eat; and I guess
we can git that up there.

"I'll load up to-night, an' start to-morrow with the first
load. It'll take me two days to make the round trip, an'
hard days at that, but I'll put on all four of the hosses and
take all I kin pile on the wagon. Then I'll get Ritchie to
help with the next load an' we'll take Johnny in the carriage
an' make it all in two trips with somebody to drive the cows.
You'd better write Jennie an' Lucy, mother, an' tell 'em to
come to Phippsburg, so's to meet us there when we go with
the last load. That'll save comin' after 'em, an' they'll be
thar to help you fix things when we git thar."

"Poor things, what a home-coming it will be to them,"
sighed Mrs. Parsons.

Nevertheless she wrote telling the girls what had occurred
and how they must take the boat on the night of the day on
which they would get the letter. They were to get off at
Phippsburg instead of the old landing and wait at the hotel
until their parents called for them on their way to the new
home up in the mountains.

This letter John Parsons mailed the next day, while his teams were eating and resting from the pull over the hills with their load of household goods.

That night he slept in the shanty upon the place which he had bought, and the following day returned to his family and the doomed cottage.

With the help of a neighbor he loaded the remainder of his worldly possessions upon the two wagons, the heavy one and the spring fruit wagon. This neighbor was to drive one team and Mr. Ritchie volunteered the use of another animal to attach to the carriage in which was Mrs. Parsons, with Johnny propped up among his pillows.

It was a sad leaving of the old home.

The muddy water was now entering over the front steps and beginning to form pools on all the lower floors. Only the topmost twigs of the apple and pear trees, which were in lower ground than the house, and portions of the evergreens in the front yard were above the deposit. Every other green thing upon the valuable portion of the ranch had disappeared entirely from sight.

Martha Parsons wept as she took a last look at the place, and yet she was at heart glad to get away.

It was like a nightmare, staying there and seeing that mass of mud and water rise day by day. And besides, however poor their new home might be, it was henceforth the only one they were to know, and she was anxious to get into it and begin the work of improvement.

As for John Parsons, he looked neither to the right nor to the left. He did not even turn his head for a last look at the old place as he rounded the hill that shut it from their view.

Pride and ambition were well nigh dead within him, and

13

he hoped for nothing beyond a bare existence for the rest of his life.

The fleeing family had perhaps placed a distance of three miles between themselves and their ruined home when from the other direction appeared two horsemen.

As they came opposite the cottage, they looked for evidences of the presence of its former inmates, but did not pull up their animals.

"Evidently they too have pulled out," remarked one of the horsemen to his companion. "I say, Jobbers, it's pretty hard, now, on the poor ranchers, and I'll be hanged if I don't wish there was some way of getting out the gold without ruining their homes. Look there now; finest ranch and finest family in the whole country. Ranch gone to the dogs and the family gone, God only knows where."

"Oh 'e's all right," returned the other. "'E'll get another bit of land some'er's and go to work again, and in a few years 'e'll 'ave it all set out with trees and grape-vines. Great country this for a man as 'as to work for 'is livin'; great country, and w'en I return to Hingland I intend to hadvise all my farmer hacquaintances to hemigrate to California."

And then the two men relapsed into silence and rode on. The next day Mr. Jobbers took the boat for Sacramento, and from there went to New York, from whence he returned to his own country, fully impressed with the idea that however rough a life it might be in the mines for gentlemen, California was a great place for men who work for a living, and is to-day probably advising every farmer whom he meets to "hemigrate."

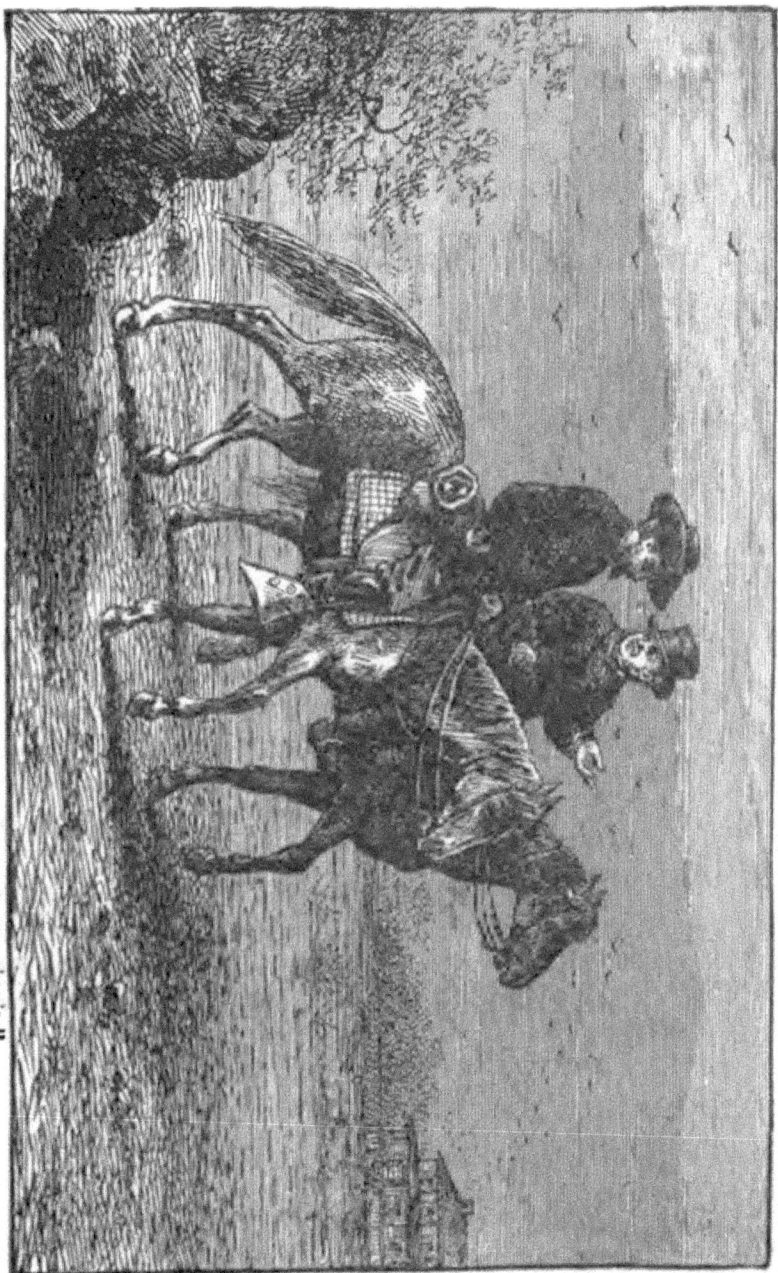

"OH, 'E'S ALL RIGHT. 'E'LL GET ANOTHER BIT OF LAND SOME'ER'S."

CHAPTER XIX.

THE MOUNTAIN RANCH.

It was high noon when our friends reached Phippsburg, and they were still fifteen miles from the new home to which they were going.

The girls had not yet arrived, the steamer on which they had taken passage having grounded upon a bar formed from the washing from the mines.*

Johnny, too, was complaining of his back, and his parents feared to take him further that day over the rough roads.

It was decided, therefore, that Mrs. Parsons and Johnny should remain at the hotel in Phippsburg while the men went on with the goods, and that on the morrow when they returned, the heavy wagon and carriage with the team which Mr. Blake was to have, should be turned over to him and the family should go on in the spring wagon.

Small as it was, the expense of remaining at the hotel

---

* SAN FRANCISCO, CAL., Sept. 15.—The rapid filling up of Sacramento River and its tributaries by débris from hydraulic mines has been brought forcibly to public notice by the dangerous sandbars recently formed, which have proved ruinous to river navigation. Just below Sacramento a big sandbar formed, so that a loaded steamer drawing only four and a half feet of water grounded this week—and only got off with difficulty. Ten years ago deep-sea vessels could pass this place, where, it is estimated, the deposits of mining débris now reaches a depth of twenty feet. Yuba River has been so filled up that the smallest boat cannot get to Maryville except when there is a flood, though formerly big boats ran there. Feather River is virtually closed to navigation all the year, because of formidable bars. Of course San Francisco Bay suffers also, and a large part near the mouth of the Sacramento has been so badly filled up as to make navigation dangerous. The "Slickens War," as it is called, is a fight of one rapidly dwindling industry against the agricultural interests of two of the richest valleys in the state and the navigation of the main inland waters. Unless something is done soon to deepen Sacramento River navigation must be abandoned and the farmers will be left to the tender mercies of the railroads.—[Special to *New York Tribune.*

was a sad draw on the few remaining dollars in the possession of John and Martha Parsons, but it could not be helped and the teams drove on and left them.

Towards evening the boat arrived, and on it came Jennie and Lucy. Mrs. Parsons could not leave Johnny to go down to the landing, but watched at the hotel window and beckoned to them as they came up the opposite side of the street.

When the girls saw their mother they hurried across the street to the hotel and into the sitting-room where she awaited them, and in another moment all three were crying upon each others' shoulders.

"Oh mother, mother, it's awful to think that the old place is lost, buried by the overflow from those mines; is there no way to save it? Can't it be floated off again?" sobbed Lucy, her whole frame shaking with excitement. "I can't bear to live and know that you and father are driven out of your comfortable home and forced to begin on a piece of wild land again. I wish you would go to town and live and let me teach school and support you. I'm sure I could do it."

"You must not take it so hard, dears," returned their mother, still holding the girls close to her. "True, it is very sad to be obliged to give up the old home, but no doubt we shall be very comfortable on the new place when we get it fixed up a little. What hurts me most is the knowledge that we may never be able to visit you if you go so far away as I suppose you will do when you are married to Mr. Annelsey."

"I'll never marry, mother, never," sobbed Lucy; "I have written Mr. Annelsey and broken off our engagement, and am going to stay with you and father and help take care of Johnny as long as I live. You need not say a word against it, for it's too late; the letter is half way to New York by this time."

To say that Mrs. Parsons was greatly surprised at this,

would be but to state the truth. To say that she greatly regretted it, would not be so true.

She had felt a certain degree of pride in the thought that Lucy would marry wealthy, and had sought to obtain comfort for the supposed coming separation in the knowledge that her daughter could want for nothing which wealth could buy, yet at times had feared that Lucy might not find happiness in the union, and wondered if it would not have been better for her to have married Erastus.

Especially since the last great trouble had come upon them, and she saw how her husband was breaking under it, she could not help thinking how much comfort it would have been to him, and to herself, if the young folks could have found their happiness in wedding each other and remaining with or near them in their old age. And now, while she scolded Lucy a little for her haste in the matter, she could not but feel thankful at heart that her child was not to go from her, at least for the present.

Jennie joined her sister in deploring the loss of their old home, and wept aloud and violently when her mother spoke of separation, but she did not offer to teach school to support her parents, and when her mother gently bade her cease to weep she wept the harder and clung the more closely.

"Come, Jennie," said Mrs. Parsons finally, "you really must cheer up, dear. It is not so bad but it might be worse. We have each other yet and no doubt shall get on nicely in the new home, and when Mr. Ensign gets ready, you and he can be married and live in San Francisco, which is not so far away but that you can come home and see us once in a while, and maybe we can visit you—why Jennie, what is the matter; have you broken with Mr. Ensign also?"

But Jennie only cried the harder and clung the closer with her face hidden upon her mother's shoulder.

Seeing the inability of her sister to speak, Lucy said:
"Jennie is married already, mother, and she and Mr. Ensign
are to start for Chicago next week.

"Mr. Ensign came to see her the night that we got your
letter telling us of the breaking of the dam, and found us
crying, and when we told him about it he urged Jennie to
marry him at once, and finally she consented and he went
and got a clergyman, and we all went down into the Professor's parlor and saw them married."

"I sh-shall ne-never forgive myself in-in the world if you
are angry with me," sobbed Jennie. "You know you-you
wrote in the letter that that we—"

"Yes, dear, I know," said Mrs. Parsons soothingly, strok-
ing Jennie's hair the while, "I wrote you that if your lovers
urged a speedy marriage your father and I would not object.
So you have done nothing wrong, and I am sure Mr. Ensign
will make you a good, kind husband, and I hope you will be
very happy.   I am only sorry that you are going so far away.
Cannot Mr. Ensign find work in San Francisco?"

At this Jennie began to check her sobs, and from the two
girls their mother learned the whole story.

Ensign had chanced to meet a gentleman from Chicago
for whom he had worked before he came to the coast, and
who now offered him a position at good wages with the prospect of a foremanship in a short time, if he would return to
Chicago and the old shop.   As wages were not so good in
San Francisco as formerly, and there were rumors of the fac-
tory shutting down entirely, he had decided to accept the
offer, provided Jennie would go with him as his wife, and
going to consult her with little hope that she would consent
to so hasty a marriage, had arrived just as the girls were in
their deepest distress over the news from home.   Taking
advantage of the situation he urged an instant marriage,

which ended in Jennie's sobbing out a consent upon his shoulder, and the young man had gone at once for the pastor of a church and had the ceremony performed in the presence of the family with whom the girls were rooming.

He was to come for Jennie in a few days—as soon as he could arrange some little matters of business, and they were to go to Sacramento by boat and from there by rail to Chicago.

"And so I am to lose one of my girls after all," said Mrs. Parsons when they had finished. " Well, if you are only happy, dear, I will try and not be sorry that you are going."

The next day when Mr. Parsons returned he hugged and kissed the girls in a boisterous manner, which he intended as a cover for his feelings over the loss of the old place and their changed circumstances.

Then he went to Mr. Blake's office, delivered up the horses, wagon and carriage, and gave him a bill of sale for the hogs and the household goods which he was to have and which had been left by agreement at a neighbor's.

In return he received a warranty deed to the new place, made by his request and without her knowledge in the name of his wife.

He did not do this for the purpose of defrauding anyone, for he owed no man a dollar, but he had lost all pride in ownership and somehow felt that honor required that, having failed to protect his own rights and guard his family from suffering, he should now resign all claim to the direction of affairs and place what little was left of their fortune in the hands of her who, equally with himself, had aided in accumulating all that was lost, as well as all that remained.

Accompanying the deed was an abstract of title signed by the recorder of deeds for the county, showing that there were no mortgages on record against the land therein de-

scribed, and that the title thereto was in the name of Mr.
Blake.

Not daring to trust to his own knowledge of such things,
Mr. Parsons took the abstract and deed to the landlord of
the hotel, whom he thought a man likely to be possessed of
some knowledge of business. The landlord looked them
over and pronounced them all right.

Determined to have no lingering doubts to worry him
hereafter, Mr. Parsons then sought out the village lawyer,
and submitted them to him also.

That gentleman glanced them over and replied:

"It's all right, sir; all right."

"Land entered by John Smith, who sells to Peter Jones.
Deed signed by John Smith and Hannah E. Smith his wife.
They sell to Thomas R. Blake. Thomas R. Blake and Mary
S. Blake deed to Martha J. Parsons.

"No mortgage appears upon the records in my office
against the above described land.

"ENOS PUTERBAUGH,

Recorder."

"That's all right. Title in your wife. Nobody can get
it away from you, sir."

"That's what I thought every time afore," muttered
John Parsons to himself as he left the office, "but they did it
all the same. But maybe as this place ain't worth much and
ain't never likely to be, they'll leave us in peace the rest of
our lives."

It was near the middle of the afternoon when the family
found themselves in the spring wagon and on their way.

The road wound round and round the hills, now up, now
down, rocky and full of gullies washed by the rains; never
being repaired except when it became absolutely impassable,
and in spite of the careful driving of his father, the rough

jolting hurt Johnny, sometimes causing him to cry out with pain.

Night overtook them when they were still several miles from their journey's end, making it still more difficult to travel with any speed, so that it was ten o'clock when they turned their tired and jaded horses off the main road into a by-track to the right, and a quarter of a mile further on pulled up in front of a cheap, unpainted board shanty—their new home upon the mountain side.

It was too late to think of doing anything except to make a cup of coffee and bunk down in the easiest way possible for the night.

Mr. Parsons, with the assistance of the neighbor who came with him the day before, had put up a cook stove and made a bunk for themselves on the floor, which remained just as they had crawled out of it in the morning. Another similar one was now made up in another corner of the room, and upon these the family slept, except Johnny, who occupied his wheeled cot, it having been the last thing packed on the wagon before leaving the old home.

When they arose the next morning the sun was shining over the mountain tops, and doing the best it could to make the scene a pleasant one.

Mr. Parsons hastily slipped on his clothes and went out to look to the horses.

Mrs. Parsons and the girls also dressed hurriedly and then stepped to the door and looked out. It had been too dark to see much the night before, and they had been too utterly tired out to try to see even the little that might have been seen, but now they were eager to know how the place really did look.

A sad enough contrast it was to the old home. Instead of a white cottage with its green blinds and wide open ve-

randahs, their dwelling was a rough shanty of boards nailed
perpendicularly to the framework, resembling in this respect
the one which they had occupied for a few days on the Suscol ranch. But instead of being sixteen feet in length, these
boards were but ten feet long, and as a consequence there
was no loft above as in the Suscol Cottage.

The interior was ceiled with cotton cloth, but there were
no little nicely made conveniences; no sink; no cupboard;
no partition; no porch over the door. All was in one room
and all was cheap and rough.

Outside, the view was no more cheering. The shanty
stood well up on the hill, or mountain. Below, and for a
little distance both in front and in the rear, was a piece of
tolerably level ground, perhaps forty acres in all, which declined gently to the west, ending in a ravine, beyond which
the earth became broken and rocky again.

Above the shanty the ground sloped upwards with a
sharper pitch for a few hundred feet and then rose rapidly,
becoming more and more precipitous, until it reached the
summit a third of a mile away.

In places portions of the solid rock foundation projected
through the barren soil, while in others, immense detached
boulders, weighing hundreds of tons, lay only slightly imbed-
ded in the earth and looking as if a push would send them
crashing down the mountain side.

Here and there stood a digger pine, its blue-green
spines looking, in the distance, like bunches of thick
smoke.

These, with a few scattering white oaks, half denuded of
their limbs by the tempests, and an occasional clump of
manzineto bushes, were the only vegetation which grew here,
except where some large boulder formed a slight protection
from the wind, and prevented the rains from washing away

the thin coating of earth below it, might be found a few bunches of coarse wild grass.

A fence of boards had been thrown around the tillable ground by the last occupants, but this was down in places, and only added to the general look of isolation and decay.

The road by which they had come the night before could be seen at one point only, and that nearly a mile distant, where it wound around a spur of the mountain and dived down into a ravine from which it emerged only to wind around other bluffs and spurs and dive down into other hollows out of the range of vision of anyone standing in the door or at the windows of the shanty.

By ascending to the summit of the mountain, a succession of lower ridges and hills could be seen stretching away towards Phippsburg and the river, with sometimes a glimpse of the valley beyond, and of a thin line of smoke from the steamers that went puffing up and down that highway of nature; but from the lower ground on which the shanty stood this view was shut out by intervening hills, and there came a feeling of loneliness, and sequestration indescribable, to the three women as they looked out upon the scene that first morning.

A thick crop of self-sown oats mixed with weeds had sprung up on the ground, untilled for two years. These the rain had beaten flat to the earth in places, while in others they still kept a half erect position and were twisted together in bunches.

The few scattering grape vines, left to themselves, had broken from their supports and run riot among the weeds and grass. The peach and pear trees showed the same lack of care, the very luxuriousness of their growth and their untrimmed appearance adding to the general look of desolation.

And this was the scene upon which Martha Parsons looked, standing in the door of the shanty with her two daughters. Contrasting it with the home they had just left, and recalling the fact that the nearest neighbor was two miles away, is it any wonder that her heart sank and that for a moment she almost wished they had gone down into the valley and rented, instead of buying this isolated and lonely place upon the mountain side?

CHAPTER XX

A GLEAM OF SUNLIGHT.

But it would not do to give way to feelings of despair. This was to be their home and they must make the best of it, and without a word she turned back and began arranging things so as to give room to set the table and get what breakfast was possible under the circumstances.

Mr. Parsons came in with his arms full of wood gathered from a fallen tree top, and soon a fire was burning in the stove and the smell of coffee filled the room.

No complaints were uttered, but all worked to get things to rights. Nails were driven into the studding of the walls and articles of clothing and many of the cooking utensils were hung up out of the way, at least for the time being.

The table was placed in the center of the room and covered with a white cloth, the frugal meal placed upon it and the family gathered about for the first meal in the new home. As they ate they talked of how best to arrange things.

If it had been the dry season they could have got on much more comfortably, but with the certainty of rain one-third of the time for months to come, the prospect was dismal enough.

However, they must do the best they could, and after breakfast Mr. Parsons helped to put up the beds, one in each corner farthest from the stove, which stood in the center at that end of the room where a single window of six small panes of glass looked out upon the mountain above them. At the other end were two windows of twelve panes each, through which could be seen the hills stretching away towards the river.

There was also a similar window on each side at the right of the doors, so the room was not dark, however much it might lack for conveniences.

Everything not needed for daily use was packed in boxes and trunks and stored away under the beds, but even with this economy of space very little room was left for moving about.

Each member of the family, however, tried to be cheerful and so cheer the rest. Lucy even went so far as to attempt a witticism, and suggested that there was no lack of room so long as none of them were obliged to leave the house in order to get space to open the stove door.

Strips of bright carpet were laid between the beds, about which were hung curtains reaching from the ceiling to the floor. The clock found a resting place upon a shelf to the left of the front door. A bureau with a mirror occupied the space between the windows at the end where the beds stood. The table, when not in use, was folded up and allowed to stand in the center of the floor ready to be opened at meal time. Upon the walls were hung a few pictures. The white curtains which had once adorned the windows of the sitting-room of the old home, were fitted to those of the new; and when all was done that could be done, the room looked so bright and cosy that the hearts of its occupants lifted a little, and but for the thought that one was so soon to leave them, whom they knew not when, if ever, they would meet again, they might have been almost happy.

Jennie did not know what day to look for her husband's coming, for he could not tell when they parted in San Francisco, how long it would take him to arrange his business, which consisted in the collection of several little sums of money owing to him, but she had written from Phippsburg, telling him where to go for directions how to find her ; and one day, about a week after the family had taken possession of the shanty on the mountain side he came, having walked out from the Landing.

Mrs. Parsons cried a little when Ensign kissed her and called her "mother." It reminded her so forcibly of the separation which his coming presaged that she could not help it. But she welcomed him warmly and made him feel that she loved him already for Jennie's sake.

From John Parsons he received a hand-shake which, hardened as his own hands were by work in the shop, came near causing Ensign to flinch. The man whose daughter he had married felt a very warm friendship for him indeed.

In comparing Ensign with Annelsey, as he had naturally done at times, when he expected both would become his sons-in-law, he had somehow come to regard him as a kind of hero, contending against odds, as he felt that all men who labored were forced to do, and that in choosing Jennie for a wife he had allied himself with those who, although giving no outward sign, were yet half unconsciously revolving in their minds some plan by which to remove the wrongs beneath which they suffered and writhed.

It was true that he had lost his pride in possession and with it all confidence in himself.

Without much knowledge of books, inclined by nature to think lightly of his own abilities, and having failed to successfully defend what he knew to be his natural rights to the wealth which he had himself created, he now felt that he had no right to offer advice upon needed reforms in society or the laws. But Ensign was young, he possessed cool courage and a spirit that would not allow him to remain supinely inactive beneath great and continued wrongs. Besides this

14

he had a fair education, and, so the girls said, had once or
twice talked to his fellow-workingmen in public upon questions affecting their interests, and there had gradually grown
up in the mind of John Parsons a feeling that Ensign was to
be instrumental in some way, perhaps as a leader, in righting
the wrongs of the people.

So long as Lucy had been engaged to marry Mr. Annelsey these feelings had been suppressed, overlaid as it were
by a fear that in encouraging them he was choosing between
his daughters, who were equally dear to him, but he had not
been able to prevent a feeling that Annelsey, being in sympathy with the cause of the losses which he had suffered,
was in some way partially responsible for them, as he certainly was a representative of the class who were the gainers
by those losses, and by the losses of the thousands and millions of other men and women who are doomed to toil all
their lives for the wretched pittance of enough food and
clothing, and hopes of better times, to induce them to continue the work of creating wealth for others.

The moment, however, he learned that Lucy had dismissed Mr. Annelsey, the thoughts which had before been
but a dumb kind of feeling, kept under by a knowledge of
the relation which the young man was likely to bear to the
family, began to take shape, and once or twice, in talking
with Jennie of the life which she and her husband would
lead in Chicago, he had even put these thoughts into words,
and now he welcomed the young man not alone as a son-in-
law, but as one who might some day help to right existing
wrongs and make the people free.

Ensign remained with the family nearly a week, and
every day endeared himself more and more to his wife's
parents. It was in order that they might become better
acquainted with him and thus not feel that they were giving

their daughter to one so nearly a stranger that he remained. During his stay he helped all he could to put the place in better shape, and as the rains did not fall during the entire week, the two men were enabled to do much towards making things look more cheerful.

A shed for the horses was built out of lumber bought for that purpose by the former owner, but never erected. The broken places in the fence were repaired; the grape vines staked and tied up, and portions of the over abundant growth of fruit trees cut away.

It was really wonderful, the change which these little improvements made in the look of the place. But then they had the sun, and the sun with a very little assistance in the way of setting leaning fences and gates upright will, in a few days, make a great change in any picture first seen when wet and sodden by long continued rains.

As the two men worked they talked,—talked of the wrongs of the farmers and the laboring and business men of the cities; of the causes of so many losses and so much poverty and suffering and of the possible or impossible remedies.

"There ought to be a law to prevent corporations from ownin' land they don't need an' can't make no use on, 'cept to make them that does want to use it pay for the privilege," said Mr. Parsons, as they were at work repairing the fence. "No man can't be really free unless he has a home of his own, and here gover'ment has gone an' give half the State to corporations, an' how is the next gineration to git homes, I'd like to know.

"An' other corporations are washin' down the mountains an' a fillin' up the valleys; spilin' the finest lands; chokin' up the river, an' destroyin' the homes of honest folks jest as ef gold was of more value than bread. I've tried hard to

14

get somethin' ahead agin old age come a creepin' on to us, and to give the youngsters a start when they left us, as Jennie is a doin' now, and here's what it all amounts to; a bit of land not much better than wild on the side of a mountain. The land God made, an' all the improvements that is on to it never cost a thousand dollars when they was new, and that ain't as much as my wife had when I married her ; so we've got nothin' at all to show fer a lifetime of hard work an' savin'.

"So fur as we're concerned, mother n' me I mean, it don't make much difference any more. We're gettin' old and shan't last much longer; but ef you an' Jennie ain't no luckier than we hev been, and there ain't no change for the better in things, I'm afeard you won't have even sich a shanty as we've got to die in, and your children won't be no better than slaves. Ye see it holds to reason that ef 'things don't git no better they must git wus, fer every year the corporations an' the rich folks is a gittin' more an' more of the land, an' of everything else, an' the more they git the easier it is to git more, an' by an' by they'll hev it all, an' them as hain't got nothin' an' can't get nothin' will hev to do as they say or starve."

"I don't exactly understand where the wrong starts," replied Ensign, "but I know there is a great wrong somewhere. The ownership of land by corporations, and by others who only wish to play at dog-in-the-manger, is one cause for the existing condition of things, but there must be others.

"Some way or other the larger portion of all the wealth which the people create gets away from them while they are exchanging it among themselves. I don't know how, but it does. If it didn't there could not possibly be rich people who have never worked.

"The merchant buys the goods of the manufacturer and sells them to those who consume them, thus saving much time which would be wasted if each individual was forced to go to the manufacturer for every article purchased. The merchant is therefore a valuable member of society—he helps the producers to make an exchange of wealth, and is fairly entitled to receive pay for what he does. But there are the national banks, I don't see how they help any; and every particle they consume or hoard up is so much taken from the wealth which belongs to those who produce it. It seems to me that those who produce wealth ought to have wit enough to devise some means of exchanging it among themselves without paying a bank for the privilege. And every once in a while there comes a panic, and thousands of business men are ruined, and thousands of laboring men thrown out of employment, and then they get desperate and try all kinds of sharp tricks to catch up again. Now if nobody is benefited by these panics, some way ought to be devised to prevent them, and if anybody is benefited by them they are the fellows that ought to be watched and not allowed to have any hand in the making of the laws, for it is natural to suppose that they would legislate in their own interest and not in that of the laboring and business portion of the community.

"Then there are the railroads; they get their charters from the people on the plea of being public highways. The people build the roads and then the companies charge just what they choose for transporting the people and their goods from one part of the country to another, and if it is goods that they transport, they usually take a great deal more of them than they leave the producers, and then bribe Congress and courts and State legislatures not to interfere with them.

"And so it goes, and I don't know how to go to work to stop it."

"Wall," replied Mr Parsons, "you're on the right track anyway, an' you jest want to keep agoin' till you think it all out. What you say about the exchangin' of wealth is sensible. It holds to reason that there oughtn't to be nothin' thrown in the way of folks exchangin' wealth. Them that works creates all the wealth there is, and if they had all the land to begin on, and weren't beat no way in the exchangin' of what they produced, it's mighty clear that ef a fellow didn't produce nothin' er help some way in the exchangin' of what others produced, he wouldn't have anything to eat very long. There ought to be some way discovered so that them that produce the wealth could trade among theirselves without supportin' a lot of fellers that don't do nothin' but stan' around an' look on.

"Ef you an' Rastus, now, could be together you'd figger it out between you in short meter, I'll wager. I tell you, Rastus is smart, and he's got the sand to back it, an' ef anybody ever goes to disturbin' him on his claim, there'll be trouble in camp dead sartin."

At last the day came when Jennie and her husband were to take their departure.

The family arose early and prepared breakfast as usual, but it was with heavy hearts and eyes wet with tears. And when it was eaten, Mr. Parsons went out and hitched the horses to the spring wagon and drove around to the door of the shanty, and helped Ensign to lift in Jennie's trunk. The smaller traveling bags followed. Then came the last kiss and clasping in arms and pledges of constant remembrance and love, over which we willingly draw a vail.

Who is there that has not witnessed similar partings; part-

ings of those whose happiness depended so much on each
other's presence, yet who were forced by the cruel necessity
of hunting for dollars to tear themselves apart, and each go
separate ways with half of the sunshine gone out of their
lives?

Will the time never come when men will understand what
the Teacher of men meant when He said, "Take no thought
for the morrow"? And is it not possible, by being just to
each other, to remove that constant, crushing weight of care
which comes from the ever-present necessity of taking
thought as to what we shall eat, and what we shall drink,
and wherewithal we shall be clothed?

I believe it will come; I know that it is entirely possible.

When good-byes had been said, John Parsons drove the
young couple to the Landing, where, with tears coursing down
his cheeks, he too, bid them good-bye and God speed, and
then, having fed his horses, again hitched up and started
sadly homeward.

CHAPTER XXI.

JOHN PARSONS GIVES ERASTUS A HINT.

When the spring came, the **level** ground about the shanty on the mountain side had been broken and sowed in grain, or planted with vegetables ; the sloping ground above set in grape vines, and a hundred added fruit trees were putting forth their buds and giving promise of the future.

John Parsons was not so young and spry as formerly, **but** he was **still in good health, and** work was his only escape from thought. **Every day** when the rain was anything less **than a regular downpour, he was to be seen at work some-where about** the premises, **and Mrs. Parsons** and Lucy lent **ready assistance.**

As the house was small, the labor of caring for it was **small also, and** on pleasant days one or both of them **were** to be found busily employed in **the** garden or vineyard.

They made few acquaintances in their new home. There was still no neighbor nearer than two miles away, and not more than a score of families within a circle easily reached for a day's visit, **and of these a** number were foreigners, who, being unable **to** speak the language, did **not mingle** with their American neighbors.

Occasionally **a** couple of women **from** some of the little ranches upon the other side **of** the mountain would come to **spend the day at the shanty,** but not often; and although **pleased to have them come, Mrs.** Parsons **and Lucy did not** always return their visits. **This was not** because they did not feel kindly towards their neighbors, but because they felt little inclination to go from home, and because they were busy, whenever the weather would admit of it, in helping to get the place in shape to produce a living for the family.

And so the spring and the summer passed, and fall came again.

They now had an abundance of vegetables; the two cows which they had brought from the old place, and which found pasturage in the hollows of the hills, supplied them with an abundance of milk and butter, and even with a small surplus to sell; and this, with the chickens and turkeys that thrived so finely and wandered at will up the mountain side and down the gorge at the foot of the level field, kept them supplied with groceries.

Of clothing they had a good supply when they came, and were not obliged to purchase, either for garments or bedding, for some time to come, and so did not suffer for anything except from a sense of their losses and wrongs, and for the want of companionship.

They heard from Jennie and her husband every few weeks. Ensign had been given the place promised him. They were living in the outskirts of the city, in a little cottage which they had bought on monthly payments, and were comfortable and happy, as young married folks who are blessed with good health and plenty of faith in each other and the future, always are.

From Erastus they heard but seldom, but knew him to be at work on his claim at the Slough.

Mrs. Parsons had written him of the destruction of the old home, and of their removal to the new, soon after its occurrence, and also of Jennie's marriage to Ensign and their removal to Chicago.

Of Lucy's breaking with Mr. Annelsey she did not write,

thinking possibly it might not be permanent, in which case it would be better for Erastus, if still feeling attached to Lucy, not to have his hopes raised to be again dashed to the ground.

Mr. Annelsey, however, did not plead very earnestly with Lucy to reconsider her action in dismissing him. It was several weeks before his reply came; and then, while he expressed regret at her decision, he did not urge her very strongly to reverse it. Knowing that his parents would oppose his marriage with a poor girl, he had not informed them of his engagement, and no comments would therefore be made at its being annulled; a fact upon which he now congratulated himself.

He had already begun to feel his affection for Lucy weaken with absence; was, in fact, becoming enamored of another young lady in whose society he had frequently been thrown since his return to New York, and whose position in wealth was equal to his own; and although he told himself that Lucy's letter had broken his heart, it is probable that after the shock to his self-esteem was over, he was rather glad than otherwise.

If Lucy expected or desired a more vehement protestation of love from her discarded suitor than she received, her manner upon opening his letter did not reveal it.

She read the letter in the presence of the family, and then calmly handed it to her mother. The next day she replied to it, reiterating her desire to be free from their engagement and asking the return of her letters.

"I shall send yours, together with the ring and other jewelry, by the same mail that takes this letter," she wrote him, and having sealed it and seen it, in company with the package, safely on its way to the office, she went about her usual duties with a cheerful, even merry air, which was a great source of comfort to her parents, and of especial satisfaction to her father.

"Ef Rastus 'ud only come back now it 'ud be all right," he mused, and feeling certain that the young man's affection for Lucy had not waned because of absence, fully expected him to come back and ask her to be his wife.

For this he waited with impatience, wondering at Erastus' delay and inventing excuses for it.

"'Spect the poor fellow hasn't jest got the money by him to come on," he said to himself.

And then again, "Maybe he's a puttin' in his crop an' wants to finish so it will be growin' while he's gone." Or, "like enough, he's a-workin' for somebody else for a spell an' can't honorably get off right away."

But as the weeks passed into months and the only evidence that Erastus had not forgotten them was a letter expressing his sorrow at the loss of their home, and a hope that he might some time assist them if they should require it, but never a word about Lucy or any intention of visiting the family, all hope of seeing Lucy married to the man whom he loved as a son and respected for his manly qualities began to die out of John Parsons' bosom.

"Rastus was always awful proud," he said to himself, "an' I reckon he can't get over the girl's preferrin' of that young jackanapes to him in the first place."

He still supposed that Mrs. Parsons had written Erastus of Lucy's dismissal of Annelsey, and it was not until months had passed and summer was giving place to fall that he learned differently.

He had never mentioned his hope that the young folks would "make up" to anyone.

Erastus knew that Lucy was with her parents, but supposed her only waiting for her affianced to come and claim her, and so worked on, striving to conquer his love but never succeeding, even for a moment.

And Lucy, although knowing that she loved Erastus, had always loved him, either supposed that he knew of her broken engagement, and knowing it, was silent because he had no love for her, or, if she suspected that he did not know, was restrained by maidenly reserve from taking any steps to acquaint him with the fact.

One day Mrs. Parsons was helping her husband in the garden, when something was said about Erastus.

"I wonder," remarked Mrs. Parsons, "what he is doing now? It is a good while since we heard from him. I wish I knew how he is getting along. Poor boy, he must have a hard time of it with no one to keep his clothes in order or do a thing for him. I wonder if he ever thinks of getting married?

"Of course he must," she added, answering her own question; "he has got a little start by this time and every young man on a farm needs a wife. I hope he will get a good one when he does marry."

John Parsons gave his clothes a little hitch, a habit he had when at a loss for a word. Then turning his back to his wife and putting an extra bit of force into the hoe he was using, said :

"I had sort o' thought maybe he an' Lucy 'd make up, now Annelsey's out o' the way, but it seems they don't. 'Pears like Rastus is too proud to take up with bein' second choice, though I don't b'lieve the girl ever cared half as much for that ar popenjay Annelsey as she did for him, even if she did promise to marry him. I wish she'd write to Rastus and tell him so. I know that 'ud fetch him. Ras ain't the fellow to get over that kind of a thing in a hurry, and I know he loved her desprit, an' it seems no more'n fair that she should take the first step towards makin' up, under the circumstances."

His manner of saying this showed that he intended it to be an argument too strong for his wife to rebut, showing reason why Lucy could, and should, let Erastus know that she had changed her mind and was ready to marry him if he still desired it.

When he paused he felt that he had not made the case as strong as it should be, but not knowing exactly how to make it stronger he waited for a reply from his wife, still keeping his back towards her and his hoe going vigorously.

But Mrs. Parsons knew that her husband had not finished what he wished to say, and she remained silent. Pretty soon he began again.

"You see, Marty, it holds to reason that Lucy should be the one to speak first. Rastus loved her, an' she knew it; leastwise he thought she did; an' knowing it she went an' engaged herself to that ar fellow from New York an' so gave Ras to think she wouldn't have him no way it could be fixed. So he went off to git away from the sight of 'em. An' now, though knowin' that Annelsey's got his walkin' papers, he don't know as Lucy 'd have him no more'n she would afore; an' Ras ain't the kind as goes spoonin' round beggin' for what folks don't want to give him. It ain't right, an' it ain't fair, when I know the girl 'ud give everything she's got in the world to have him back, that they should be kept apart jest because it's customary for the man to speak first. He has spoke first once an' now it's her turn."

All the time John was speaking Martha Parsons was thinking. She believed that Lucy loved Erastus and was secretly in hopes that he would yet return to her, but she was not sure, and she saw the delicacy of the situation more clearly than did her husband, who had never been able to

discover any necessity for the concealment of the true feelings of either party to a love affair.

When her husband had ceased speaking she was silent
for a moment and then said simply:

"Are you sure Erastus knows that Lucy has broken with
Mr. Annelsey?"

John Parsons suddenly stopped hoeing and turned quickly
around facing his wife.

"Didn't you write him that, when the girls first come
home?" he asked in surprise.

"No, I did not; I was not certain that she cared for him
and feared to awaken anew, hopes that, after all, might be
useless. It was not certain that Lucy's engagement with
Annelsey might not be renewed, or that because she dismissed him she loved Erastus, and I thought it best to let
him learn of it by accident. I supposed he would find it out
through Jennie or someone else, but I do not think he has."

Her husband made no reply but resumed his hoeing and
the subject was not referred to again. Indeed very little further conversation occurred between them during the entire
afternoon, both appearing busy with their own thoughts.

At the supper table that evening Mr. Parsons proposed
that the two women should go to town the next day with
some butter and eggs and such other articles as they could
spare, and make an exchange for family supplies.

"Johnny and me'll keep house while you're gone," he
said; "we're capital at keepin' house, ain't we, Johnny? And
mother'll bring you some candy or somethin'."

There was nothing very unusual in this proposition. Mrs.
Parsons and Lucy had made similar trips on several occasions,
leaving Johnny and his father at home.

John Parsons hated to "peddle," as he called it, and his
wife always got better prices for the butter and eggs and

chickens than did he; besides which she knew better how to invest the proceeds economically in necessities for the family, and there was need of economy now. And as neither of the women liked either to go to town alone, or to stay alone with Johnny while the other went with the husband or father, it had become the rule for both to go and leave Johnny to the care of his father, and so they decided to do now. Accordingly such vegetables as they were to take were gathered and placed in the spring wagon. A hunt was made for eggs, which were carefully packed, small end down, in oats, to prevent their breaking, and the bit of butter which they had saved was taken from the well where it hung by a rope, and rewrapped in white cloths.

When it became dark they went with a lantern and caught two dozen chickens and put them in a crate, previously made and kept in which to take fowls to market; and bright and early the next morning the horses were hitched up and they started.

When they were gone, John Parsons washed the dishes, which the women had not stopped to do, tidied up the house the best he knew how, talking to Johnny all the time, and then went into the garden to work, taking the boy with him, as was his almost invariable custom when the weather was fine, and placing him, in his wheeled cot, where they could talk together as the father worked.

The fresh air and sunshine did the child good and he amused himself in many ways. The chickens and turkeys learned to regard him as a friend and would come around him, often jumping upon his cot for some bit of food which he had brought, some of them becoming so tame as to permit him to handle them.

When noon came the man and boy returned to the house, where the father prepared and they ate dinner. Then, when the dishes had been washed and Johnny had dropped off to sleep, as he always did after dinner in the long days, John, Sen., went to the bureau and rummaged around until he found some writing paper and finally a pen and a bottle of ink.

These he brought to the table, drew up a chair and sat down.

"I'll jest give Rastus a hint," he was saying to himself, "an' if he's still of the same mind as he used to be, he'll be here in less'n two weeks an' mother an' Lucy'll never know what fetched him.

"Wimin's curis about some things; I never did understand 'em very well. There's Marty, now; best woman livin', tender hearted as a chicken, an' Lucy's jest like her; but they're a-lettin' Rastus an' her break their hearts fer each other rather than to speak up an' tell him how the land lays; but I ain't goin' to 'low it."

He dipped the pen in ink and then let it slip through his fingers and make a great blotch on the white table cloth.

This was unfortunate; it would be a tell-tale spot informing the women of what he had been doing in their absence.

He arose and wet the dish rag and tried to remove the ink spot, but only succeeded in making it larger. Finally he carried the pen, ink and paper to the bureau, took off the table cloth and hung it in the window to dry, brought back the writing materials and again sat down to his task.

It was a long time since he had written a letter; he tried to think how long, and could not remember of having done so since the family came to the coast. Erastus was a tolerable penman, and good at composing, and had, at Mr. Parsons' request, written the few business letters that there had been a necessity for, and since he had left, there had been no business letters to write, and until now John Parsons had contented himself with simply sending his love or supplying some bit of news for Lucy or her mother, when they wrote to either of the absent ones on family affairs.

But now he had an object to accomplish and must write, and he squared himself to the task.

Again he dipped the pen in ink, but discovered that he had forgotten the day of the month and got up and consulted the almanac which always hung on a nail, driven into the window casing near the clock.

When he had the date safely down he began:

" DEAR RASTUS:

"Yer mother and Lucy hav gon to town with some chickens and things and are goin to bring back some groceries.

"Lucy aint a goin to marry Mr. Annelsey after all; she's give him his walkin papers fer good.

"We are gittin long purty well considerin, though this place aint quite so comfortable and nice as the old one was. There aint no young folks around here much, and Lucy dont act like she wanted to hav anything to do with any of the young fellers that does come. Hadn't you better come home and make us a visit. Your mother and me wants to see you awful bad and so does Lucy; leastwise I think she does.

"We're gittin the place fixed up some better than it was when we came here. Built a porch over the front door last week and the wimen has set out some rose bushes on both sides of it; you know Lucy always was terrible fond of roses.

"Johnny is bout the same as when you left. He and I hav been at work in the garden this forenoon, but he's asleep now thats the reason I'm writin' you. You see I dont want the wimen to know it, they are so awful curis about such things. I spect Lucy ud think it wasn't proper if she knew it. I reckon she thinks you cant never forgive her, er love her

15

any more, cause she went and engaged herself to that feller Annelsey, fore she knew what she wanted.   You see a woman thinks she mus'n't chirp even ef her heart is a breakin.

"Wall, they'll be comin back fore long an I must quit writin and get ready for em.   When you come up you needn't say anything to Lucy or mother bout my havin writ to you, cause you see it wont do em any good to know it, an Lucy might not like it; might think you come out of pity fer her er somethin.   They're awful curis critters, wimen is.

" This from yours affectionately,

"JOHN PARSONS."

He read the letter over slowly and carefully, and then added:

"P. S.   It was Lucy's doins breakin off with Annelsey, an I dont see why she should have done it ef she hadn't loved somebody else better."

The letter finished, he sealed it up, directed it and placed it in the inside pocket of his vest.

He had yet to get it to the post-office without the knowledge of the family, and he was at some loss to know how to accomplish this, as it was fifteen miles to the Landing, and he could think of no excuse for going there immediately after his wife and Lucy had purchased all needed family supplies; but he determined to bring it about somehow.   "Maybe they'll forget something," he said, mentally, as he replaced the pen and ink in the bureau.   "I hope they will; ef they do I'll jest lope a horse an' ride over there to-morrow an' mail this letter, fer I'm bound to give 'Rastus a hint of how the lead runs."

CHAPTER XXII.

THE LOVERS' MEETING.

Although having said, in his letter to Erastus, that he expected his wife and daughter soon and must prepare for their coming, John Parsons did not really look for them yet for some hours.

It was fifteen miles to Phippsburg over a hilly road, and it required the whole of a long day to make the trip, dispose of the articles taken, and return; and it was not yet the middle of the afternoon when the letter was finished. Yet John Parsons had no intention of telling a falsehood. Liars and cowards were his especial detestation, and this slip of his from the path of truthfulness, like nine-tenths of the white lies so common among all classes, was the result of an inability to readily command language in which to express his thoughts.

He had given the "hint" which was the purpose of his writing, and could think of no proper way in which to close his letter and at the same time tell Erastus not to mention, to Lucy or to Mrs. Parsons, the fact of his having been written to. The whole affair was intended to be a fine stroke of diplomacy by which the father hoped to reunite those whom he loved, and whom he believed were warmly attached to each other, without wounding the modesty and self-respect of his daughter.

It was dusk when Mrs. Parsons and Lucy returned.

The husband and father met them at the gate which opened into the enclosure where the shanty stood, and

15

kissed as he helped them, dusty and tired, to descend from the wagon. Then he handed out the bundles and packages which they had purchased, after which he cared for the horses while the women entered the house.

They found the fire burning brightly, the tea-kettle simmering on the stove, and the table set. The ink-spot on the table cloth was not visible, for it had been carefully covered with a broad dish; and if Mrs. Parsons noticed it when she removed the cloth and shook out the crumbs that evening, she was wise enough not to mention it, and in the morning a clean one was substituted and the stained cloth thrown into the wash.

Johnny was of course anxious to see the various packages unwrapped, but was persuaded to defer seeing all except the articles purchased especially for him, until they had eaten and cleared off the table, when they would all take a look at them.

As the family sat at supper they talked of the day's journey, the prices received for chickens and eggs and vegetables, and what they had purchased with the proceeds; of what those who remained at home had done, and of what they would do with the money to be obtained from the next bit of produce which they would have to spare.

"Just as soon as possible we must put up the addition to the house of which we have been talking," said Mrs. Parsons. "It won't cost much, and will add more to our comfort than anything else we could get with that amount of money."

"Did you ask the price of lumber at the Landing?" asked her husband.

"Why, no; I did not suppose we could buy it now, and so did not think to ask."

"Well, I d'know; we've got a few dollars laid up now,

and by sellin' the calves we might scrape up enough to buy the lumber and get it home before the rains set in. The roads 'll be too bad for haulin' after that. If we had the lumber home, then we'd get the nails and other things along as we wus able, and I could do the work myself durin' a clear spell in the winter."

" But can we sell the calves for a fair price? Who is there to buy them ? "

" Bob Meeker, over on t'other side o' the mountain 'bout four miles, said the other day he'd buy 'em, an' pay cash, ef I'd bring 'em over any time within a week. I guess we'd better let him have 'em an' git the lumber. It'll be mighty unpleasant bein' cooped up here all through the wet season agin', an' ef we had the lumber I'd manage the rest of it some way."

So it was decided to sell the calves and buy the lumber for an addition to the shanty, and the next day John Parsons took them over to Mr. Meeker and got the money for them.

On the way home he stopped at another neighbor's and borrowed a heavy wagon, and the day following started to town bright and early with the letter to Erastus still carefully concealed in his inside pocket.

" Bet that'll fetch him home on a run," he mused as he dropped it into the office at the Landing just in time to have it get into the mail bag as it was being got ready for the down boat. " He'll be here in a week ef that letter goes straight, er else he ain't as good at takin' a hint as I think he is."

Mrs. Parsons noticed that her husband was unusually jolly that night when he returned home, and all the next day and the days that followed after it.

He had always tried to appear cheerful in the presence of

his family, and had never failed to respond to any effort of
Johnny's to get up a laugh, though it often caused him an
effort to do so; but on this particular evening, although it
was late and he must have been tired, he really felt jolly,
and he joked Lucy about one of the clerks at the store,
where she and her mother had traded when in town, and
also about a neighbor's son, who had shown a disposition to
seek her society, but who, not receiving any encouragement,
had decided that she was "stuck up," and so informed the
other young people of his acquaintance.

The letter was three days in reaching its destination,
and then lay in the post office several days more before
being called for.

Erastus had no correspondents other than the members
of Mr. Parsons' family; and as there had been little that
was pleasant to write about on either side, letters had not
been frequent between them of late, and the young man
seldom went to the post office.

One day as he was working with several of his neighbors
upon a ditch which was to be the means of irrigating their
claims, another neighbor, who had been to town, rode up
and, stopping his horse, called out:

" Here, Hemmingway; here's a letter for you."

Erastus was in his shirt sleeves in the ditch, shoveling,
and the horseman leaned from his saddle and handed him
the letter.

" If that's from your girl, she don't write a very purty
hand," he said, with a wink at the other ditchers, who had
stopped work and stood leaning on their spades.

Glancing at the superscription, Erastus saw that it was in
a strange hand. The post mark, however, proclaimed it to
be from Phippsburg, and his first thought was that something terrible had again happened to Uncle John and his

family—that they were all dead, may be, and a stranger had written to inform him.

So many terrible things had happened Uncle John's family, there had been so much of suffering and loss to them all, he instinctively felt that anything unusual could only portend additional evil.

Hastily tearing off the envelope, he looked at the signature and saw the name, "John Parsons," in stiff, awkward letters, at the bottom of the page, and it flashed over him that Lucy was married and that Uncle John had written to tell him of it because no one else liked to do so, and the blood rushed to his heart, which beat so that it seemed his companions must hear it.

But no ; the letter said, " Lucy and her mother had gone to town."

Then she was not married yet. The blood began to return to its proper channels.

" Lucy has given Annelsey his walkin' papers."

Could it be possible that she was not going to marry the New Yorker after all !

And if not, what then ?

The letter seemed plain enough to be understood without possibility of mistake, yet he read it the second time before its full import came to him, and then the blood rushed to his heart even more violently than before.

" Lucy might yet be his—that is what Uncle John meant," he said to himself. " If she had not loved some one else better she would not have dismissed Annelsey." And "she did not encourage any of the young men there "—that was what the letter said, and it said he was to come at once.

He had climbed out of the ditch and was brushing the dirt from his overalls with his hands.

"Mr. Johnson," he said, addressing the neighbor with
whom he boarded, "will you let me have your roan horse

for a couple of weeks and use my colts while I'm gone ? I'm
going home and want to make the trip as quickly as possible, and neither of the colts can stand a hard jaunt under the

saddle very well. I'll take good care of the roan and promise not to hurt him. If I do you may take your choice of
the colts to pay the damage."

"What's up?"

"Folks sick?"

"Why don't you go to 'Frisco and then take the steamer?"
came from one and another of the crowd.

"The fact is," replied Erastus, with his usual straight-
forward honesty, "I have not got money enough. You fellows know how it is yourselves. Money don't grow on these
sand ridges until they are irrigated; but I can ride through
in four days by traveling late and early and resting in the
hottest part of the day, and not hurt the horse a bit if Mr.
Johnson will let me have him, and it won't cost half as much
as it will to go by the cars and boat."

"You can have the horse if you want him," replied Mr.
Johnson. "I know you won't hurt him; but you haven't told
us yet who is sick or dead."

"There's no one sick or dead, boys; but I'm going, and
going to start to-night."

"Girl run away with another fellow?" asked one of the
men, with a grin.

"No, my girl hasn't run away with another fellow,"
replied the young man, with a laugh that some way reminded
him of what he had often called the "giggling" of the
girls.

How could he help it when reminded so forcibly of what,
up to the moment, he hardly realized; that instead of running away with another fellow as he had expected her to do,
his girl had dismissed the other fellow because of her love
for him.

The rough joke sounded irresistibly funny, and withal
brought such a delightfully warm feeling to his heart that it

is no wonder he laughed, or that the laugh was just a trifle hysterical.

What a terrible mistake there had been. What a wretch he was not to have spoken up when Annelsey first came courting Lucy, and so have saved all this suffering.

How tender his heart grew, thinking of her who had suffered so,—who must have suffered so terribly all this time.

Such were the thoughts that passed through the young man's mind as he walked rapidly towards his boarding place.

But what if Uncle John was mistaken?

He was half-way to the house when this thought came to him, and he stopped and stood perfectly still for some seconds, but not stiller than his heart seemed to have become.

"At any rate I'll know the truth," he said aloud, and then mentally, "I played the coward once, I'll not do it again. Uncle John certainly meant me to understand that Lucy loved me well enough to be my wife, and I would be a craven indeed not to ask herself now."

Going directly to the shed where the roan horse stood, he groomed him carefully, then went to the house and to the low room up-stairs where he slept.

Here he bathed and changed into his best suit, being careful to see that the few dollars in money which he possessed were in his pocket book and in his pocket.

Meantime Mr. Johnson had left the ditch and gone to the little patch of ground a quarter of a mile away, which his wife cultivated as a garden, where he knew her to be at work.

When told that Erastus was going on a visit to his old home and would start at once, Mrs. Johnson hurried to the house and began preparing a meal before he should go.

Neither of them asked the young man any questions as to the cause of his sudden going, but both guessed that it was in some way connected with a love affair and were anxious to assist him in every way possible. Mr. Johnson offered to loan him all the money he had, which was less than two dollars, and Mrs. Johnson fluttered around, trying to get something a little extra for him to eat, helping him with his necktie, and offering to do a dozen other things as if he had suddenly become a child, or what appeared more likely—was going to see his sweetheart, if not, indeed, to get married. And all the time she was trying not to say anything that would show how very anxious she was to have him confide in her, yet hoping greatly that he would do so.

Erastus, in the first flush of his new found joy, was only restrained from showing Mr. Parsons' letter and making a clean breast of the whole affair by a lingering fear that Uncle John might be mistaken.

It was really very hard for him to keep from telling. Mr. and Mrs. Johnson were the best friends he had here at the Slough, and he knew they thought a great deal of him, and he wanted to tell them what a lovely girl Lucy was, but could not quite bring himself to do so even when Mrs. Johnson remarked, as she fixed his necktie, that she "supposed he would soon have someone else to do it for him now," and so he left them wholly in doubt, and mounting the roan rode away in the direction of the foot-hills of the Sierras.

He curbed his own impatience and the desire of the spirited roan at the start, well knowing that time would be lost and not gained by fast riding for the first hour or two.

The sun had long since set, when having put thirty-five miles between himself and his starting place, he dismounted, tethered his animal in a spot of wild oats a little off the road, rubbed him down with dry leaves and grass, and rolling himself in a blanket lay down upon the ground.

If his body was weary he was not aware of it, for his

heart was filled with the sweetest hopes; and what sustains the physical powers like hope?

As he lay looking up at the stars, and watching the full moon coming slowly up from behind the distant hills and climbing a sky that had not known a cloud for weeks and weeks, he recalled every incident of his life from the time when Mr. and Mrs. Parsons had taken him, a poor, outcast boy, to their home and their hearts.

He thought upon every act of Lucy's which appeared in any degree to indicate her feelings towards himself, and tried to place one against another, the unfavorable against the favorable, in such a way as to enable him to strike a balance and determine just what his chances were. But in this he was conscious of failing, for there were many little instances —acts or words—the meaning of which he was utterly unable to determine, which he yet felt certain had a meaning if only he knew upon which side of his love account to place them. Besides, it was so very pleasant to fancy that the favorable ones outnumbered the others, if indeed there were any others, that he could not avoid going off into blissful waking dreams of the future, when he should have got his place at the Slough irrigated, and set in fruits, and have a cottage built.

He would have a cottage just like the one in the foot-hills, where they had all spent so many pleasant days, he thought; the cottage now abandoned and going to decay. Lucy would be by his side always, and Uncle John and Aunt Martha should bring Johnny and live with them, their honored and beloved guests, and all the misunderstandings and suffering of the past should be forgotten.

And thus he lay and drew bright pictures of sweet days to come, until from waking dreams he passed to dreams which come in sleep, but they did not greatly differ from each other; the music and the words were just the same—were love and Lucy; love and Lucy.

Although the sun was not yet up, there was no dew upon his blanket or in his hair when he awoke in the morning; for dew seldom falls in this portion of California during the dry season.

The roan horse had risen from his bed in the tall oats, and had stretched himself and begun again to eat of the rich herbage.

Erastus led him to drink at a creek which they had crossed but a little way back the night before, again rubbed him down, and leaving him eating, walked to a rancher's shanty, a quarter of a mile away, in quest of his own breakfast.

He found the family just sitting down to their own meal, explained to them that he had ridden late the night before and had camped out, and was given a cordial invitation to " draw a chair up to the table and help himself," which he very promptly did.

Breakfast eaten, he offered to pay, but was refused; gave thanks instead of money, and hurrying back to the place where he had left his horse, fastened his blanket to the saddle, placed both upon the roan, and mounting, resumed his journey.

Just before noon he stopped at a little town, put up at the hotel, fed and rubbed down his steed, got his own dinner; and did not mount again until the greatest heat of the day was over. Then he pushed on at a rapid pace until an hour after sunset, when he again tethered his horse and slept upon the ground, as he had done the night before.

The day following was a repetition of the one which preceded it, but its close found him well up in the foot-hills, and he put up at the cottage of a rancher, with whom he had

stayed over night when on his way to the Slough the year
before.

In the morning he arose with one thought throbbing in
brain and heart, "to-night I shall see her; to-night I shall
know my fate."

He fed and groomed his horse as usual, but could
scarcely wait for breakfast, which was not yet prepared when
he returned from the stable. He had eaten a cold lunch for
supper, but his impatience conquered all desire for food.
He was counting the hours now, and the moments would
drag themselves so until he was in the saddle again.

Rather than appear discourteous or strange, he waited for
the morning meal to be prepared, but was off almost before
his host had arisen from the table.

He had ridden seventy-five miles the day before, and had
feared the roan might feel a little stiff and sore at starting,
but when he saw him come out of the stable with head up,
apparently as anxious as himself to be off, this fear vanished,
and he determined to push through the remaining forty
miles without halting. But he found the roads not so good
as he had anticipated.

He was now in a part of the foot-hills with which he was
unacquainted, for he no longer followed the road over which
he came the year before, but struck across the country by a
route which left the old home off to the left, and threw him
further up towards the mountains, and when noon came he
was still, from the best information he could get, fully fifteen
miles from John Parsons' shanty, and compassion for his
horse induced him to stop at a rancher's for feed and rest;
so that with this delay and the trouble which he experienced
in learning exactly where the shanty was, even when within
a few miles of it, the afternoon was well nigh worn away
when he reached the point where the by-road which led to

it turned off from the main track; and even then he was not certain of this being the place.

He had stopped his horse and was debating with himself whether to turn off or follow the main road yet further, when he saw coming around the spur of the mountain and into the road over which he had just passed, her for love of whom he had come, and the sight sent all the blood in his body surging to his heart, and for the moment he could neither have spoken nor moved.

Evidently Lucy had not seen him pass, and was not now aware of his presence.

She had gone to find the cows and drive them home to be milked, and was following along behind them as they lazily moved homeward.

She was dressed as Erastus had seen her oftenest in the olden time, in a light print dress and sun-bonnet. In her hand she carried a little crooked stick, which she had picked up to drive the cows with, but was paying very little attention to them. Instead she was gazing off upon the hills which stretched away and away, one above another, until they became snow-capped peaks that in the light of the falling sun looked like amethysts set into the cerulean blue of the heavens.

Had not the cows paused at sight of the man and horse standing in their path she might have reached his side before becoming aware of his presence, but when the cows stopped and stood with their great eyes staring with the least bit of surprise at what was not a very common sight to them in their mountain pastures, she raised her stick and bid them "go-long." Then seeing for the first time a gentleman standing by the roadside holding his horse by the bridle, she blushed a little beneath her sun-bonnet, and dropping her eyes, followed closely after the cows, which had again lazily taken up their line of march.

The blush which suffused her cheeks was not, however, owing to her having recognized the horseman, for she had not done so. She had only glanced at him and then dropped her eyes with a feeling of embarrassment, for she seldom met gentlemen now, and however much poets may sing the charms of milkmaids in calico dresses, they will never be able to convince any member of the sex that they look their best in that rôle, any more than can be taken from them their womanly desire to appear well in the eyes of one of the opposite sex, even though he be an entire stranger, as she supposed this one to be who stood waiting for her approach, presumably that he might inquire the way to some neighboring rancher's shanty, or possibly if her parents would entertain him for the night.

When within a few paces she raised her eyes and turned her face towards him.

As she did so he spoke her name and took a step towards her.

"Lucy!"

She stopped suddenly and the little crooked stick fell to the ground while both hands went to her face pushing back the sun-bonnet.

"Lucy, don't you know me? I've come all the way back to see you; started the moment I got your father's let—that is the moment I learned you were not going to marry Mr. Annelsey. I love you, Lucy—love you better than anybody or anything in all the world. I have always loved you ever since we were children together, and I want you to be my wife."

And she only said: "Oh! Ras!" and put her hands to her face and began to cry.

"Lucy, Lucy, can't you love me?" pleaded her lover. "I know I am not rich like HE was, but I'll love you always, love you better, it seems to me, than anybody else can love you. Can't you love me Lucy?"

She put out one little sunburned hand and laid it on his arm. With the other she continued to hide her face.

"Oh, Ras," she sobbed. "I—I—do love you; I always d-did, but I thought father wa-wan-wanted me to marry HIM, and that you l-loved Julia Ennis and then I didn't care. Oh, Ras, I'm so glad you've come."

And she buried her face on his shoulder.

With his arms about her, telling her over and over again how dear she was to him, and how it was because he thought she could not love him as he wished that he had gone away, the two might have stood there until the sun had hidden itself from sight behind the mountains and the night had come up from the valley below, but that the roan horse, in his efforts to nibble at the grass by the roadside, jerked so hard upon the bridle which Erastus held upon his arm as to bring them back to a knowledge of their surroundings.

Then they started slowly homeward along the by-road that wound around the rocks, and over the stones, and in and out of gulleys washed by centuries of rainy seasons.

So slowly in fact did they go on, that the cows, lazy as they were, had got home and been milked, and Mrs. Parsons had looked many times in the direction from which they came, and in which she knew Lucy had started in search of them, hoping to see her coming   Finally, a little worried at her long absence, she suggested to her husband that he go up the mountain a little way and call, and he, quick to take the alarm, was on the point of starting when he saw the lovers approaching; the roan horse following the length of his bridle rein behind.

For a little space John Parsons stood in doubt, then raised his hand to his eyes as if to gather more of the failing light.

Only an instant he stood so, and then bringing his hand down upon his thigh with a slap, he exclaimed:

"I knowed it! I knowed Ras could take a hint! That's him, Marty, that's Ras, an' he an' Lucy hev made up. Don't ye see? he's a-holdin' of her hand."

"I KNOWED IT! I KNOWED RAS COULD TAKE A HINT! THAT'S HIM,
MARTY, THAT'S RAS, AN' HE AN' LUCY HEV MADE UP. DON'T
YOU SEE? HE'S A-HOLDIN' OF HER HAND."

16

CHAPTER XXIII.

THE COTTAGE AT THE SLOUGH.

A very happy little group it was that sat under the new porch of the shanty until long after the stars came out that night.

So many changes had taken place; there was so much to talk about, that it was ten o'clock before they once thought of the time, and still they talked on for another hour before retiring—the family to their beds and Erastus to a bunk on the floor.

The young man remained three days with them, and during that time they talked over all matters relating to family affairs—past, present and future.

Mrs. and Mr. Parsons of course gladly gave their consent to the engagement of the young people, but it was necessary to postpone the wedding until Erastus could get his place irrigated and in shape to produce a living.

It seemed very hard to part again so soon, but since he could not take Lucy with him, every day spent away from his own ranch delayed their marriage that much the longer.

And then there would be the pleasure of writing and receiving letters, which of course they would do every week at the farthest.

The project of selling the mountain ranch and all going to the Slough to live was talked of, and Mr. and Mrs. Parsons agreed that when Erastus got his place irrigated and was ready to marry, if he was satisfied with the country and the prospect, they would sell their own home and buy again as near him as possible, and if not they would both sell and go elsewhere and buy together.

And thus all were comforted by the thought that Lucy's marriage, when it should occur, would, instead of separating her from her parents, reunite them all with Erastus, and it is probable that for these three days the inmates of the shanty upon the mountain side were as happy as it often falls to the lot of people to be.

Certainly John Parsons was happy.

Lucy and Erastus wandered about the place, and through the gulch and up the mountain side together.

Together they went for the cows, as Lucy had done alone the night Erastus came.

Erastus helped Mr. Parsons sprout the grape-vines, and Lucy helped Erastus; and if occasionally, as they worked together at a vine, their hands met and their fingers intertwined it was no more than the tender tendrils of the vine they were trimming did.

If, as they walked hand in hand over the mountain, or sat to rest in some quiet nook his lips sought hers and drank deep of love's nectar, they only followed the example of the birds that near them billed and cooed, and talked of where their next year's nest should be.

And have not you, dear reader, done the same? Then have you not known the sweetest and the best thing that life has to give?

I will not describe the parting, when at last the day and the hour came, and the roan horse stood ready to be mounted at the door.

There is enough of sadness and suffering in this true story without dwelling upon the parting of those loving hearts.

It was noon when Erastus started on his return; it was

night on the fourth day when he led the roan into his stall at the Slough and ate supper with Mr. and Mrs. Johnson, to whom he frankly told the purpose and result of his visit, and from whom he received hearty congratulations.

The next morning he went back to work on the ditch, and if his companions were ready with their jokes, he was in far too good humor with the world and all things in it to be offended at what he knew was kindly meant.

For months he worked early and late at the ditch, and when it had been completed, and the water, in its slow seeping through the soil, had rendered it capable of sustaining vegetable life, he began planting of trees and vines, and breaking the soil for future crops. When the year closed he found his place beginning to look quite like living.

He had intended going again to visit Lucy and her parents at this time, but his place still lacked a dwelling, and the little it would cost to make the journey would aid just that much towards buying the material towards the cottage which he had planned, and he finally decided not to go, but instead to take his team and work a month for the rancher who had pastured his colts during two dry seasons; and thus, instead of spending what little he had, obtain enough more to enable him to get the material to begin building with.

When this was done he procured the assistance of a neighbor who had a few carpenters' tools and some knowledge of the trade, and together they framed and sided up the cottage.

Then he worked at night to finish it.

Often when thus engaged, after a hard day's work in the field, would he take from his pocket one of Lucy's letters, and sitting upon the work-bench or a saw-horse, re-read the lines he already knew by heart, or lose himself in dreams which those lines gave rise to; then, rousing himself, take up his tools and **work far into the night, that the cottage** might be the sooner **completed and the face and form** which he now saw only in dreams, be ever present **with him in** reality.

At last the cottage **was finished and ready for occu-** pancy.

A plain cottage it was; not **unlike the one on the moun-** tain side, only a little longer, **and wider and higher.**

There were two rooms below **and one** above, and **there was a little porch over the** front door—not long or broad, but sufficient to shade the room from the **sun a little and** give relief from the bare and inhospitable look which a dwelling without any projection always has.

He meant **to add a larger structure in front in a few** years, when **his ranch should be fully irrigated and in** cultivation, and so reprodu**ce the cottage in the foot-hills in** accordance with the plans he had laid the night he slept under the stars on his hastily made visit the time he **won** Lucy's **consent to** be his wife; but for this he must wait yet a while.

And so, with a heart filled with hope and **courage, and** running over with affection for her who was to return with him as his bride, he took a long look about the cottage, and going out, carefully **closed the** door behind him that it might not become **unfastened during** his absence.

Standing in front of his cottage, he **cast his eyes over** his ranch with a feeling of pride and satisfaction.

That which three years before had been **a bit of desert** was now a farm, with an orchard and vineyard **and fertile** fields; none of them very large, it is true, but everything there was the work of his own hands, the result of his own energy and economy, and it **was something of** which he might well be proud.

When he had taken it all in—the cottage **and the green**

fields and the young orchard and vineyard—as a picture which he could hold in his memory until he returned, and could describe to Lucy and Uncle John, and Aunt Martha, and Johnny, he turned and walked rapidly away in the direction of Mr. Johnson's.

He was to start early the next morning, and was to drive his own team; the colts now fully grown and hardened to work.

He had decided upon this after conferring by letter with Lucy and her parents.

Mr. and Mrs. Parsons desired to give as much as possible of the furniture necessary to start the young folks in housekeeping, and they could do this to some extent out of what still remained of that brought from the old home in the foot-hills, and it was just as cheap and a good deal nicer, these lovers thought, to make the journey this way, in their own conveyance, with their household goods packed in the wagon, than to first transport them fifteen miles to Phippsburg, ship them by boat and cars, and then go a long distance after them at the other end of the route.

Besides, in thus going across country they would have a whole week to spend in each other's company; in which to talk of their love and lay plans for the future.

It would be almost as good as a real wedding tour, Lucy decided.

And so one afternoon the dwellers on the mountain side saw a wagon drawn by a pair of bay horses, whose driver was a dust-covered young man with a sun-tanned face and sandy mustache, wearing a wide-brimmed straw hat, coming up the by-road which ended at their gate, and knew that the bridegroom had come to claim his bride.

The place had changed considerably since Erastus had seen it two years before.

The addition to the shanty had been erected, and with the little porch in front fairly raised it to the dignity of a cottage.

The rose bushes which Lucy and her mother had planted had grown as all things do grow in that climate and soil; had clambered all over the porch and were in full bloom, having been watered and tended by loving hands.

Back of the cottage and on either side great hollyhock bushes, with purple and white and yellow blossoms stood "thick as people in a street," and over the low windows, and reaching clear up to the eaves, Madeira vines mingled their soft, green leaves with those of the morning-glories, that in the early hours of the day were sprinkled thick with beautiful, bell-shaped flowers.

In front were long beds of pinks, and verbenas, and larkspurs, and great crimson-hearted dahlias, that lifted up their faces and bloomed and nodded in the breeze; bent low as if to inhale the fragrance of the mignonette that looked up from the borders of the beds in which they all grew.

The grape-vines upon the sloping ground above the house had added two years of growth to their stems; and although yet unable to stand erect without the supports to which they were tied, their symmetrical arrangement in rows, together with the richness of their foliage, formed a background that brought out the coloring of as pretty a picture of simple home life as one may hope to see in a long drive in the mountains or foot-hills; and it is in the mountains and the foot-hills that beautiful pictures are to be sought for.

Outside of the inclosure and a little further up the mountain, the cows which Lucy had driven home on that blissful evening two years before when Erastus had told her of his love, were quietly chewing their cuds beneath a scraggy, low-branched oak.

Below, brown in the October sun, lay the stubble field from which the grain had been harvested, and which now stood in a rick near the shed where the horses were munching at their feed.

Beyond the cottage was the young orchard of peach, and pear, and apple-trees, and over all the cloudless blue sky of California.

More than a hundred turkeys wandered at will through the orchard, down into the stubble-field, and far up on the mountain side. Or they clustered about the shed and rick of grain, or came with the chickens at feeding time to the bare bit of earth near the kitchen door to receive their portion of the food thrown to them by some member of the family dwelling within the vine-wreathed cottage.

And here, one morning a week after Erastus' coming, a little party, composed of neighbors and their families, gathered to witness the marriage of the young couple who had plighted their faith two years before, standing in the road while the cows went lazily home without them.

It was not an assembly such as would have graced a fashionable church in a great city. Not one among them all, perhaps, but would have felt ill at ease in a richly furnished parlor of a brown-stone front in New York or Chicago.

They were common country people—husbands and wives who gained their living as John and Martha Parsons gained theirs—by the tillage of the soil and the raising of fruits, and grain, and poultry. Young men and maidens, the sons and daughters of these people in the common walks of life, dressed—the girls in cheap, light-colored lawns, with maybe a bit of bright ribbon at the throat or about the waist; the young men in suits of linen or some other light and not costly fabric, and all of them with hands and faces tanned by the sun, but with hearts that throbbed as quickly at whisperings of love, or capable of feeling as keenly the stings of unjust criticism as if they were robed in velvet, with diamonds sparkling upon soft, white hands.

Before these friends and neighbors, Lucy, dressed much as the other maidens were dressed, only that her robe of pure white was of finer material, and without ornament except some roses upon her breast and in her beautiful dark hair, stood up with Erastus and gave the responses that made them husband and wife as they were propounded by the gray-haired minister whose services had been secured for the occasion.

The kisses and congratulations over, and the tears which would come in spite of her determination not to let them, dried upon the cheek of the bride, they all sat down to a meal at which there was a bride's cake, of course, and a cold roast turkey, and great mealy potatoes, and the most beautiful bread.

There was fruit also ; the first borne by the trees and vines planted, since coming to the place, by the hands that sought out and plucked these, the occasional first offerings found scattered here and there among the foliàge.

And afterwards there were kisses and hand-shakes again, and foldings of the bride to the bosom of father and mother, and tears in the eyes of all, and fervent "God bless you's."

And then Lucy was helped to a seat in the wagon, over which a canvas cover had been stretched and into which the little store of household goods which formed her dowry had been packed. Then her husband climbed up by her side and amid wavings of handkerchiefs and more "God bless you's," they drove down the lane and out upon the road which led away over the mountain and the foot-hills towards the new cottage which awaited their coming at the Slough.

Oh, what a **happy, happy** journey was **that for seven whole** bright October days; traveling by easy stages during the day, and camping out, sleeping in the wagon at night!

What beautiful bits of scenery they pointed out to each other! How they laughed over the little incidents of the journey or the camp, as the tipping over of their coffee-**kettle** while getting their evening meal in **some quiet** little grove, after the **day's drive.**

What memories of the longer journey **across the plains when they were children came** back to them **as they watched** the camp-fire smouldering **in the darkness, and the twink-**ling of the stars overhead; **and what** beautiful secrets they disclosed to each other as proofs of their mutual love and confidence! And when, on the evening of the last day's journey, they drove up to the Johnson shanty, what a hearty greeting Mrs. and Mr. Johnson gave to the young bride who had come to make glad **the home of** her husband, and **to be a neighbor and** friend **among neighbors and** friends!

And when, after a hearty meal of the best that could be found in the house, they **went to take a look at their** own home, walking hand in hand across the fields, **with** what pride Erastus pointed out the boundaries of his own claim; to the vineyard, and orchard, and fields, made fruitful by **the** water that, coming through the open ditches cut by his own hands and those of his neighbors, was fast turning the desert into a garden.

And the cottage; how pleased Lucy professed to be—really **was—with** its appearance and conveniences! What pleasure they **took** in deciding just where each piece of **furniture should be placed!** They would have a carpet on the larger **down stairs** room, and the bureau and the best

chairs should go in that ; and the small table, with a few
books, should stand near the center of it. Lucy's guitar
should hang on the wall with Erastus' flageolet, and just as
soon as they could they would get a few pictures to help
make the room look still more bright and tasty. Their bed
they would put up stairs, and until they could build larger,
would eat in the kitchen, or, in pleasant weather, out of
doors, and so keep the best room always cosy and nice.

And so, still planning for the future, yet perfectly happy
in the present, they returned as they came, hand in hand
across lots to Mr. Johnson's, where they were to spend the
night.

On the morrow Mr. Johnson helped Erastus to unload
the few heavy articles and place them in the cottage and
then went away, and together the young couple put down
the carpet and arranged the furniture, returning to Mrs.
Johnson's to dinner as that lady insisted that they should do.

Indeed, she would have had them remain with herself
and husband for a week, "until they got rested from their
journey," as she said, but to this they could not think of
consenting.

They were both anxious to get into their own house, that
they might together take up the work of making still more
beautiful and productive the spot upon which they expected
to remain all their lives.

.

CHAPTER XXIV.

THE THREATENING WHIRLWIND.

The year that followed was a very happy one to the young couple, working away upon their claim at the Slough.

True, they were poor, and were forced to live very economically; but what was poverty when they had love, and health, and the assurance that poverty would be vanquished in a very few years more?

It lacked less than two years of the time when they could "prove up" and get a government patent to their land under the homestead act, and by that time they would have almost as fine a fruit and vegetable ranch as the state afforded; for here the frost never comes, and with all fear of drouth banished by the certainty of an abundant supply of water from the river through the irrigating ditches, prosperity seemed assured beyond any possibility of failure.

Then, too, a branch of the Southern Pacific railroad was being built near them, and would be completed, and furnish means of transportation for everything they raised, by the time their trees and vines were in full bearing.

And they had good neighbors, which added much to the pleasantness of their surroundings; for though never content to be separate from each other, even for a day, our young friends enjoyed having their acquaintances drop in on them, and often visited among their neighbors, spending the evening or Sunday afternoon.

They heard regularly from Lucy's parents, and quite frequently from Jennie and her husband, who were still in Chi-

cago and doing well.   At least Ensign had steady employment, and they were comfortable and happy.

Mr. and Mrs. Parsons had now fully decided to sell their
home on the mountain at the first opportunity, and move to
the Slough; their out-of-the-way location alone operating
against the ready sale of the place.

Meantime Erastus and Lucy worked on.

The size of orchard and vineyard was increased by the
planting of other trees and vines.   Rose-bushes were set out
at the corners of the porch and beneath the windows, and
evergreens and flowering shrubs in the front yard.

The main irrigating ditch having been completed the year
before, the work of carrying the water wherever needed, by
means of small side ditches, was comparatively easy and rapid,
so that some pretty broad fields of grain and grass were
beginning to stretch away on every side of their cottage.

But now came a terrible rumor.

It was told doubtingly at first, as something that could
hardly be possible—that the Pacific Railroad Company laid
claim to the lands about the Slough, and would compel payment of their present market value, all improvements
included, or evict the homesteaders from possession.

The settlers quite generally laughed at the tale, as being
started by someone for the purpose of giving them a fright.

"What!" they said, "the railroad company claim our
lands! Why, the land was absolutely valueless, thought not
to be worth paying taxes on, until we irrigated it and built
houses and put out orchards and vineyards.

"Besides, the land grant by Congress was made to a company whose charter fixed the line of their road more than a
hundred miles away, on the other side of a range of mountains; and even this grant the company has forfeited long
ago, the time in which the road was to be built in order to

obtain the land having expired two years since, and the road is not built yet."

It seemed absurd for anybody to talk about a railroad company having a claim to their lands, when they had redeemed them from the desert, and were almost ready to prove up on them under the homestead and pre-emption laws.

Yet there were those who were less easily disarmed of fear.

They knew that in Iowa a railroad company had dispossessed settlers who had actually proved up and received deeds to their homes from government.

There were those among them, too, who had suffered from the overflow of hydraulic mines, others from the Suscol Ranch, and yet others who had suffered from the encroachments of corporations in other states and other portions of this state, and these were prepared to believe that nothing was too preposterous for the railroad company to claim, if its officers thought there was the remotest chance of enforcing it, either by fair means or foul.

When Erastus Hemmingway heard the rumor his heart sunk, for he had seen too much of the heartlessness and greed of corporations not to fear the worst, and he at once took steps to ascertain the truth.

He wrote to the headquarters of the company, repeating what he had heard, and asking if there was any truth in the statement that the company professed to have any claim to the land in the vicinity of the Slough.

In reply he received a letter and also a circular.

The letter was signed by Leland Stanford, president of the railroad company, and was to the effect that the company hoped to be allowed the original grant of lands made by Congress in aid of the road, but the boundaries of the grant

17

had not been determined, and probably would not be for some time.

Meanwhile, the letter went on to say, the settlers could be assured that in no case should they be the losers, as, if it should eventually be determined that the land which they occupied was within the limits of the grant to the road, the company pledged itself to transfer it to the occupants on payment of the government price, and attention was called to the accompanying circular, copies of which, the letter said, were being issued and distributed all over the state for the purpose of inducing people to take up land at the Slough. This circular also contained a pledge that if found to be within the grant of Congress to the road, the company would transfer the land to whoever had improved it, immediately on payment of the government price.

This letter, taken in connection with the circulars, which were scattered freely among the settlers, if it did not remove all feeling of fear from the minds of Erastus and a few others, did serve to allay the general alarm, which was before on the increase, and improvements went on as usual.

The circulars of the company sent to other portions of the state had the desired effect, and very soon other families began to come in in considerable numbers, all taking up claims and relying upon the printed pledges of the company that in no case should the land cost them more than the price asked by government for wild land.

So time sped on.

And now those who came first to the Slough began to reap abundantly of the fruit of their labor and perseverance.

The work of turning a veritable desert into a garden had been accomplished. It had been done, too, without capital, and by men who were forced to support themselves and their families while the transformation was being made.

Orchards and vineyards were loaded with fruit. Olives and apples, peaches, plums, apricots, pears, pineapples, lemons, pomegranates, nectarines—all the semi-tropical fruits, and some which grow nowhere else outside of the tropics themselves, were to be found in full bearing upon the irrigated lands of the settlers at Mussel Slough.

Green fields grew broader and greener. Little flocks and herds of cattle and sheep were to be seen feeding on the rich vegetation which came with the water that overspread the land from the system of irrigating ditches; and as the result of all this, new and pretty cottages were taking the place of the wretched huts in which nearly all had been forced to live during the first years of their residence; and it was in the midst of this prosperity, when want had been banished by years of patient, persevering toil, and they were rejoicing over troubles past, and the thought that for the rest of their days they could take life easy, that the stroke came which turned all their joy into mourning, and changed the current of their blood from the peaceful flow of quiet, happy hearts to a seething flood in hearts made hot with fear and hatred.

This was no rumor from an unknown source that reached their ears, awaking doubt in some and ridicule in others. It was not the faint murmuring of a distant storm that might never reach them, but the sudden rush of the whirlwind; the flash of the lightning, the falling of the thunderbolt from a sunny sky. It came as a notice from the railroad company to each settler, informing him that he was a trespasser on the lands of the company, and must immediately vacate unless he was prepared to pay the value of the lands occupied by him, which had been carefully appraised, so the notice read, by competent judges, whose estimate of the value of each quarter-section accompanied the notice.

17

This appraisement ranged from ten to thirty-five dollars per acre; that of Erastus Hemmingway being thirty dollars per acre, or a total of four thousand eight hundred dollars, which he was asked to pay to the railroad company for the land he had redeemed from the desert; or failing therein was ordered to at once vacate the premises.

The excitement which the receipt of these notices caused can be imagined.

Threats of vengeance upon the officers of the company were both loud and frequent, and had they been present, there is no question as to what their fate would have been. Death in some form would unquestionably have been meted out to them.

But they were careful not to be present.

They had deliberately laid, and were now executing, a plan to rob these people of their homes, and they were too cunning to come within reach of their victims while the first hot flush of righteous anger was upon them.

With the power which their immense wealth, the gift of Congress, gave them, they did not fear the courts or the state authorities.

They already controlled these, and were prepared to bribe or threaten, as they deemed most likely to accomplish their ends, any official who stood in the way of their plans for wholesale robbery.

The leaders in the plot stood high in social and political circles.

Stanford, the president of the company, had been Governor of the State, and it was while filling this exalted position that he first began to lay plans for the subjugation of the people, and in Huntington and Crocker he had able partners and unscrupulous allies.

The settlers had small means of making the outrage upon

their rights known, and their cause was, indeed, desperate, and it is small wonder, when in every dwelling at the Slough were women whose eyes were red with weeping, that there should be men whose lips uttered curses, and whose muscles twitched with eagerness to lay hand upon the authors of their woe.

Only a few days before the notices to pay or vacate reached the settlers, Erastus and Lucy had received a letter from Mrs. Parsons saying that they had at last found a probable purchaser for their place.

They would know in a few days, she wrote, and if they sold they should pack up and start for the Slough at once, as they did not wish, even if the purchaser of the property would permit, to remain on the mountain through the winter. It would seem more lonely than ever when the place was no longer their own.

The only thing that would delay their coming, if they sold, was Johnny's health.

The boy had not been as well as common the past summer, and had been quite sick recently, but was getting better now, and she thought would be able to be moved, and if they sold she would take him and start at once by boat, leaving Mr. Parsons to drive across with their household goods, as Erastus and Lucy had done.

The reception of this news had caused much pleasure to the young couple, who were both desirous of having their parents near them.

Lucy was especially anxious for the presence of her mother at this time, and hastened to reply, urging that they sell if they could get anything like a fair price, and that they come at once.

But when the determination of the railroad corporation to rob them of their own home became known to them, they felt it would be better for their parents not to sell, at least for the present; and Lucy again wrote, telling her parents of the difficulty they were in, and that if they had not sold, it might be better not to do so.

It was a hard thing to do, and the poor young wife had often to pause and wipe away the tears that blinded her eyes as she wrote of their troubles—thinking, too, of the sorrow it would bring to the hearts of the old people upon the mountain side.

She was expecting to become a mother soon, and all the sweet joy with which she had been looking forward to the coming of the babe, had given place to a terrible fear of what the future might have in store for them all.

Erastus had not been loud in his threats, as had others. Indeed he had not threatened at all; but he was not a man of many words. And she had not forgotten how at the Suscol Ranch, when but a boy, he had taken her mother and Mrs. Ritchie with the children, of which she was one, to a place of safety and then returned to defend the cottage with his life. And now the thought kept coming to her, "What if the company should actually attempt the eviction of the settlers and Erastus should again defend their home, and be killed?"

She tried to put the thought from her, but it kept coming back, each time with increasing strength, until it came almost to be a conviction. She knew, or thought she knew, that if efforts were made at an eviction, her husband would call upon his neighbors to defend their homes with their lives, and would set them the example.

It was a horrible thought. But it came and it clung to her; and though she tried hard not to make her letter to her parents be without a gleam of hope, she yet felt when it was written and sealed that she had failed, and was still further depressed by the thought of the effect it would have upon those to whom it was to be sent; and especially upon her father, who she knew would bear the blow even less stoutly than her mother.

Meantime the verbal sale of the mountain ranch had been concluded between Mr. and Mrs. Parsons and the gentleman of whom Mrs. Parsons had written.

They were to receive two thousand dollars cash down and to give immediate possession; and on the morning but one following that on which Lucy's second letter was mailed, John Parsons started to town with the deed made out, and signed by his wife.

He was to meet the purchaser at the court-house in Phippsburg, deliver the deed and receive the money, provided the title was found to be clear, of which there was no doubt in the minds of either party ; the abstract, which Blake gave to Parsons when he bought the property, having been shown as proof of that fact when negotiations for the purchase and sale were first begun.

The sky looked cloudy and threatening when he left home, but it would not do to fail of being at the appointed place on time, and he kissed his crippled boy and his wife and left in good spirits, promising to be back by dark.

On reaching town he put out his horse, saw that he was properly fed, and then started for the court-house.

On his way there he had to pass the post-office, and stopping to inquire if there was any mail for him, was handed Lucy's letter to her mother.

He recognized the post-mark and opened it at once,—not a common proceeding with him, for his eyes were no longer good, and even where letters came addressed to himself instead of his wife, he usually preferred to wait until he got home and then have her read them aloud while he ate supper, or smoked his pipe and rested.

But now something impressed him with the thought that he had better open the letter. He had a feeling that perhaps all was not right at the Slough.

Perhaps it was because it had been only a few days since they had received a letter from there, and so were not expecting another so soon.

Tearing off the envelope he began to read, but had not proceeded far before his hand trembled so that he could not hold the paper still enough to see the letters, and he folded it up and put it into his pocket.

He had read enough, however, to understand what had befallen his children.

He knew that they were to be driven from their home, as he and they had so often been before, by the merciless greed of soulless corporations, or combinations of rich men whose hearts had turned to stone beneath the weight of their immense wealth.

For a moment it seemed to him that he should die right there, and those who were looking saw him stagger like a drunken man, but he rallied at once and went out without a word.

The thought that the cottage on the mountain side was still theirs, and would afford an asylum for the children, had come to him, and he was hastening to tell the would-be purchaser that under the circumstances they could not let him have the place.

It was fortunate that the bargain was not closed, he thought. How lucky that he had opened the letter instead of waiting until he got home !

They could all live comfortably in the cottage together, and he and Marty should have those dearest always with them the little while they should continue to live, and by them to close their eyes when they died, and no one would disturb them on the mountain side, which was so secluded and lonely that hardly anybody appeared to want to live there. Yes, it was very fortunate that the bargain had not been closed, and he would pay the man for his trouble and ask to be released.

He half paused in his rapid walk as the thought occurred to him that the other party to the deal might not think it honorable in him to back out after once giving his word for the sale of the place, but the intensity of his desire to have the matter settled and all possibility removed of his family being again without a home hurried him forward.

Entering the court-house he went directly to the recorder's office.

The gentleman whom he expected to meet was already there, and in company with the recorder was looking over the records.

Without so much as bidding them good morning, John Parsons began to say that he had changed his mind and wished to be released from his verbal contract, but before he could make his meaning understood the gentleman who had contracted for the place said:

"How is this, Mr. Parsons? I find a mortgage on your place. I understood you to say it was clear of all incumbrances."

"A-a mortgage!"

The words came in a whisper from lips that were bloodless, which the other did not notice, for his eyes were upon the volume of records, and he answered:

"Yes. A mortgage for fifteen hundred dollars with interest for six years, unless it has been paid; making a total of about the amount I was to pay you for the place. The

mortgage seems to have been given by Mr. Blake to a Mr.
Jones, of San Francisco, and—"

But he did not conclude the sentence, for at that instant
the two men at the desk heard a groan, and turning, saw
John Parsons fall to the floor.
They picked him up and laid
him on a bench, and one of.

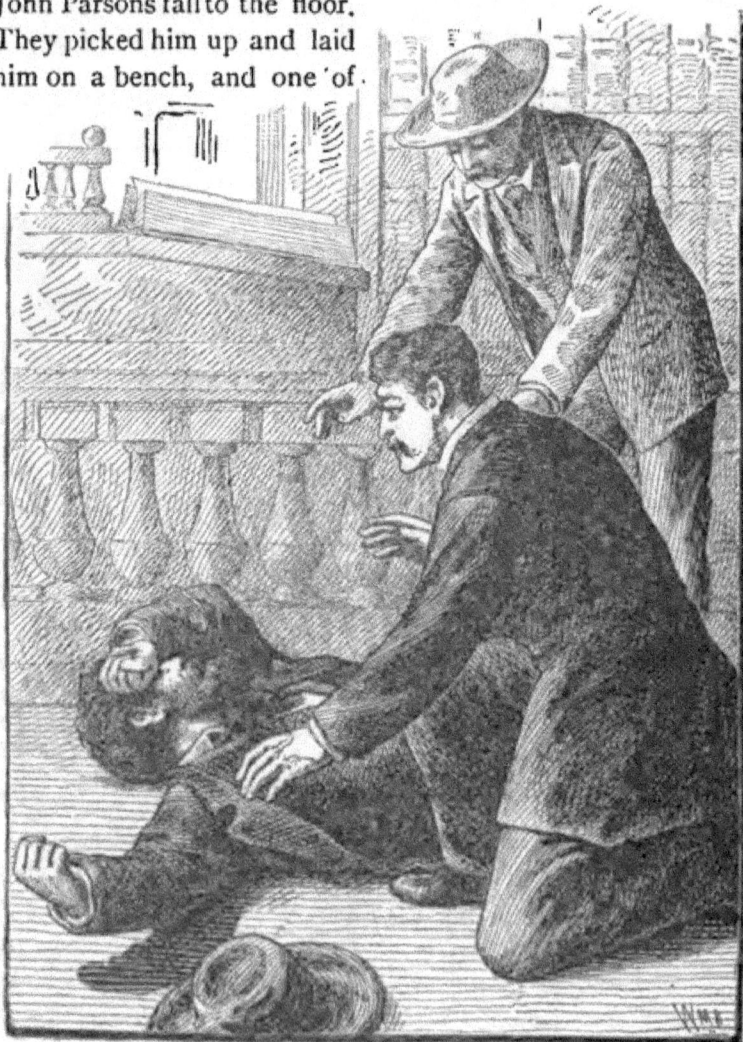

them ran for the doctor, while the other attempted to pour some whiskey down his throat from a flask.

In a moment he revived, and when the doctor came running in, followed by a crowd of business men and idlers, was sitting up with his head leaning upon his hands, his elbows upon his knees. As the crowd entered he looked up for an instant and then resumed his former position, but that instant sufficed to show to those present a face so haggard that not one among them all recognized it as the face of John Parsons, the owner of the mountain ranch.

The doctor advanced and laid a hand upon the wrist of the stricken man, as if to feel his pulse.

Then John Parsons again raised his head, and with an effort arose to his feet.

"It ain't no use, Doc.," he said, recognizing the physician as one who had attended Johnny in his recent illness. "It ain't no use," he repeated, "it's the heart that's ailin' an' there ain't no medicine that'll do it any good; leastwise nothin' you kin give. The children is bein' robbed of their home just as their parents has been afore 'em, and there ain't any hope, and there ain't anything left to live fer.

'I thought when I read the letter jest now that we could all live together somehow on our own little ranch, but it 'pears that it is to be tuck from us too—though I don't know how it comes. I have an abstract that I got out of this very office when I bought the place and it says there weren't no mortgage onto it then, but now there 'pears to be one for all it's wo'th, an' they'll take it of course, an' there ain't no place left where an honest man kin take them as is dependent on him. It would be better if we was all dead, an' I 'spect we will be purty soon.

"The railroad company'll turn Erastus an' Lucy out, an' the girl'll die, maybe, for want of a shelter, when her baby comes to be born, an' her father won't have any shelter to offer her; fer ef they were mean enough to mortgage the place and then sell it, they'll be devils enough to turn an old man an' woman an' a crippled boy out the minute they want possession."

All this was said in a tone of voice and manner that showed, even more than his words, how utterly broken and hopeless the man was, and when he ceased speaking he staggered again, and those about him thought he would have fallen; but he gathered his energies, made his way through the crowd, which opened to let him pass, went to the stable, and replacing the saddle on his horse, mounted him and turned his face toward home.

The moment he left the recorder's office, a dozen voices were heard eagerly demanding to know the details of the affair.

The man who was to have bought the place could tell nothing beyond the fact that on examining the records he had discovered a mortgage against it for about the value of the property.

"It seemed strange," he said, "that the mortgage should be there and have escaped the eye, not only of Mr. Parsons himself, but of the maker of the abstract which he received from Mr. Blake. There is evidently a mistake somewhere. Possibly the mortgage has been paid and the mortgagee has neglected to cancel it on the books in the office; if so and it can be proved, it can all be made right yet."

Then somebody suggested that Mr. Parsons be called back and an effort made to ascertain the facts.

"It is a pity to let the old man suffer so, if it is only a mistake and the mortgage has been paid," they said; and a half dozen of them started at once to call to Mr. Parsons to stay and try to learn all the facts, but the recorder, who had remained silent during the discussion, now spoke:

"It's no use, men," he said, "the mortgage is there, and there is no doubt but it will take the place, unless the old man can raise the money to pay it off.

"You know I have only been in office less than a year. When I came in here I got to looking over the books back a piece and I found things a little bit mixed, and set to work to straighten 'em up. Among other things I stumbled onto this mortgage. It was recorded all right, but it wasn't indexed, and you know a man might hunt for a week through these books and not find a thing that wasn't in the index. Besides, no one would ever think of doing so, as every mortgage is supposed to appear in the index under the name both of the maker and the mortgagee.

"I thought at the time that like enough trouble would come of the blunder, which is the fault of old Puterbaugh, who was recorder at the time it occurred. He was never sober two days at a stretch, and ought never to have been elected, but he managed somehow to get the nomination, and then we had to vote for him or go back on the party ; and you know we couldn't do that.

"Well, as I was saying, I thought like as not Parsons never knew of that mortgage being there, but I hadn't the heart to mention it, and it wasn't any of my business anyway, and I really hoped it had been paid and would never give him any trouble. But about a week ago a fellow was here from Frisco—you remember him, Jo?" he said, interrupting himself and addressing the landlord of the hotel, who was one of the crowd—"that fellow with a stove-pipe hat and a suit of brown velvet clothes. He stopped with you ?"

"Yes," replied the landlord, "I remember him. He was there to dinner and supper and left on the down boat."

"Well," continued the recorder, "that was Blake's brother-in-law. I don't know whether he is as big a rascal as Blake was or not, but anyway it seems that Blake got hard up and borrowed fifteen hundred dollars of this brother-in-law and gave a mortgage on that place up there for security.

"It was more than the ranch was worth at the time, but I reckon Blake was in a fix where he had to have that amount, and as that was all the security he had to give, his brother-in-law let him have it. Maybe he never went to look at the place at all, but just took Blake's say-so for what the property was worth.

"Well, after a bit, Blake, who was always looking over the records to see if he couldn't strike a lead of some kind, happened to stumble onto the fact that old Puterbaugh hadn't indexed that mortgage, and he made up his mind to sell the place to somebody else and leave the country.

"He knew no one would be likely to see the mortgage in making an abstract, and if they did discover it, why he would say it had been paid and destroyed, but the party had neglected to cancel it on the records. Then he would bluster around, pretending to be looking for the party who had held it in order to have the matter fixed up, but would never be able to find him, and pretty soon the man who was going to buy the place would get sick of waiting and go off somewhere else, or buy another place, and the whole thing would be forgotten.

"At least, that's the way I figure it all out, and I reckon I ain't very far from right."

"But how does it come that this brother-in-law hasn't put in a claim for his interest money all this time?" asked one of the bystanders. "If his claim on the place is good, he has been losing a pile of dust by not collectin' his interest from year to year."

"Well, maybe so, and then again maybe not," returned the recorder. "You see, the improvements Parsons has put on the place is worth a good deal more than the interest. Besides, this brother-in-law may not have known that Blake had sold the place, and was just making it easy on Blake, as he supposed.

"Anyway, the mortgage is there, and if you'll step over to Tom Anderson's office I guess you'll find that he has the job of foreclosing it in the next term of court, which begins the second Monday of next month, and that he has already sent notice to the *News* for publication, as required by law."

"It's an outrage on the old man with the crippled boy," remarked one, as the crowd dispersed, "and Blake ought to swing for it. If he was back again, I'd be one to help do it."

"And I," "and I," "and I," echoed a dozen voices.

But Blake was not there, and will doubtless take good care never to go back. If living still, he is probably to be found in New York, or some other great city, running some swindling institution by means of which he obtains a living. He may even have amassed a fortune, and if so, should be looked for, if wanted, among the presidents of savings banks, or managers of some corporate monopoly, robbing the people under the shelter of the law.

CHAPTER XXV.

OVER THE RANGE.

It was three o'clock on a short October day when John Parsons left Phippsburg on his return to the cottage where his wife and crippled boy awaited him.

He did not call it home—did not think of it as such now. Another held a claim against it for all it was worth in money, and his past experience led him to expect no mercy.

He had not stopped to ascertain who held the mortgage, or anything about it, further than that it existed and was for a sum greater than he could, by any possibility, raise.

He had no hope that it might prove a mistake in any way; that it might have been paid and not canceled. He accepted it as what he ought really to have expected would happen sooner or later, for he had come to believe that the poor, those who labored in any way for a living, were looked upon as legitimate prey by a set of men who had by some means obtained control of the courts and of State and National legislatures, and who in one way or another—but always under the guise of law—would rob the people just as men rob the honey bees, taking the honey, but letting the bees live, in order that they might store up more honey for the robbers when their turn comes for being robbed again. And so from the first mention of a mortgage he gave up all hope, regarding it as but another of the ways—of which experience had taught him that there were many—of taking from him and his their little accumulations; and but one thought, one impulse remained—to get back where his wife and crippled boy were and die in their presence and with them.

His brain seemed incapable of thought. There was a numbness about his whole body that made it difficult for him to retain his seat in the saddle, and several persons who saw him pass, swaying to and fro in his seat, thought that for once he had been drinking and had taken more liquor than he could well carry.

But he was not drunk. He was crushed.

All hope had fled, never to return again. No ray of light came to him from any source.

He paid no heed to the inquiring looks of those whom he met as he passed through the streets of the little town and took the road leading up into the mountains; no attention to the guidance of the animal which he rode.

He had no clearly defined idea of what he should do or say when he reached the spot where his wife and Johnny were, or of how they could bear the terrible news.

He felt isolated from the entire world; was unconscious of what was passing around him or of the rapidly gathering storm overhead.

His one dim idea was to get to where his wife and boy were; and I think he really expected that once there they would all go away out of the cottage and out of the world— that they would all die together, and at once.

There seemed to be no place in this world for them, and yet they were ordered to "move on." Where else could they go to except to the other world; and who else but Death was to point the way, or be their guide upon the journey?

And Erastus and Lucy were to go too, and would take the little baby that was not yet born, for they were without a home also—they, too, had been ordered to "move on."

1

Then he wondered if Jennie and her husband were to go with them, and he was not quite sure about it. They would follow pretty soon, of course; for all who tried to get their living by work would be ordered to "move on" sooner or later; but it did not appear that they were to die at once, as he and Martha and Johnny, and Lucy and Erastus and the baby must do.

When the clouds, which had been gathering all day, broke at last, and the rain poured down in torrents, he did not seem to know it.

He was wet to the skin in an instant, but he was not conscious of it. His rubber coat remained tied to the back of the saddle, where he had fastened it in the morning before starting.

The water ran from his person and filled his boots, his horse placed his nose close to the earth and plodded on blindly in face of the storm, but his rider sat the same, one hand upon the loosened rein and the other hanging idly at his side; his eyes fixed upon the ground just in advance, but seeing nothing, taking no note of anything.

Left to his own will, the horse plodded on through the mud and rain at a walk. Before they were half way home night had set in—night as black as clouds and falling rain could make it.

Soon the water, still falling in torrents, began to fill the gulches with floods of the color of clay; floods which bubbled, and seethed, and roared their way down the hillsides and across the road, forming a frothy line of white, the only thing visible in the pitch darkness.

And still the horse plodded onward, fording the streams as he came to them; scrambling up the steep and slippery inclines where the road wound round the mountain side, avoiding, either by instinct or that peculiar power of seeing

in the dark which some **horses possess, the deep gullies cut**
by the rushing **water in the clay of the** roadbed; and still
the rider **sat** motionless—save as **he swayed to and fro** with
the movements of the animal which **he rode—and looked**
straight forward into the night.

Suddenly, when they were about two-thirds of the way
up the mountain, there came a flash of lightning, followed by
a clap of thunder which seemed to rend the very earth, and
echoed and re-echoed from peak to peak, and then went
rumbling **down the ravines** and **gorges,** finally dying out
miles and miles away among the foot-hills.

Many people have lived for years in California and never
heard a clap of thunder or seen a vivid flash of lightning.
A friend of the author's who lived for twenty years, a part
of the time in the foot-hills and a part in the valley, informs
him that never but once in all that time did she know the
elements to be thus at war.

It is no wonder, then, when the flash of lightning came,
and the mountains shook with **the roar of** the thunder, that
the steady **old horse which John** Parsons **rode** should be
frightened into **springing suddenly to one side, throwing his**
rider, and with **his nostrils** distended **and head and tail in**
the air dash **away in the** darkness, leaving **him lying stunned**
by the roadside.

How long he lay there John Parsons never knew; nobody
ever will know, unless the angels who watch over each of us
have made a record of it as part of the account against those
whose greed sent a fellow mortal on that **journey up** the
mountain through the worst storm known for years, with his
brain turned by the knowledge of his loss, and all the blood
in his body congesting about **his heart. And if** the angels
do keep such account, there must be added to it the sufferings of Martha Parsons, as she watches by the cot of their

crippled child—grown dangerously ill **since morning—watches**
and waits, **and listens in vain for some sound that** shall tell
her that, through the storm **and** the darkness, her husband
is safe at home **at last.**

Johnny, **as his mother** had written Lucy, had been growing **weaker for** some months, and had finally appeared so
bad that his parents had taken alarm and called a physician;
but as the lad seemed to rally under the prescription left him,
they had ceased to fear any serious results. But now that
the effect of the medicine **had spent itself the patient again**
began to sink rapidly.

In the excitement of making and signing the deed the
day before, for which purpose a justice of the peace had come
to the cottage in person, and in the **departure** of Mr. Parsons
with the **deed in his** pocket with the **intention of consummat-**
ing **the sale of the place, the change** in Johnny's condition, if
any, had not been observed; and the lad made no complaint,
having come to accept his crippled and weakly condition as
something which could not be changed. Her husband had
not been long gone, however, before Mrs. Parsons noticed
that Johnny had a slight fever, and at once began to censure
herself for not having observed it sooner and asked John to
have the **doctor** come out, or **at** least send another prescription.

It was now too late to do this and she must do the best
she could alone; perhaps after all the fever would soon pass
off.

She prepared and gave the child some simple household
remedy, sponged his person with tepid water, and sought
to amuse him by **talking of** the coming journey to the Slough,
where Lucy and Erastus **were,** and the pleasant time they
would **have when they** got there.

But the fever did not go down; on the contrary it became higher as the hours passed, until finally **Mrs. Parsons became** greatly frightened.

She **prepared** a note **to Dr.** Brenton, asking him to come **at once.** Upon the envelope she wrote a request that any one going to town would deliver it into his hand.

She then fastened the letter to a stick, one end of which she sharpened with the butcher knife, and telling Johnny she was going **into the** yard and would be back in a few moments, **ran down to the** big road and stuck the stick, with the letter **attached, into the** **ground** **where anyone passing** would be almost certain of seeing it. This done she returned to the **house as quickly as she had gone, and waited, and watched** the one point of the road which was visible from the window, hoping to see **pass a team** or a horseman, **as an assurance** that the message had found a carrier.

One team she saw going in the opposite direction, but if the driver of it saw the letter he made no effort to forward it to its destination, fancying, perhaps, that someone going **to town would soon** pass and take it.

As the afternoon came on, a new cause for alarm to the watcher by the cot of the sick boy appeared.

The clouds were gathering in a way that betokened a long continued and heavy rainfall. What if John should be detained until **late** by the business on which he had gone; would he be able to return at night in the midst of **the storm** which was approaching? If not, how should she get through the night all alone with the sick child?

Or, what if John should attempt **to come** through the darkness and rain and should **meet with an** accident?

She felt certain that he would make the attempt to reach home that night, no **matter what** the weather might **be; but** would he be able to get through? Would not the ravines fill with water and make the road dangerous, if not absolutely impassable?

She could not tell, she could only wait and hope for the best; but every moment seemed an hour, for hours before she had any reason to expect her husband's return, even if he was not delayed by the storm.

It was but a little after three o'clock when it began to rain; but so thick were the clouds that it seemed as if night were already at hand.

Johnny had dropped off into a light sleep and she sat by the window that commanded a view of the garden, the level ground with the ravine below, and the hills stretching away towards Phippsburg and the river.

The rain came down in torrents, and she noticed how quickly little rills formed and ran down between the rows of vegetables in the garden, and lost themselves in the stubble field beyond.

The turkeys and chickens, deceived by the unusual darkness, had all sought their roosts, except here and there one who had been late about getting in and now stood with drooping tail feathers and a generally demoralized look beneath the thick leaves of some shrub or vine.

Then it occurred to her to save for washing purposes some of the water that was falling, soft water being a luxury during half the year on the mountain; and she threw an old shawl about her head and shoulders and went out and set the wash tub and boiler under the eave spout, and saw them filled almost before she could turn back into the kitchen.

And now Johnny had wakened and was calling her.

She went to him and felt her heart give a great throb as she noticed that his fever was higher than ever, and that his eyes had a strange look about them.

She preserved her calm appearance, ministered to his

wants, and when he asked for his father, told him that he had not returned and that they must not look for him yet awhile, but that he would come by and by.

During a partial lull in the storm she ran out to the shed and milked the cows, which had come up of their own accord, and were contentedly chewing their cuds beneath the shelter. The horse left at home stood in his stall, and kept turning his ears back and sideways, as if to catch the sound of his returning mate, and she set her milk pail upon the ground and threw him a bit of hay.

Returning to the house she lighted both of the lamps and took them into the sitting-room where Johnny lay, in order to make it seem as cheerful as possible.

She had kept the wood box full of dry wood all day, and now she prepared everything for the starting of a fire in the cook stove, and a little later, started it, and put the tea-kettle on.

Although it was quite dark now, she did not much expect her husband just yet, but wished to have everything ready to get him a cup of hot tea the moment he did come. She also brought out a suit of dry clothes and hung them by the fire ready for him to put on.

She could still see a little distance through the deepening gloom, and she observed that the water had cut bits of gulleys between the potato rows, and that the stubble field below had the appearance of having become a lake.

The rain, too, instead of decreasing as the night set in, was, if possible, falling faster than ever; and she could hear a faint roar coming up from the ravine, and knew that soon the water would be rushing through it in great volume, and with a force that would overwhelm any living thing caught in its path; and a half dozen such ravines crossed the road over which her husband must pass in coming from Phippsburg.

She shuddered as she listened, and turning away, went and sat down by Johnny's crib and tried to interest him by reading a little story from a child's paper.

But the boy was too sick to care for hearing her read; he wanted his father, and kept asking when he would come, to which she could only reply that they might look for him any moment now, but that the rain might make him late, and they must be patient.

And so the hours wore on and the rain continued to fall, while every moment the weight at her heart grew heavier and more oppressive.

Johnny slept fitfully, waking every few moments and always asking "if father had not come yet," or if his mother "thought father would come pretty soon now," until the sudden clap of thunder came, at which he was seized with an awful fright and screamed again and again with all the force of his weak lungs.

Even his mother was startled into an involuntary exclamation by the suddenness of the concussion, and for an instant she thought the cottage had been caught in a land slide. She controlled herself at the sound of the child's cry, and bending down, lifted him tenderly in her arms, cuddling his poor wasted form to her breast as if he had been but a babe.

It was only with difficulty that she checked his screams, and even then he was so fearful and nervous, and sobbed and begged so piteously for his father, that it was only by calling to her aid all the fortitude which she possessed, that Martha Parsons was herself enabled to keep from breaking down.

It was an hour before Johnny was sufficiently calm to be again laid in his crib.

As soon as she could leave his side for a moment she went to the window and tried to peer out into the darkness.

She had placed one of the lamps in the window some

hours before, hoping that it might prove a beacon to guide her husband if he was still living, which she was almost ready to doubt, so utterly desolate all things seemed.

Pressing her face close to the glass she endeavored to penetrate the awful gloom; but could only see for a few feet into the darkness.

The rays of light from the lamps had power to penetrate no farther.

It seemed to her, as she stood there, straining her eyes in a vain effort to see, that the darkness was a living thing and that it devoured the rays of light bodily, or contended with them and slew them as they strove to make headway against the night.

When the lamp burned low for an instant, and the light sent out through the window was less strong, she was almost sure she saw the darkness put out its hands and grasp the rays of light and strangle them.

Mingled with the steady swish of the falling rain, the roar of the water rushing through the ravine now came clear and distinct, and knowing it was all one's life was worth to attempt to cross it, she gave up all hope of seeing her husband that night, if ever again, and only prayed that he might be in a place of safety, and out of the reach of the elements that appeared as if about to swallow up the mountain.

It was a little past midnight, and Johnny had again dropped off into a light sleep, when from the direction of the gate opening into the enclosure came the sound of a horse neighing.

The watcher within listened intently, and with new hope springing up in her breast.

Was it possible, after all, that John had returned; that he had passed safely through the darkness and the floods and reached home at last?

Yes, there was the sound of the horse walking past the window at the upper end of the house, where Mr. Parsons was in the habit of riding through to the stable.

"Poor dear, what an awful time he must have had coming through the storm," she said softly, as she rose hurriedly and went to light the lantern.

Opening the kitchen door she held the lantern in a way which she hoped would afford her husband some assistance in putting out his animal; if not, would at least help him in getting to the house.

She heard the whinny with which the horse in the stable welcomed his returned mate, and expected every moment to hear the stable door open and close, and the footsteps of her husband as he made his way towards her.

After waiting several moments and hearing nothing further she began to be frightened and finally called softly,

"John! John!"

Getting no reply, she caught up an old garment of some kind, threw it about her shoulders, and holding the lantern above her head made her way through the rain to the stable.

The horse which her husband had ridden stood at the door waiting to be let in, but she could see nothing of his rider.

She listened a moment and then again called—low at first and then with all her might,

"John! O-oh John!"

The weary, drenched and mud-bespattered horse lifted his head and gave a low whinny, but no other answer came to her call,

"John! O-o-oh John!"

She listened; but only the swish of the rain, falling in literal sheets, and the dull roar of the swollen waters in the ravine below, reached her ears.

And now she noticed that the horse's bridle-rein was dragging. .

Had he thrown his master, or had John dismounted in order the better to keep the road, and by some means permitted the animal to escape him?

She examined the bridle-rein and found it broken, and she felt certain that the horse had thrown her husband and afterwards stepped upon the rein and broken it.

Then John was dead. The father of her crippled boy, her companion for so many years, was drowned, it might be in the angry waters that even now were pouring through the gorge with the roar of a demon. Or he was lying in the road, cold and stiff, with his lifeless eyes staring up into the blackened heavens, the pitiless rain beating upon his face.

Such were the thoughts that burned their way through the brain of Martha Parsons as she stood dumbly looking at the broken rein by the dim light of the lantern.

The impatient pawing of the horse, demanding to be let under shelter, recalled her to a knowledge of her surroundings, and quite mechanically she opened the stable door. The horse entered, rubbed his nose against that of his fellow and began at once to eat from the bin in front of him.

Mrs. Parsons followed him in, removed the saddle and bridle, and taking the lantern from the floor where she had set it, retraced her steps through the storm to the house.

Fortunately, Johnny had not wakened sufficiently to note her absence, and was unaware of the return of the horse without his father, and she could sit down and think what to do.

What could she do?

Over and over again she asked herself this question.

It was two miles to the nearest neighbors, and between

ran the gorge, in attempting to cross which, perhaps, John
had lost his life.

It was too dark to see more than a **few feet ahead of one,**
even **by the aid of a** lantern, and if that were **to go out, it**
would leave her in utter inability to return.

Besides, there was the sick child, who would scream himself **to death if** he wakened and found himself alone in the
house.

And just then **he did** waken, and she went to him **and**
gave him the water he asked for, and induced him to again
close his eyes and sleep, doing it all without showing the terrible agony at her heart, or saying a word about the return
of the horse without his rider.

When she thought **Johnny asleep, she** arose and went into
the **kitchen. She did not dare to remain in the** room with
the child lest he should suddenly open his eyes and see the
agony which she felt she could no longer suppress.

There was nothing she could do for her husband, living or
dead, except to keep the lamp burning in the window as a
beacon, in case, as was just possible, he had been thrown
after crossing **the** gorge, and was now wandering about in the
darkness.

But for Johnny she **would have set out to** follow the road
back towards town, hoping to find some trace of her husband,
but to do so and leave Johnny when there was so little chance
of any good coming of it, was **not to** be seriously thought
of. She must wait until daylight, and then—even then what
could **she** do? If the rain should cease it would still be
days and maybe weeks before any one would be likely to
visit the cottage.

But this fact **did not change** matters. There was positively nothing she could **do** except to wait and keep the lamp
in the window burning as brightly as possible.

For many moments she sat motionless, and then stole quietly to the side of her child, whom she found much as he had been for some hours past—sleeping uneasily and with considerable fever.

As she was slipping from the sick room again, she heard a noise as if some one were fumbling at the kitchen door in a vain endeavor to find the latch.

She listened with a feeling of returning hope, mingled with a horrible, superstitious dread; the latter born of her excited condition, and the terrible dreariness of her surroundings.

The sound continued until she could not be mistaken; it was someone trying to open the door, and who else could it be but her husband? With a feeling of faintness, as if she had suddenly been caught as she was about to drop into a horrible abyss, she hastened to lift the latch.

As she did so, a form covered with mud, hatless, and with a look of death upon his face and in his eyes, entered.

For an instant she did not recognize the form as that of her husband, but when he staggered forward into the light and sank upon a chair, she saw that it was he, and in an instant she was at his side, striving to remove his storm-soaked garments.

"Tell me where you are hurt, John; tell me what to do, quick," she said. "Are you wounded anywhere, or only terribly bruised by your fall? Tell me quick, so I can help you."

But he only stared at her and made no reply.

"John, John," she cried, now doubly alarmed, "what is it? where is it? tell me, dear. Is it your head that hurts?"

He looked at her so strangely that she thought he must have been crazed by a blow upon the head.

Slowly he raised his hand at last and drew it across his forehead.

" I d'know, Marty," he said in a hesitating tone, " I reckon—I d'know—exactly what is the matter."

He still sat gazing at her with that strange look in his eyes, as if he was not certain of where he was.

Mrs. Parsons hurriedly placed the tea-kettle back on the stove, where it instantly began to sing, and a moment later had a cup of tea prepared.

Then she came and put her arm about her husband's neck, paying no attention to his filthy garments, while she held the cup to his lips.

" Drink this, dear," she said, " and then I'll get your wet clothes off and get you to bed and you will feel better."

He took a sip of the tea and then, looking up at his wife as she bent over him, asked:

" Do you think they'll let us stay till mornin'? "

And Martha Parsons tried to keep her voice from trembling and make it sound cheerful as she answered: " Oh yes, dear, they said we could stay until morning."

She saw that he was out of his head and knew that the better way was to humor any fancy of his brain, and hoping that if she could get him to bed and apply hot draughts to his person, he might recover his mind in a few hours.

" Then I reckon we had better stay," he said. " It'ud be mortal hard on you an' Johnny to hev to leave in this storm. I hope they'll let Lucy an' Rastus stay till mornin', too."

She finally succeeded in undressing him and getting him into bed, where he lay staring at her as she moved about, preparing hot draughts and placing them upon his head and feet, and across his chest.

Johnny had awakened when his father came, and tried to call him, but being told by his mother that his father had

"DO YOU THINK THEY'LL LET US STAY TILL MORNIN'?"

fallen from his horse and was hurt, and that he must keep
quiet, he had done so, though his eyes were big with fear,
and with the fever, which had come up higher than ever.

Occasionally, as she worked over her husband, chafing
his limbs and changing the cloths and vessels of hot water
with which she had surrounded him, he would mutter some·
thing about "the mortgage," or "the mines," or about "Lucy
and Erastus," and once she thought he spoke the names of
Jennie and her husband, but she gathered nothing from what
he said of the loss of their home, and supposed that his condition was the result of a fall from his horse, and of being so
long exposed to the storm.

His limbs were cold and she feared he was going into a
nervous chill, and worked with all her might to restore the
circulation, but in spite of her efforts he continued to sink.

His eyes would close for a few moments and then open
again suddenly, but never with any sign of a clear perception of his condition or surroundings, but only to mutter
something about "campin' out," and "the mines," and "the
children," until just before day began to break, when he
aroused from the lethargy into which he was fast sinking,
made an effort to rise, fell back, tried again and succeeded
in getting upon his elbow, stared about the room, and at
Johnny's crib, and then with the wild look in his eyes and
upon his face changing to one which showed that he recognized his surroundings, he again sank back upon his pillow
and made a sign for his wife to come closer.

As she bent over him he strove to speak, and finally said
brokenly:

"'Tain't — no — use, Marty.   My — my — lead — is — is
worked out, and our—our claim's been jumped agin."

He struggled for breath, his eye-balls turned upward and

he choked, but seemed to rally his expiring energies for a farewell message, and added:

"I—I'm goin'—goin' over the range, to—to stake out a new claim, an' you an' Johnny an'—an' the rest will find—find me waitin' when you come."

A great shiver shook his frame, his breast heaved with a long drawn sigh, and the spirit of John Parsons had gone ahead to prospect for a home for his loved ones in the other country, of which we know so little and hope so much.

CHAPTER XXVI.

"TAKE ME UP, PAPA!"

Daylight came at last; came slowly, as if it were forced to contend with the unwilling darkness for mastery; and even then the clouds did not lift, or the rain cease its steady down-pour.

Martha Parsons never knew whence came the strength that enabled her to close the eyes of her dead husband, or to continue existence when she had done so.

One was dead, but one yet lived, and living, needed her care. While that life continued she felt that her strength would continue also, and beyond that she neither thought nor cared. When his father's spirit took its flight, and afterwards, while she was caring for the dead body—straightening out the limbs and folding the arms across the breast—Johnny lay in his cot and watched his mother without a word or a cry, but with a look half of awe and half of surprise, as if he had seen the flight of the spirit and understood why and whither it had gone. And when all was done and the cot in which he lay had been wheeled into the kitchen, where the fire burning in the stove, gave a little more cheerful look to the room, he still asked no questions and made no complaint.

His mother found herself wondering if Johnny knew that his father was dead, but could think of no way of ascertaining without herself imparting the information if he did not already possess it, and this she feared to do lest it should cause his spirit to follow that of his father.

19

" If only we could both go," were the words that kept swelling up in her heart, and seeking utterance at her lips.

Then remembering what Lucy had written; that if possible her mother should come to them before her babe was born, that she might be with her in her hour of trial, she felt anew that she must live for the sake of her children.

But what was she to do ? How could she obtain help to bury the dead, or a physician for the sick child ?

The rain might continue for a week, and already communication was cut off with all who lived below, if not with those on the other side of the mountain, and she dared not leave Johnny to go for help, even if she could make her way through the floods.

She did leave him for a few moments, long enough to go to the stable and throw feed to the animals. She did not milk the cows, did not dare leave the child long enough for that, but the horses she must feed, for she might need one to ride for help, and he must be strong to contend with the torrents which would have to be crossed if she did go.

Johnny's fever had gone down a little again now. She watched him with all possible care and tried to appear cheerful, and even to talk with him as usual, but he answered her with such a strange look of questioning, making no reply in words, that she was still in doubt if he knew what had taken place, and finally ceased to talk to him except to ask him to take medicine or food.

The medicine he swallowed without opposition, but the food he rejected utterly and could not be persuaded to take a mouthful.

· About noon she made a cup of tea for herself and tried to eat, but found it almost impossible to do so, although she had eaten nothing for twenty-four hours, and it was only by telling herself that she must eat in order to keep up her strength until help came that she was enabled to swallow anything.

She dared not think how long it might be before help came; but, come it late or early, she must keep up until that time.

She tried to think of some way of hoisting a signal of distress, as she had read of shipwrecked mariners doing at sea, but could not.

She watched the one place in the road which could be seen from the kitchen window, but she saw no one pass.

No one could pass the gorge, now a roaring, noisy torrent, with a depth and power that made fording it a matter of impossibility.

And so the minutes and the hours dragged slowly by, and the rain continued to fall.

Night closed in early, owing to the darkened heavens, and she lit the lamps, placing one in the room with the dead, the other on a stand near the cot of the living, and sat down by the side of her child to watch him die.

That he would die before the morning came she knew, and she wondered at her ability to act coolly, or to act at all.

All through the fore part of the night she sat watching every movement of the hands, every rise and fall of the chest, every trembling of the eyelids, utterly unconscious of any weariness in her own frame.

She kept a fire burning in the stove, and every little while gave the dying child a few drops of some liquid preparation which she had made, as the only thing she could do to prolong life.

The child slept almost continually now, and when he awoke, made no effort to speak, but the questioning look which had been there since his father's death, had not left his eyes.

As midnight approached, she saw the increasing evidences of approaching death, and knelt by the side of the cot with one arm under the pillow on which her child's head lay.

His breathing was less regular now, and weaker, coming in little quivering sighs and half-formed sobs.

He was awake, and had been for some moments. At last his eyes were open and he seemed to be looking at her, but when she asked him if "there was anything mother could do for her poor sick darling," he only smiled the faintest little smile possible, and made no effort to speak.

She remained kneeling for more than an hour, now raising now lowering his head a little as seemed to make his breathing easier, until just as the clock struck one, a look of surprise overspread his face, and slowly raising one arm, he placed it about his mother's neck, allowed it to rest there for an instant, then slowly removed it, lifted both hands as if to someone unseen by her, murmured faintly, "Take me up, papa!" sank back into his mother's arms, and was gone.

When again the daylight came, two dead bodies were lying in the best room of the cottage on the mountain side; one upon the bed, with a white counterpane drawn about it, and one in the little cot, clothed in a white robe of some soft stuff once worn by the living, but which had lain unused in the bureau drawers for years, and which the mother's hands had fashioned into a shroud during the hours which had intervened.

Very peaceful was the look on either face as they lay there. All trace of suffering and care had fled, and in their place was a look of rest and perfect peace.

At least so thought the weary, loving woman, who, bending down to kiss each in turn, felt strangely comforted, although her heart seemed breaking.

When daylight had fully come she went out and fed the

animals and fowls, and milked the cows; leaving the dead where they lay, and as her own hands had cared for them.

She felt compelled to do this, partly out of sympathy with the dumb brutes who must suffer without human care, but more from a feeling that John would have her do it. For had she not always cared for the animals when he chanced to be away and there was no one else to attend to them? And now that he was absent never to return, she did not feel that it made any difference; he would still want her to care for them.

When this was done she returned to the house, made a cup of tea and forced herself to eat a little, for her work was not yet finished and she must have strength.

Then she went about putting the house in order, and in taking down the clothes which her husband had on when he came home wet and dying, Lucy's letter fell out and she picked it up and read it, and reading, understood all, or thought she did.

It was the knowledge that their children were to be driven out as they themselves had so often been that had killed John; that and some trouble about their own home. She did not know what this trouble was, but finding the deed in his pocket she knew that the place had not been sold, and putting that knowledge with the words muttered by her husband in his delirium, she guessed that someone laid claim to the cottage in which she watched her dead.

But nothing now had power to add to her sufferings. Her cup was already full and could contain no more; so these added wrongs, whatever they might prove to be, could not make her sorrows greater.

She put the letter in the bureau drawer where all letters from the children were kept, finished tidying up the house, kissed again the cold faces of her dead and went out, carefully closing and fastening the door behind her, and going to the stable, saddled a horse and prepared to ride in search of help.

It was still raining, but in a mild kind of way, as if each particular drop half repented of having decided to fall upon the already water-soaked earth.

The gullies upon the mountain side had been widened and deepened, and new ones had been cut through the cultivated ground below.

The grape-vines were half denuded of their foliage, and what remained hung listless, as if drowned in the flood. The rose leaves lay scattered beneath their draggled bushes, the fruit trees drooped their slender twigs, and all nature seemed as if it had had a surfeit of weeping.

The waters filled the ravine below, and overflowing, had covered the stubble field and extended half way to the cottage.

A few turkeys and chickens, weary with their long confinement, were strolling about in a disconsolate kind of manner, and with a look that seemed to say that they were tired of life and ready to be eaten if anybody could get up an appetite in such abominable weather.

Leading the animal she had chosen to ride to a block near the kitchen door, she mounted him and rode away.

At the main road she turned to the right, knowing that it would be folly to attempt to ford the ravine, and having decided to go further up the mountain and try to reach the cottage of some people living on the other side of the divide, reasoning that the higher up she went the less would be the volume of water in the ravines.

She found the road almost impassable in places, and once was nearly carried away by the force of a stream which she was compelled to cross, but finally succeeded without injury to herself or horse in reaching the shanty of a settler, and told the object of her coming.

She wanted help to bury her dead, and she wanted some one to go to the nearest post-office and mail a letter to Erastus and Lucy, and another to Jennie and her husband.

These letters she had written during the night after Johnny died, sitting in the room where her dead lay.

They were brief, for no words came to her in which to tell of her sorrow, or her awful loneliness; but in a few sentences she had told what had occurred.

She found heartfelt sympathy and ready help in those of whom she had come to seek it.

They would have had her remain there while they, with other neighbors, cared for the dead; but she would not listen.

So long as anything remained to be done for her loved ones she would help do it. She could not leave them even to the care of those who had known and respected them while living, and despite all they could say, rode back alone, while the neighbor went to secure other assistance, and his son prepared to make an attempt to reach some point from which to mail the letters.

When she reached the cottage on her return she put her horse in the stable, unsaddled him and fed both him and his mate, and then went into the house.

A few moments later several neighbors, both men and women, came and remained until the next day, when the bodies of her husband and child were placed in the vehicles in which they were to be conveyed to the little burying ground on the other side of the mountain.

The gray-haired minister who had married Lucy and Erastus two years before, again came to the cottage to say a few words over the bodies of the dead, trying to find language which would convey a little comfort to the one lone mourner who was so dear to them while living; but she scarcely heard his words, and did not at all comprehend what he was saying.

She had no thought but that her dear ones were better off.

Her husband, she knew, had been an upright man, and had followed Christ's teachings in that he always preferred to suffer rather than do wrong to another; and Johnny surely could have done no grievous wrong.

No, she was not fearful of their condition in the life upon which they had entered, but now that the hour was approaching in which she could do no more, even for their dead bodies, she felt her strength giving way, and when they had been laid side by side in their one grave, and the words "dust to dust and ashes to ashes" had been spoken and the few neighbors present turned away, they saw her falling to the earth unconscious, and kindly and lovingly they carried her in their arms to the nearest house.

Before reaching there she had revived and insisted on being carried back to the cottage whence her beloved ones had been taken, and only the lateness of the hour, and the dangerous condition of the roads after night-fall, induced her to relinquish her design.

Even this would not have deterred her had they not made her feel that she would risk other lives than her own, since they would not permit her to go alone if nothing could induce her to remain.

Thus urged, she consented to remain until morning, but nothing that could be said could induce her to stay longer. No offer of any one to make their house her home until she heard from Erastus and Lucy would she accept.

Erastus would come as soon as they got her letter, she

knew, and she would wait for him at the old place on the mountain side.

So they took her there, and two of the neighbors remained through the first day and night, and when they went away, they sent an elderly woman of the neighborhood, noted for her kindness in sickness and in death, to remain with her until Erastus should come.

This, she told them, was unnecessary; she did not fear being alone, and was quite able to do what little there was to be done in taking care of the stock and poultry.

But they would not listen to it, and so the woman staid, and every day others came to see if there was anything that the two needed, but there was seldom anything that they could do.

Mrs. Parsons had learned from others the full extent of the misfortune regarding the mortgage, and knew that the place must go, but this did not worry her.

If she had still possessed it, Erastus and Lucy could have come and lived with her, but since she did not, she would go to them, that was all the difference.

And if they were forced to leave their own ranch, why, they would find shelter somewhere else; it did not greatly matter where. A part had gone on ahead to the country beyond the grave, and the rest would follow before very long. All her thoughts were centered there now, and it mattered little what became of earthly interests.

It was a full week before Erastus came.

The letter had been delayed a few days on account of the flood, and then had remained another day uncalled for in the office, for while the dead were being laid away upon the mountain side, a new life was being ushered in at the Slough.

The same day on which the letter was received saw Erastus start; Lucy and the baby, both of whom were doing well, being left in the care of Mrs. Johnson and another neighboring woman.

He reached Phippsburg by the morning boat and had no difficulty in finding means of getting out to the cottage, for the calamity which had befallen the Parsons family was in every mouth, and there were numbers who were ready to offer assistance to one who came to care for the lonely woman who had endured such suffering.

Mrs. Parsons saw him coming up the lane and met him in the yard in front of the cottage.

Up to this moment she had not shed a tear, and not a sob had choked her utterance, but great black rings about the sunken eyes, and a stooping of the form as she went about the house and yard, told plainer than tears could do, how heavy was the grief at her heart.

She had herself wondered that she could not cry, but she could not; and when she would have done so, her eyes grew hot, but no tears ever came to quench the flames that seemed to consume them.

But when Erastus came, and putting his arms about her, kissed her cheek and brow, and smoothed her hair, in which the gray had grown suddenly prominent, she put her head upon his shoulder and wept as if she never would cease.

And so, with his arm about her, and his own tears falling fast, he led her gently into the cottage, and when she grew calm, told her of the birth of her grandchild.

Then they talked of what it was best to do, and as Erastus was determined not to yield up his place at the Slough without first exhausting every effort in defense of his rights, it was decided to leave everything which Mrs. Parsons did not wish to take with her, in the care of a neighbor, to be sold, while she returned with Erastus to the Slough, and to Lucy and the baby.

Accordingly, the wearing apparel and a few household goods, including the little wheeled cot in which Johnny had lain so long, and which Mrs. Parsons could not bear to have go into other hands, was packed and loaded, and the next afternoon a neighbor drove them to the Landing, and the cottage upon the mountain side was left desolate.

CHAPTER XXVII.

CONSPIRATORS.

A close carriage drawn by a splendidly matched pair of bay horses rolled up California street, in the city of San Francisco, and on Nob Hill stopped in front of a palatial residence, the home of a man who, not very many years since, was the possessor of but little if any money or property, but who is now a railroad king and the possessor of millions.

As the horses were brought to a stop, a liveried servant climbed down from his perch, opened the door of the carriage, and a heavy, dark-complexioned man in the prime of life descended and approached the mansion.

As he reached the broad marble steps, the door opened, and four boy pages in dark livery ranged themselves on either side of the steps, returning to the hall to await orders only after the heavy man, their master, had passed on in advance.

Once inside, the heavy man turned to the right and entered a large room, the furniture of which was of rosewood and mahogany, and of European manufacture. The most costly of Axminster carpets was upon the floor, and the heaviest of damask and finest of lace draped the windows. Costly pictures were upon the walls, marble statuettes adorned the mantels and the corners of the room, while solid silver chandeliers of many hundred pounds weight depended from the ceiling.

From this room the heavy man passed through an archway with massive sliding doors to another room of similar size and ornamentation, and from this to a smaller one furnished as a library.

Magnificently carved cases of rosewood held artistically bound and beautifully illustrated works of the best authors in fiction, in history and travel, but none of these were of much interest to their possessor, who, without pausing, passed onward, and at the left entered another room supplied with a small table, a desk, a sofa, and a few chairs—the private room of the railroad king and holder of the title deed to the mansion.

Seating himself at the desk, he drew a key from his pocket and, unlocking one of the drawers, took therefrom a bundle of papers, which he ran over carefully, noting down an item or two from each. After an hour spent in this manner, he desisted from his work, replaced the papers, locked the drawer, and, turning half round in his chair, touched a button in the wall. Almost immediately a servant in livery appeared and stood waiting for orders.

"Bring me a lunch,—some fruit or something, and a bottle of wine."

Again the servant bowed and retired. A few moments later he re-entered with a tray, on which was a bit of cold chicken, some grapes, apricots, peaches, a bottle of wine and some glasses. These he deposited on the table, which he wheeled around in front of his master's chair, and was about to retire, when the railroad king again spoke:

"Tell Barnes to come here."

The servant bowed and disappeared. The heavy man poured himself a glass of wine, set it beside the tray, and then devoted himself to his lunch.

He was still eating when the door opened, and a man in middle life, well dressed, and with a look which indicated both persistence and cunning, entered.

"Peters said you wished to see me," he said, bowing slightly.

"Yes," replied the heavy man, "I want you to see the merchants and business men of the city and give them to understand that we don't want any of their interference with our business, and that we shall find a way to make it unpleasant for them if they do."

Barnes, who was a kind of private detective to the railroad king, and accustomed to all kinds of work requiring cheek and impudence, did not change his expression or move a muscle while receiving this order, but remained entirely passive while the other was speaking and for a few seconds after he had ceased. Then, with a movement as if turning to go, he said, in a tone which was intended to indicate only a desire to fully understand his orders :

"Anything you want especially emphasized ? "

"Yes," replied the other, taking up his wine glass and setting it down again with force; " yes," he repeated, "there is. I want you to make them understand that we can take care of our own affairs, without any assistance or advice from them, and that if they have any sympathy with the outlaws who are claiming homestead rights on the land which Congress gave to us, they had better keep it to themselves, unless they know of some better way of shipping goods than over our lines of road."

"All right. I only wanted to know just what you wanted done, and how far I was to go in the matter."

"You can go far enough to make them understand that we are not in the habit of arresting grangers for the pleasure of seeing them bailed out of jail by the business men of San Francisco, and we don't propose to form any such habits at this time. Hello! is that you? Well, come in," he said, suddenly changing his tone, and addressing a man about his own age but much less given to flesh than himself, who appeared at the door and stood as if waiting for an invitation to enter. Then again addressing himself to Barnes, he said :

"You can go now. You have got your orders, and understand what you are to do."

As Barnes passed out the other entered, shook hands cordially with the heavy man, and, seating himself in a chair which the latter set for him, reached over and helped himself to a glass of wine, saying, as he did so :

"Just got back on last train. Called at the office ten minutes after you left; found our noble partner there, and as he wanted to talk over matters, we thought we'd come over to your house. They told me you were in your private room, and I took the liberty of coming unannounced."

"That's right," replied the heavy man, "glad you came. Was anxious to see you. Where's he now ?"

"He'll be along in a few moments. Some old fellow from down below, some homesteader I guess, was trying to talk him into giving up our claim to his land, and as I didn't care to listen to the old fellow's lingo about how hard he had worked to improve his claim, and how tough it was to be turned out of house and home without anything to start on again, I came on ahead and left him to follow as soon as he could get rid of his visitor."

'That's it," replied the heavy man. "They are everlastingly whining about being turned out of their homes. Why don't they go somewhere else and begin again ? They ought to know by this time that they can't fight a rich corporation, such as we are."

The thinner man laughed. It was not what one might call a hearty laugh. Neither was it exactly forced. The person of the party emitting it shook just a little, as much at least

20

as a person with that amount of flesh could be expected to
do.   Evidently the thinner man saw something mirth-pro-
voking in the suggestions of the other, that these men whose
lands they were seeking to possess themselves of, should go
elsewhere in the State and preëmpt again ; and he looked
at his companion with a kind of quizzical expression, as if
he would have said :

"Suppose you suggest some place in the State where
these men can find land open for preëmption that we do
not claim, and perhaps they will go there."

The other evidently understood the look, for he winced
a little beneath it, and then said, in a petulant kind of
way :

"Well, let 'em stay where they are, then, and work for a
share of the crop.   All the more reason why they should, if
they can't find any land to preëmpt anywhere else in the
State.   Anyhow," he continued, in a more determined tone,
"if they are going to whine, I propose to give them something worth whining about.   I was just ordering Barnes, as
you came in, to notify the business men that they had better keep their fingers out of our pie if they don't want to get
them burnt."

"Anything new ?" asked the thinner man, with a sudden show of interest.

"Nothing special ; only, if we conclude to have any of
those pretended settlers arrested again, and let 'em lie in
jail awhile, until they come to their senses, we don't want
anybody coming forward with offers to go their bail."

The thinner man laughed again, the same quiet kind of
laugh as before.

"Well, governor," he said, "I guess you can manage
that without any assistance, and I am willing to leave it to
you as long as you do it properly.   It has to be done, of

course, for the land we must have, but I own that I prefer buying congressmen and senators to driving those poor devils out of their homes."

"Oh, yes, that's all very nice," replied the other, "but what is the use of buying congressmen and senators, if we are not to reap the benefit of the purchase? It isn't the senators and congressmen that we bought, either. They did the selling. The thing bought was the land, and it isn't our fault if the men that are on the land have got themselves into such shape that they go with it; and, besides, if we are going to be squeamish about taking what we have bought, we might better have kept our purchase money."

The thinner man smiled. Then he leaned back in his chair, stretched out his legs, ran both hands deep into his pants pockets, and gazed up at the ceiling.

"All right, governor," he said. "I'm not going to moralize about the right of congressmen or courts to sell the land or the men that work it. We went into this thing to win, and of course we are going to see it through. If the people have no more sense or spirit than to sit still and let us gobble up the country, they are only fit for slaves, and slaves they shall be. If we can keep them quiet a few years more, until we get our plans all laid and in operation, get possession of the water transportation as thoroughly as we have of the railroad facilities, their whining won't count for much; and you can depend on me standing by you until the thing is done. I was only saying that I like better the work of paying congress and the courts to let us take what we want, than I do the work of turning those poor devils out of their homes, after congress and the courts have given us permission to do so. Now a congressman or a judge is well fed and generally well satisfied with himself and the world at large, and so is not given to unpleasant reminis-

20

cences or predilections, while at the same time they are generally sufficiently ready to turn an honest penny to make
them anxious to make themselves agreeable to anyone who
is known to have a little matter that he is willing to pay for
having attended to — at least that has been my experience.
All of which helps to make the work of getting their consent
to our little schemes very pleasant; at least a good deal more
pleasant than listening to the complaints of the poor
wretches of grangers whose homes have been disposed of
without their consent, and who, when we have driven them
off, bag and baggage, with their wives and young ones, will
begin again somewhere else, with the certainty that the same
thing will be done to them again as soon as they get enough
together to make it an object for anybody to do it."

"That's it," replied the heavy man. "If we don't do it,
somebody else will ; and, besides, we have paid for the privilege, and so have the best right to make the first assess-
ment. And while we are about it we may as well make it
large enough so no one else will be tempted to trouble them
for a while at least. But here he comes. Come in," he
called, in response to a rap on the door, and a gentleman
entered, nodded familiarly to the heavy man and his companion, and, drawing a chair up to the table, sat down.

Nodding sideways towards the thinner man, he said :
" He came in just after you left, governor, and as we knew
you would want to hear how things were looking at the Capital, we concluded to come up and let him make his report
to us here.'

"That's right. .Glad you came," replied the heavy man.
I am anxious to hear just what shape affairs are in at Washington, and what the outlook is. It is of the utmost importance that our friends there stand by us now. Do you
think," he added, addressing the thinner man, "that we can

depend on enough votes in the House and Senate to pull us through ? "

" I don't see why we should fail," replied the thinner man. " The president of the Senate has kindly permitted the use of the room directly back of his desk for our private lobby, so that we can watch matters and have a consultation with our friends at any moment. I think everything is all right there now, but if need be we can fix a man or two at the last moment.

" In the House matters have not progressed quite so far, but there is time enough yet. Congressmen are not becoming any more virtuous or hard to approach as the years pass, that I can see; but the contrary. There's a difference, to be sure, but it's a difference of price. When we first began we had to satisfy only a few of the party leaders, and the rest followed ; but of late they have all dropped to our racket, and either kick out and refuse to vote with us on any terms, or they demand to be paid for their votes the same as the leaders, which makes it rather expensive getting what we want. Still it's a good investment."

" How much will it take, according to your estimates ? " asked the heavy man.

" How much ? Oh, well, that's hard to say exactly. You can judge about as well as I. Congressmen this year range all the way from five thousand dollars up to fifty thousand, and senators proportionately higher, and we must have a majority of both houses.

" Of course we can count on getting some votes on the plea of the public good, and the necessity for more railroads to open up the country and to provide competition. Then there is a certain number of members who are afraid to vote with us, but who can be persuaded that they need a vacation about the time the bill comes to a vote, and can be got rid of for the day for the cost of a trip home or to New York, with provision for a good time after they get there. Then a certain other number can be sent off on committees of investigation, and the number who must be paid directly be greatly reduced in that way. I should say it would cost about half a million to get what we want."

"Half a million," echoed the heavy man with a sigh. "Congressmen at five to fifty thousand dollars—what is the country coming to?"

As neither of his companions ventured a prediction, the heavy man continued : "When we commenced business here on the coast we could get all the help we wanted from members of Congress by placing a few thousand dollars of our stock in the hands of the right men. And down South, before the war, they say able-bodied niggers used to sell for a thousand dollars apiece, the best of 'em." And the heavy man lay back in his chair and looked grum and disgusted.

"You don't look at the thing in the right light," returned the thinner man, laughing. A thousand dollars apiece for niggers is high, is way up, compared to what we pay for white men. At a half million dollars for the lot, there are already enough squatters on the land we are after to bring the price to five hundred dollars for a whole family, with several million acres of land thrown in, enough for several pretty good sized plantations, I should say."

"I wish you wouldn't always put things in that disagreeable kind of a way," remarked the third man. "It is but a few years since we fought to set the negroes free in this country, and I don't like to hear about making slaves of white men. It don't sound well."

"Oh, well, just as you like. It's only a choice of terms," replied the thinner man, good-naturedly. "By the way, you say 'we fought;' I don't remember ever to have heard the number of your regiment and company? What State did you enlist from?"

"Come, come," interrupted the heavy man. "What's the use of your sparring each other? If none of us went to war ourselves, we did all we could to induce others to go, and so helped sustain the government. As governor of the State during that time, I did everything I could in support of the administration. It was conceded at the time that to my efforts was due the fact that the Pacific coast remained true to the Union. We both understand your way of putting things, of course, and it's all right with us; but it wouldn't do to let outsiders hear you talk that way. They might think you were in earnest."

"Never you fear for that, governor. I am not going to give the thing away. Why, you ought to hear me expound the matter to members of congress. I actually get eloquent sometimes, I do believe, dwelling on the advantages which our enterprise will be to the country; opening up its resources and laying bare its great natural wealth to the energy and enterprise of the people. Why, I'll contract to keep any congressman or senator who votes the way we want him to, in arguments to prove himself a patriot and statesman. I do that regularly with lots of our fellows, besides writing whole columns of matter for the newspapers, setting forth the desirability of the thing from a commercial standpoint. Maybe you didn't know that that great speech of Thompson's in the House last week was written by me. Well, it was. That is, I furnished the figures and outlined the argument. Thompson put the thing into shape a little; rounded off the periods so they would sound well, and then shot it off to the country. It made a big noise, too, I tell you.   The associated press reported it, and all the big dailies had it next morning with double headlines."

"I hope Thompson succeeded in convincing the rest of the members of the House that our enterprise has been a great benefit," remarked the last comer.

"I should say so.   Why, benefit is no word for it.   Considering the fact that we invested exactly eleven thousand five hundred dollars in this thing to start on, and now own half the coast, with a prospect of gobbling up the other half, I should say it had been a benefit, with a big B."

"Oh, come, now, I'm tired of your nonsense; let's talk business.   Give me the names of the men whom you have seen and the price they can be had at, and anything else of importance, so we can decide what to do at once.   I suppose, though, we will have to pay them their price, whatever it is, but we must get it down as low as possible, for we may have to fight the thing in the courts, if not in the departments, after we get the bill through.   And election is coming on, and we have to take care of our friends, or some of 'em may get left, and it's cheaper and safer to help those to a reëlection whom we know to be friendly, than it is to trust to new men who may not be of our way of thinking."

"That's true," returned the other.   "It is always harder to approach a man the first time than the second or third. Your new man may be either afraid to deal, or what is quite as likely, afraid of selling too cheap, not being posted on the price of votes.   Or he may possibly have too exalted an opinion of the position of Congressman and law-maker to make it safe to approach him with a business proposition. Such men are not common in Congress now-a-days, but occasionally one gets there by accident, and we have to be cautious and feel our way. And it all costs. Wine is higher in Washington than it is in California ; and a champagne supper, about as good a thing to bring men together and get acquainted and friendly as any, will spoil a thousand dollar note.

" How about the third House?" asked the last man in.

"The Lobby? Oh, well, we have to use the lobby, of course. It is generally safer to deal through a third party. Gives one a chance to swear he did not authorize anything of the kind, you know. The trouble of it is one can't always tell how much the go-between is beating him. I expect them to keep a good big per cent. of what passes through their fingers, of course. One can't expect them to act from disinterested motives entirely, but it isn't exactly pleasant to learn, after the deal is closed, that some fellow to whom you paid ten or twenty thousand dollars to do certain things with, has kept the whole of it and trusted to luck to prevent your finding it out. However, I flatter myself that such things don't occur very often. Anyway, one must take the bitter with the sweet in life."

" I suppose that's so," replied the heavy man, "but I hope you don't allow them to beat you out of such sums often. But come, get out your memorandum, and let's get down to business at once. I want to know what the whole thing is going to cost us."

The three men drew close about the table, the tray with the bottle and glasses being shoved to one side. The thinner man produced a small morocco-covered memorandum book with a gold clasp, in which were written the initials of certain lobbyists, members of Congress and the Senate of the United States. Opposite to these initials were the amounts in pencil which he had either formally contracted to pay for the service which he desired at their hands, or which he believed would be required to induce them to comply with the wishes of the corporation which he represented.

The three conspirators spent a half hour in examining these. Then followed a discussion of who among the candidates for congress should be aided and who defeated, not only upon the coast, but in other States and portions of the Union, after which the two men last introduced arose to go. As they did so, the heavy man poured out three glasses of wine. Passing one to each of his companions, he raised the other to his lips.

" Let us drink to the success of our enterprise," he said.

"And to the confusion of the people," added the thinner man.

The third man scowled slightly, and glanced about him with the least sign of nervousness, as if he feared that the reckless language of the other might reach ears for which it was not intended ; but he drank his wine and said nothing.

The heavy man emptied his glass at a gulp, refilled and again emptied it. "To the confusion of the people," he said, repeating the words of the other.

Then following his guests to the door, he bowed them out into the hall, and calling a page, bade him attend them to a carriage in waiting, and returned to his private room.

CHAPTER XXVIII.

CONSUMMATE VILLAINY.

When Erastus and Mrs. Parsons reached the Slough, they found Lucy very sick; the shock received at learning of the death of her father and Johnny, while in her feeble condition, having still further prostrated her and brought on a low fever, from which her recovery was slow.

From the hour of her arrival, Lucy's mother became her nurse, waiting upon and watching her with all a mother's solicitude, and the new demands thus made upon her affections and sympathies, forced her in a measure to withdraw her thoughts from the dead and fix them again upon the things of this life, and so very probably prevented her from sinking into a condition where morbid watchfulness for death, as the only release from the memories of the past, would have slowly consumed her life.

Then, too, there was the baby. A wonderful baby it was. All babies are; at least in the opinion of their mothers and grandmothers.

If there was ever, anywhere, an exception to this rule, the writer never heard of it, and certainly this was not one.

The youngster was as fat as three-weeks-old babies ever are, and of the same beautiful color.

He had a fine head of hair—in prospect—and had already made two weak little attempts to put his toe into his mouth, which everybody said was very remarkable and showed wonderful genius in one so young, and Lucy "just knew he was the sweetest baby that ever lived; so he was."

She first thought of calling him Erastus, after his father, but finally decided to name him John, after her own father and little crippled brother, now dead and at rest upon the mountain side.

After the arrival of the few household goods belonging to Mrs. Parsons, the baby was placed in the little wheeled cot that he might be the more easily cared for during his mother's illness, and seeing him there, by degrees there came to the breast of Martha Parsons a feeling half as if this was her own Johnny made well again by the angels, just as he was when he first came to her.

But this could not remove wholly the awful sense of loneliness and loss, and the gray in her hair became more and more prominent, and the stooping of her form more and more noticeable as the days went by.

When Lucy's health was finally restored she again took up her round of household duties known to every farmer's wife, only permitting her mother to do such portion as seemed a pleasure to her, and both she and Erastus sought in every way possible to fill her declining years with comfort.

Meanwhile the contest between the Southern Pacific Railroad Company and the settlers continued.

Although having notified the settlers to vacate their homes unless they were prepared to pay their full value, including all improvements, the railroad company made no immediate attempt to force compliance with their demands.

To do so would bring the whole matter prominently before the country and raise such a storm of indignant protest from the whole people as not only to force the company to relinquish their claim to the homes of the settlers, but to the entire grant of many millions of acres.

The conspirators well knew that they had complied with no portion of the terms required in the grant, and that until they did so they could have no legal or equitable right thereto.

They had decided, however, to obtain the land without complying with the terms of the grant, and their policy was to harass the settlers by threats, and in every way possible to incite them to such acts of violence as would bring them in conflict with the state or local authorities, while the officers of the company stood ready to appease any public sentiment that might be stirred up against themselves by asserting their readiness to submit to arbitration or the decision of the courts, and it was in pursuance of this policy that they made no immediate attempts to enforce their orders to pay or vacate.

When it became evident that they were to be forced into a long and expensive contest in defense of their homes, the settlers had formed themselves into a league, for the purpose of employing counsel and taking whatever other steps were possible for the protection of their rights.

An appeal was made to O. H. Browning, then Secretary of the Interior, at Washington, for his decision regarding the claims of the company and of the settlers.

Mr. Browning examined the matter carefully, listened patiently to the arguments of the attorneys of the railroad company and decided that the company had not built their road upon the line specified in their charter, but had instead built one hundred and fifty miles distant from that line, where they had no authority for building, and consequently could have no possible claim to any portion of the grant.

At the same time that he rendered this decision Secretary Browning ordered the land commissioners to consider the lands in California claimed by the railroad company open for settlement, and to allow those claiming them under the homestead and pre-emption laws to prove up and obtain their patents from the government.

This decision was received by the settlers at the Slough with glad and grateful hearts.

It secured them in their natural and acquired rights, and was accepted as proof that the authorities at Washington were beyond the power of the corruptionists, and that the general government would continue to respect the rights of the humblest of her citizens equally with those of the wealthy and powerful.

With their love for and pride in their country and its institutions strengthened by the justice of this decision of one of its officials, those who were in a condition to do so at once prepared their papers for proving up, but before they could secure their patent from the government word came that Mr. Browning had withdrawn the lands from market and that they would not be permitted to receive their patent until further notice.

The cause of this action on the part of the Secretary of the Interior was the receipt of a request from a prominent politician, who was a major-general in the Union army, whom the railroad company had induced to intercede for them, asking that further opportunity of presenting evidence to show that they were entitled to the land in question be given them.

This was but a trick of the conspirators to obtain time, prevent the settlers from at once receiving their deeds from the government, and give themselves opportunity to learn where an influence could be found or purchased sufficiently powerful to secure a permanent reversal of the decision of the Secretary.

The Presidential campaign was coming on and they

hoped for a change of some kind that would enable them to accomplish their dishonest purposes.

The settlers, although anxious and uneasy in their minds, believed that the government would ultimately deal justly with them, tended their orchards and vineyards as usual, and added new fields to the territory already irrigated.

The election came and passed.

Grant was elected President and J. D. Cox, of Ohio, was made Secretary of the Interior in place of Mr. Browning.

To Mr. Cox the officers of the railroad company applied for a favorable decision upon their right to the lands in question, bringing every influence possible to induce him to do so, but without success.

Mr. Cox decided as Mr. Browning had done, that the company had no right whatever to the land, and ordered it again opened to pre-emption and homestead, and this decision was sustained by the Attorney-General of the United States, Hon. Charles Devans.

It is probable that Stanford, Crocker, and Huntington, the leading conspirators and owners of the Southern Pacific Railroad, had anticipated the nature of the decision and decided in advance upon their course of action.

By means which may sometime be better known to the public than at present, they procured the introduction into the United States Senate of a joint resolution authorizing the Southern Pacific Railroad Company to build its road "as near as may be" on the line specified in their charter from the State of California, and providing that when the road should be built in compliance in other respects with the law making the grant of lands, the Secretary of the Interior should cause patents for the same to be issued to the company, "expressly saving and reserving the rights of actual settlers."

This resolution was referred to the Senate committee on Pacific Railroads, whose chairman was friendly to the road, and who immediately wrote to Secretary Cox, suggesting that he withdraw his order permitting the settlers to prove up on their claims until the committee could report, and the Senate and House act upon the resolution.

Mr. Cox complied with the request, again withdrew the lands from market and again the Mussle Slough settlers were refused permission to present their proving-up papers and receive a title to their homes.

No sooner was this accomplished than the attorneys for the railroad company, in the Senate, in the House, and in the Lobby, began the work of securing enough votes to pass the resolution.

The settlers protested and petitioned against its passage, but little attention was paid to their pleadings for justice.

The member of congress from the district through which the road was being constructed was either incompetent or in the pay of the road, and made but feeble efforts to defeat the schemes of the corporation, and the Senators from California were equally derelict in their duty.

Finally the settlers raised money among themselves and sent an attorney to Washington to plead their cause for them.

He returned with a Federal appointment in his pocket and without having accomplished anything for those who sent him, and the resolution in favor of the railroad company passed both Houses.

The people at the Slough were now greatly discouraged, but still not without hope.

The resolution plainly provided that the rights of actual settlers should be respected, and they could not see how any one could dispute the fact of their being such. Indeed it was only by asserting that their rights were secured by that clause of the resolution that enough members of the House and Senate who were not absolute tools or partners of the conspirators, were induced to vote for the resolution to secure its passage.

Besides this, the railroad company, when its officers first decided to make an effort to seize upon the land in the vicinity of the Slough, had issued circulars urging people to come and take up land there, promising them that as soon as the company received patents for the land from the government it would deed to the settlers, upon payment of the price of wild land ; or at two and a half dollars per acre for barren plains, such as most of the land at the Slough was ; and that in no case would a price exceeding ten dollars per acre be charged, even for timbered land.

A large portion of the settlers now at the Slough had come in compliance with this invitation and agreement on the part of the railroad company, and they still relied upon the promise of the company, or thought the courts would compel it to comply with the promise set forth in its circulars—a promise which became a binding contract when the settlers, acting upon it, came upon the land and began to improve it.

The officers of the company had, however, no intention of complying with the promise, and their success in bribing congress led them to feel that there was nothing to be feared from the courts.

They demanded the full value of all lands, including improvements, and claimed that the words "actual settlers" in the resolution of congress, referred to such as government had granted patents to before the passage of the act making the grant of lands to the company; which was before the first settler came to the Slough, and was of lands along the line proposed in their charter, distant one hundred and fifty miles and on the other side of a range of mountains.

During all this time the settlers had held frequent meetings and endeavored in every legal manner known to them to defend their rights.

Erastus Hemmingway was always in attendance upon these meetings, and although he said but little, what he did say was always to the point, clear and forcible, and he came to be regarded by all as one whose judgment was of value, and who was ever prompt with his portion of the money found necessary to be raised from time to time in defense of their homes.

At last, and after repeated meetings and much discussion, it was decided to make an offer to compromise with the company as the cheapest way out of the difficulty, and a letter was addressed to its chief officer, stating that while they did not recognize either the legal or equitable claim of the company to their lands, yet for the sake of being at peace they would all pay the prices which those who came by invitation of the company had been promised the land at; or the price which a disinterested committee would say the lands without the improvements were now worth; or the price at which the company was now offering to sell raw land of similar quality.

This would compel those who took homestead and preemption claims before the company made any pretense of being entitled to the land—while it still professed to be intending to build its road and take the lands upon the line laid down in its charter—to pay from two and a half to ten dollars per acre for what they should have had for nothing as homesteaders, or on payment of one dollar and a quarter per acre to the government in case they claimed as pre-emptors. But all were weary of the long contest and preferred peace at any price short of bankruptcy, rather than a continuation of their troubles.

In reply to this offer of the settlers the president of the company responded saying that they were willing to do what should appear right, and requesting the settlers to select a committee from among themselves to come to San Francisco and confer with the representatives of the company.

This letter was read at a regular meeting of the Settlers' League, and a committee immediately selected and authorized to act for the whole. ·

Among those chosen for this duty were Erastus Hemmingway and his neighbor Mr. Johnson.

The committee proceeded to San Francisco, put up at a hotel and notified the railroad officials of their presence and readiness to confer.

Instead of proceeding to the conference, however, one of the officials went before the authorities, swore out warrants and had them all arrested and conveyed to jail, where they were locked up and forced to remain until morning, Barnes having performed the work assigned him by the railroad king as told in the previous chapter, and notified the business men of the city that it was the will of the railroad company that no one should go bail for the arrested men, and that the company would ruin the business of any one who dared to do so.

After lying in jail all night they were taken before the court and dismissed without a hearing, and in spite of their protest and demands to be given an opportunity to explain to the court the circumstances of their arrest, and so were forced to return to their homes and their waiting neighbors and report that no mercy was to be expected from those who

21

had conspired to reduce them to serfdom upon their own lands.*

Still these men retained possession of their homes, and though they had ceased making improvements, were able to obtain subsistence therefrom.

Time passed, and the railroad company obtained from the government patents for the amount of land specified in the original grant.

The road was not completed as the law making the grant required that it should be before the patents should issue, one hundred and ten miles of it being then, as now (1884), untouched, and no portion of it being upon the line specified in their charter, which was the only line upon which they had the right to build a road, much less to claim a grant of land for building, even under the resolution of congress, it being plainly absurd to say that one hundred and fifty miles was as near to their original line as it was possible to build.

The settlers were now powerless in the hands of the corporation, which played with them much as a cat does with a mouse before craunching its bones for the final act of swallowing.

Their first act after having completed the road through the Slough and formed connection with a road leading to San Francisco, was to place the price of freight so high as to consume the entire profit of all labor upon the irrigated lands, thus seeking to prevent the settlers from obtaining further means with which to continue the contest and transform them into the serfs of the company.

The outside world during all this time remained in almost

---

* PUBLISHER'S NOTE.—This part of the story may seem incredible; but the imprisonment of the committee that went to San Francisco upon the invitation of the railroad authorities, the appraisement of the lands at the price of farms, the attempted eviction and the murdering of the settlers on the 11th of May, 1880, occurred as related.

absolute ignorance of the desperate attempt being made upon the rights of a portion of our citizens.

The greater part of the press of the Pacific coast wore the muzzle of the corporations, and only the most meagre reports of these matters were sent out through the Associated Press, and such as were sent were tinged with the coloring furnished by the conspirators.

The first year after the completion of the main irrigating ditch the settlers had set apart the eleventh day of May as a day of general rejoicing, and thanksgiving for the harvest which followed the coming of the waters, and through all their troubles they had regularly observed it, their festivities usually taking the form of a picnic, which was attended by everybody, regardless of age or sex, and it was this eleventh day of May, this festival day in 1880, that the corporate conspirators fixed upon for the consummation of their scheme for possessing themselves of the homes of these people.

In order to secure fit tools for this purpose, the company had made pretended sales of the homes of a portion of the settlers to men of known desperate character, among others to one named Crow, a noted desperado and crack-shot; and it was these men whom the United States marshal was ordered to take upon his raid of eviction.

The marshal left San Francisco before day and arrived at Hanford, the station nearest the Slough lands, at seven o'clock in the morning.

Here he was met by Crow with his gang of desperadoes armed to the teeth, and all started together in wagons.

Crow carried two bulldog revolvers and a knife in his belt, and had a repeating rifle and a double-barreled fowling piece in the wagon in which he rode, and all bristled with deadly weapons, principally revolvers and knives.

As was anticipated by the marshal, they arrived at the

first house in the Slough settlement after its occupants had left for the picnic.

Without ceremony the door of this peaceful dwelling was broken down and everything in it pitched into the highway.

This done, they placed three No. 10 cartridges upon the doorstep as an indication of the fate which awaited the honest settler and his family if they dared replace their household goods and resume the occupancy of their home.

They then started in the direction of the next settler's claim, intending to proceed in the same manner with each of twenty-five houses against whose owners the marshal had writs of ejectment.

But they were not destined to proceed so far.

Unknown to them the gang had been seen to leave Hanford by one who, surmising the nature of their errand, hastened to notify the settlers of what was about to be attempted.

Mounting a horse he rode with all speed, and, approaching the picnic grounds, came first upon several parties who had driven a little way back from the immediate scene of festivities in order to find a suitable place for leaving their teams and wagons.

Among them were Erastus Hemmingway and his neighbor, Mr. Johnson.

To these men he communicated what he had observed, and his belief regarding the intention of the marshal and his gang of desperate characters.

All listened eagerly to the information brought by their friend, and then held a hurried consultation among themselves.

Erastus, Johnson, and one of the others, were armed with a single revolver of small calibre each. The rest were without weapons of any kind.

They did not like to return to the picnic grounds and

frighten the women and children with an announcement of what they believed was taking place; neither did they propose that their homes should be ravished and they make no effort to defend them.

It was finally agreed that Hemmingway, Johnson, and those who were with them, should hurry across country to a point in the road about a mile away, over which the marshal and his crowd must pass, while the friend who had brought the information should quietly notify others and leave them to follow or wait for a report from those who were in advance, as they thought best.

Hurrying across the fields, this little body of men came out into the road by which the gang were proceeding, just in advance of the marshal and his party, as they approached the cottage of the second victim marked upon their list for eviction.

Seeing them, the marshal halted and got down from the wagon in which he was riding. Crow and the others did the same.

Approaching to within a few feet of the marshal, Erastus demanded to know if it were true that they had come to evict the settlers, and was told that they had.

"You will not be allowed to do so," replied Hemmingway; "we redeemed these lands from the desert and gave them all the value they possess. They belong to us and we intend to hold them."

The marshal replied that "he was doing only what the law and the court required of him, but that rather than use force he would abandon the attempt."

But Crow and his gang thirsted for blood, and had been ordered to prevent any abandonment of the object for which they were sent.

Scarcely had the words of the marshal issued from his

mouth when Crow drew his revolver and fired at Erastus, thus giving the signal to the others of the gang, who at once followed his example and emptied their revolvers into the bodies of the innocent and almost defenseless men in front of them.

Crow's first shot was aimed at Hemmingway's heart and missed it by but a few inches. The bullet entered his left breast and passed entirely through his body, but though mortally wounded he succeeded in drawing his own revolver, and, firing, killed one of the desperadoes on the spot.

One other of the gang was wounded by a shot fired by Johnson, who was himself instantly killed by the second volley of the desperadoes.

Two others of the settlers were killed outright and three wounded; the latter by shots from the fowling piece of Crow, who fired at them as they fled, and but for the fact that the horses attached to the wagon, in which lay the villain's revolving rifle, took fright and ran away, not one of them would have escaped death.

Terror-stricken the bleeding men sped on in the direction of the picnic grounds, but had gone but a little distance when they met a score of neighbors, who, having been told the rumor of attempted evictions, had not waited for word from the first party, but followed on after, leaving their panic-stricken families to hitch up the teams and follow by the longer way of the road.

To these men the news of the awful tragedy just enacted was communicated, and a portion hurried forward while others returned to find the families of the dead and wounded men, if perchance they had not yet left the grounds, and prepare them as best they could for the worst that could occur.

BUT THOUGH MORTALLY WOUNDED, HE SUCCEEDED IN DRAWING HIS OWN REVOLVER, AND, FIRING, KILLED ONE OF THE DESPERADOES ON THE SPOT.

Meantime the marshal and his brutal allies had beat a hasty retreat.

The former avoided Hanford and reached another station, where he took the train for San Francisco.

Crow, attempting to follow on after his horses, was found next day dead by the roadside, a bullet through his heart, one hand clasping a bulldog revolver and the other his double-barreled shotgun.

Erastus Hemmingway and the other murdered and dying victims of the conspiracy were tenderly lifted from the ground and carried to their homes.

Lucy, with her mother and two children—a second child, a girl, having been born to them—reached home in advance of those who brought her wounded husband.

They had heard the most terrible rumors, and were tortured by the most horrible fears, but were in ignorance of what had actually occurred until the men came bearing the bleeding body with its unconscious face and laid it at their feet.

To those who cannot imagine the agony of these loving hearts no description which the writer can give would convey any meaning whatever.

Erastus lived until morning.

He was unconscious during the whole time, and died without a word or look of recognition of those about him, while wife and mother and children poured forth their anguish in tears and sobs as they watched the pulsing of the heart grow fainter and fainter and felt the hands which they clasped become colder and colder, as the death-damp gathered upon the brow of him they loved.

When he was buried these two lone and widowed women, the one in the prime of life, the other bowed and broken and gray with years and sorrow, but more with sorrow than with years, returned to their desolate home to clasp two fatherless children to their breasts, and weep and moan, living in daily fear of other attempts at eviction and other tragedies until such time as death shall come to them, or until the whole people shall waken from their slumbers, throw off the fatal spell which binds them, and demand that justice be done, and reparation made so far as may be.

Walking down one of the principal streets of Chicago one day recently I met Ensign, the husband of Jennie Parsons.

He was not as well dressed as when I last saw him, and his greeting had less of self confidence and manly independence than formerly.

In truth, I think he intended to pass without speaking, but I stopped him and held out my hand.

"How do you do," I said; "and how is Jennie and the babies?"

"They are well, or as well as could be expected under the circumstances," was the reply.

I feared that all was not exactly right with them, but could not well appear to be inquisitive. I have a high respect for Ensign and his wife, and had no intention of permitting them to drop from my list of friends, and I said:

"I am coming out to spend an evening with you before long if you will allow me. I suppose you are still living in the same cottage on C—— street?"

"No," he replied, "they foreclosed and took that from us more than a year ago; after we had more than half paid for it, too. You see I was thrown out of my place by the failure of the company I was at work for, and could not keep up the payments on the house and lot, and so lost all we had saved since coming here, together with what little we had when we came."

" And where are you living now ?" I asked.

He hesitated a little and then said:

" After we lost our place I got another job at one of the mills, but was sick with the fever for a time, and when I got up again I could get no steady employment, and we were forced to rent some rather poor rooms on —— street, fronting on the railroad track. Well, the railroad company claimed the ground that this building and others stood on and wanted possession, so they ordered us put out without ceremony.

" I came home from a long tramp after work one day and found Jennie and the children on the sidewalk with what few household goods we had left, crying their eyes out with fear and anxiety."

" And then what ?" I asked, seeing that he hesitated again.

"Well, I was out of money, and rent had to be paid in advance, and as we had nothing to pay with, and could not borrow, we moved into an old building with another family down by the river, until I can find work and rent a better place. We don't call it living; it isn't living; it's only just a camping; but what can a fellow do? I assure you there are hundreds of other families in the city who are equally bad off."

The story " Driven from Sea to Sea " is finished,—no, not finished. John Parsons and Erastus Hemmingway are dead. One sleeps with his crippled child upon the mountain side ; one lies buried in the valley, side by side with his neighbors, who fell like him, the victims of the rapacious greed of corporate conspirators on that fatal morning of

May, 1880 ; but Martha Parsons and Lucy Hemmingway still live, and living still contend with a corporation for the shelter above their heads and the heads of orphaned children. With them battle others whose homes and farms are in jeopardy from the same source.

Occasionally some settler, driven from his home, made desperate by long-continued suffering, by wrongs oft repeated, takes vengeance upon the immediate author of his woes ; and some man, some tool of the corporation sent to hold possession of the land from which the settler has been evicted, is found dead upon the spot where the wrong was done.* Even as you read these lines and wonder if such things are possible, honest settlers, not alone in California, but in any of a dozen different States, it may be, are being

---

* The following article from the *San Francisco Daily Examiner* of November 13, 1883, shows that this terrible conflict is still going on :

THE LAST MUSSEL SLOUGH TRAGEDY.—It is not surprising that another tragedy has been added to the dark history of the Mussel Slough country. It is simply another chapter in the old story of the conflict of might against right ; of a long succession of deep and deadly injuries ripening in a harvest of blood ; of the oppressed striking at the oppressors ; of the victims of injustice and cruelty turning, as even a worm will turn, and stinging the feet that trample on them. It has been so in every land under the sun, and will be so as long as the world lasts. Traced to its source, the bitter enmities engendered flow from railroad greed and avarice. The conflict is simply one wherein organized wealth has sought to rob the settler of his home, for the railroads will pillage the farmer of his home and lands as readily as they rob the merchant and the tradesman. Everything is fish which comes to the railroad net.

It is not necessary for the *Examiner* to relate the history of these contests. They are familiar to the people of the State. Such robberies have been so common as to have lost even the semblance of novelty. Now and then the picture of remorseless greed, of unsated avarice, is deepened with a tragedy, as in San Joaquin County recently, when Patrick Breen lost his life. He took possession as a railroad tenant of lands on the Moquelemos grant, dispossessing a settler of his home. Who killed him it is not necessary to inquire. He drove away those who should have enjoyed these lands in peace. And now the scene has shifted to the Mussel Slough country, memorable for similar tragedies in the past. Two men, named McAuliffe and Riley, were the other day put in possession, as railroad tenants, of settler Cockrell's property. Yesterday McAuliffe was found dead, shot through the heart. He was the instrument of the corporations, and their victim as well, since they are responsible even more than the outlaw whose rifle has laid him lifeless on his new domain. The law, if it can find the homicide, may hold him to account. But there is sometimes a sentiment of rude justice which rises in conflict with the law, and this will justify men in defend-

driven from their homes, their altars overthrown, their household gods destroyed, their lives sacrificed, their wives widowed and their children made orphans.

No, the story is not yet finished; but so far as told it is a true story. All of the main incidents have taken place substantially as related. They are part of the history of our country; have occurred to our own citizens, beneath the shadow of our own flag.

Had it been other than a true story it might have ended with a brighter picture; with the brightest and best of all pictures—the picture of a loving and honored old couple enjoying the last years of their well-spent lives amidst scenes of plenty and beauty, the work of nature and their own hands; with loving children and laughing babies, the children of their children about them.

As it is a true story it could not be told otherwise than as it has been, and if the pictures presented have been sorrowful instead of pleasant ones, and if the reader has been forced to weep, when, like the writer, he would prefer laughter to tears, it is not the writer's fault.

If sometime the people shall make it possible to write a story in which, without being untrue to life as the great mass of the people live it, the pleasant pictures shall crowd out and force us and them to forget the sorrowful ones, then will the writer of this be only too glad to write the sequel of " Driven from Sea to Sea; or, Just a Campin'."

ing when it is possible, and avenging when it is not, their violated rights and pillaged homes.

Breen and McAuliffe were but instruments of the corporations—deceived and betrayed, no doubt. It is to be lamented that they foolishly undertook the tasks assigned them. It is deplorable that they have lost their lives. If railroad rapacity is insatiable, and violence results, it is a pity that the mere agents become the victims.

It is time for this wretched state of affairs to end. Too long have the grasping corporations persisted in their dishonest work. They are deliberately breeding in this State a spirit of vengeance that bodes them terrible evil. If it is possible for them to learn wisdom, they will halt in their career of rapine and enter upon a policy of honesty and peace.

PART II.

BODIES WITHOUT SOULS.

CHAPTER I.

THE DANGERS THAT THREATEN US.

In order that the attention of the reader should not be drawn from the story, the foot notes in " Driven from Sea to Sea; or, Just a Campin'," were necessarily very short, giving but an imperfect idea of the facts upon which the story is based. Feeling that the people should fully know the extent to which these evils have been carried, it has been decided to give in the following chapters notes of warning, coming from the highest reliable sources, together with documentary proof that the most corrupt practices alone have enabled our railroad corporations to procure laws that have made it possible for such outrages to occur as are related in the story. Many other alarming facts exist in regard to the corrupt practices of railroad corporations which lie outside of the range of the story, but which it is deemed not inappropriate to speak of in this connection. The title "Bodies Without Souls" is suggested by the soulless action of these corporations

There is great danger that the masses of the people, through the cunning designs of this growing power, will be lulled, by the idea of a free ballot, into a feeling of security that will cause them to slumber until our liberties are undermined. Already this condition has nearly been reached on the Pacific coast. The publishers of this work have recently received two letters from California, one from one of the largest houses in San Francisco, and one from the editor of a newspaper, in both of which the writers tacitly admit their fear of the railroad power. It is alarming to witness the abject fear to which these people are made subject on account of the consolidation of the railroads of the state into an unrelenting corporation, whose policy it is to have it plainly understood that they will crush any one who opposes them.

The conventions that assume to prescribe how the ballot shall be cast, from the national to the primary, are largely manipulated by this power. They care but little as to which party shall win so that men are nominated whom they can control. Jay Gould's testimony, given in a subsequent chapter, and other evidence, proves this and gives an insight into the adroit manner in which their work is done in managing our politics. An eminent writer has recently said :

" Practical politicians, all over the United States, recognize the utter hopelessness of contending with the railroad power. In many, if not in most, of the states, no prudent man will run for office if he believes the railroad power is against him. Yet, in a direct appeal to the people, a power of this kind is weakest, and railroad kings rule states where, on any issue that comes fairly before the people, they would be voted down. It is by throwing their weight into primaries, and managing conventions, by controlling the press, manipulating legislatures, and filling the bench with their creatures, that the railroads best exert political powers. The people of California, for instance, have voted against the railroad time and again, or rather imagined they did, and even adopted a very bad new constitution because they supposed the railroad was against it. The result is, that the great railroad company, of whose domain California, with an area greater than twice that of Great Britain, is but one of the provinces, absolutely dominates the state. The men who really fought it are taken into its service or crushed, and powers are exerted in the interests of the corporation managers which no government would dare attempt. This company, heavily subsidized, in the first place, as a great public convenience, levies on commerce, not tolls, but tariffs. If a man goes into business requiring transportation he must exhibit his profits and take it into partnership for the lion's share. Importers are bound by an 'iron clad agreement' to give its agents access to their books, and if they do anything the company deems against its interests they are fined or ruined by being placed at a disadvantage to their rivals in business. Three continental railroads, heavily subsidized by the nation under the impression that the competition would keep down rates, have now reached the Pacific. Instead of competing, they have pooled their receipts. The line of steamers from San Francisco to New York, via the Isthmus, receives $100,000 a month to keep up fares and freights to a level with those exacted by the railroad, and if you would send goods from New York to San Francisco by way of the Isthmus, the cheapest way is first to ship them to England. Shippers to interior points are charged as much as though their goods were carried to the end of the road and then shipped back again ; and even, by means of the agreements mentioned, an embargo is laid upon ocean commerce by sailing vessels, wherever it might interfere with the monopoly."

The same men control the Associated Press. It is simply a " wheel within a wheel ;" so that the news furnished to us in our telegraphic reports from day to day, comes to us through men who have a personal interest in suppressing all facts that would arouse the indignation of the people against them. There can be no question that this is done. It was done in the case of the Mussle Slough Massacre. There are comparatively few people that have ever heard of that outrage. It is natural to suppose that anything of a similar character, or anything else

22

that the managers wish to suppress, will be kept out of the dispatches. We have come to depend very largely for our general information upon this medium. How can we retain our intelligence if the news can be manipulated and distorted to subserve the interests of a few designing men? By thus controlling the news, and by the arbitrary manner in which a few men are allowed to fix and change rates of transportation and travel, and to grant rebates to favorites, millionaires, who do little but scheme, are springing up all over the country. In proportion as their wealth increases they are absorbing the products of our farmers and others, who are creating the real wealth of our land.

The people themselves are to blame, as a mass, for tolerating a system of laws that turns the larger portion of the fruits of honest labor into the hands of the shrewd schemer, leaving the toiling millions of real producers to suffer for the very things which they have produced.

CHAPTER II.

OPINIONS FROM HIGH SOURCES.

The following opinions, considering the sources from which they come, are entitled to the most careful consideration. We give them concisely without comment.

Hon. David Davis, formerly Judge of the Supreme Court of the U. S., says:

"The rapid growth of corporate power and the malign influence which it exerts by combination on the national and State Legislatures, is a well grounded cause of alarm. A struggle is pending in the near future between this overgrown power, with its vast ramifications all over the Union, and a hard grip on much of the political machinery on the one hand, and the people in an unorganized condition on the other, for control of the Government. It will be watched by every patriot with intense anxiety."

Again he says:

"Great corporations and consolidated monopolies are fast seizing the avenues of power that lead to the control of the Government. It is an open secret that they rule States through procured Legislatures and corrupted Courts; that they are strong in Congress, and that they are unscrupulous in the use of means to conquer prejudice and acquire influence. This condition of things is truly alarming, for unless it be changed quickly and thoroughly, free institutions are doomed to be subverted by an oligarchy resting upon a basis of money and of corporate power."

Governor Gray, of Indiana, in a message to the Legislature of that State said:

"In my judgment the republic cannot live long in the

atmosphere which now surrounds the ballot box. Moneyed corporations, to secure favorable legislation for themselves are taking active part in elections by furnishing large sums of money to corrupt the voter and purchase special privileges from the Government. If money can control the decision at the ballot box it will not be long until it can control its existence."

The Attorney-General of the State of New York, in commenting upon an extraordinary proceeding in the Supreme Court, June 3, 1881, to thwart proceedings instituted by the State to protect the public interest in the case of the New York elevated railroads, stated that he was :

"Amazed now at the power that corporations seem to have to embarrass necessary legal proceedings taken against them ; that the increase of the influence of corporations in this country, and their ability to thwart the supervisory proceedings taken against them by the public authorities to prevent great monopolies or to subject them to proper restraints, are among the most alarming characteristics of the time, and constitute a danger to which all the people must be aroused before long if we would preserve our free institutions."

On the twenty-seventh day of January, 1880, Mr. Gowen, then President of the Philadelphia and Reading Railroad, in an argument before the Committee on Commerce of the House of Representatives of the United States, in Washington, said :

" I have heard the counsel of the Pennsylvania Railroad Company, standing in the Supreme Court of Pennsylvania, threaten that Court with the displeasure of his clients if it decided against them, and all the blood in my body tingled with shame at the humiliating spectacle."

United States Senator Windom, in a letter to the President of the Anti-Monopoly League, said :

" The channels of thought and the channels of commerce, thus owned and controlled by one man, or by a few men, what is to restrain corporate power, or to fix a limit to its exactions upon the people ? What is then to hinder these men from depressing or inflating the value of all kinds of property to suit their caprice or avarice, and thereby gathering into their own coffers the wealth of the nation? Where is the limit to such a power as this? What shall be said of the spirit of a free people who will submit without a protest to be thus bound hand and foot?"

Hon. Jeremiah S. Black, ex-Judge of the Supreme Court and ex-Attorney-General of the United States, recently said:

"All public men must take their side on this question There can be no neutrals. He that is not for us is against us. We must have legal protection against these abuses. This agitation once begun, and the magnitude of the grievance being understood, it will force our rulers to give us a remedy against it. The monopolies will resist with all their arts and influence, but fifty millions of people, in process of time, will learn the important fact that they are fifty millions strong."

The third semi-annual report of the railroad commissioners of the State of Georgia, submitted May 1st, 1881, says:

"The moral and social consequences of these corruptions are even worse than the political; they are simply appalling. We contemplate them with anxiety and dismay. The demoralization is worse than that of war—as fraud is meaner than force, and trickery than violence. Aside from their own corruptions, the operators aim directly at the corruption of the Press and the Government." * * * "Worse even than a purifying storm is this malaria in the air, which poisons all the body politic, and corrupts the youth of the country by presenting the highest prizes of society to its most unscrupulous and unworthy members."

The Hon. David Agnew, ex-Chief Justice of the Supreme Court of Pennsylvania, in an address which he delivered on the 15th of June, 1881, used the following language:

"A remarkable fact attending all the great railroads of the United States is the immense wealth of their leading officials. It is confined to no State, and is exceptional to all other employments. The grandest talent and greatest learning, in law, physics, and other learned avocations, accumulate a few thousands in a lifetime; but railroad officials, often rising from mere clerkships, roundsmen, ticket and other agents, with salaries running from hundreds to a few thousands, eventuate as possessors of many millions. It is no uncommon thing to see a railroad president, rising from the humblest station, in the course of fifteen or twenty years, become the owner of five, ten, or even twenty millions, at a salary which would not average, for the whole time, over ten or twelve thousand dollars. These are mysteries that the common people cannot understand."

The National Board of Trade, at its convention in 1881 adopted a report which declared that :

"The degree to which the great powers of steam and electricity have been allowed to pass into corporate hands, which employ them as a means to tax the public unduly for their use, is at this time forcing itself upon the attention of our statesmen, and there is a widespread feeling that the public welfare demands that the power and privileges of corporate grants shall be limited in the future."

In 1879, a committee of the Legislature of New York, Mr. Hepburn, chairman, after an exhaustive examination, declared that the charge of *flagrant abuses* in railroad management has been *fully proven*, and adds :

"The mistake was in not providing proper safe-guards to protect the public interest, and hold the railroads to a strict accountability for their transactions ; thus, through the laxity of our laws and the want of governmental control (measurably excusable, considering the unforseen possibilities of railroad development at the time of the enactment of those laws, but no longer pardonable in the light of the evidence herewith submitted), have crept in those abuses hereafter mentioned, so glaring in their proportion as to savor of fiction rather than of actual history."

James A. Garfield said :

"The modern barons, more powerful than their military prototypes, own our greatest highways and levy tribute at will upon all our vast industries. And, as the old feudalism was finally controlled and subordinated only by the combined efforts of the kings and the people of the free cities and towns, so our modern feudalism can be subordinated to the public good only by the great body of the people, acting through their government by wise and just laws."

In the report of the N. Y. Board of Trade occur these words :

" Honestly and equitably managed, railroads are the most beneficent discovery of the century, but perverted by irresponsible and uncontrolled corporate management, in which stock-watering and kindred swindles are tolerated, and favoritism in charges is permitted, they become simply great engines to accomplish unequal taxation, and to arbitrarily re-distribute the wealth of the country. When this state of things is sought to be perpetuated by acquiring political power and shaping legislation through corrupt use of money, the situation becomes more serious. "

H. C. Lord, ex-President of the I. C. & L. railroad, writes the following to the *Locomotive Engineer's Journal :*

" We have had a civil war, wonderful in its proportions, its terrible cost of life, human suffering, treasure, and national credit ; and yet, in spite of all pride and boasting, how do we stand to-day? I put the question most honestly and earnestly, and future history will answer it. Is not capital realized through devious ways and by means of unjust methods reveling in luxury while labor is comparatively unrewarded, deferred, often unpaid and too often despised ? Is not this an era in this country in which mediocrity, pride and public corruption are holding high carnival ; can railway managers accumulate great fortunes in half a score of years except at the ultimate, if not the immediate, expense of labor? If not of it, of what ? It must strike every thinking man that the pride and avarice of our country is growing too rapidly and without any sufficient cause, and it will be better to put the brakes on in time. Let my readers commence, if they please, at Washington or New York, and prosecute their investigations over and through the railways spanning this continent and connecting the waters and commerce of the Atlantic and Pacific, and tell me when and where public integrity has prevailed against both political and financial corruption, or where capital and greed have not taken an unfair advantage over the rightful property and labor of the people."

CHAPTER III.

OPINIONS OF THE PRESS.

Many volumes could be given from papers that have had
the independence to speak their real sentiments on a subject so
vital to the interests of every American citizen. But as it is
deemed important that more space shall be given to the documentary evidences of corruption, as contained in following
chapters, extracts can be given from but a few of our leading
journals.

"THE COMING CONFEDERACY."

From the New York Times, Dec. 6. 1880.

"Scarcely a week goes by without some announcement of a
movement for the consolidation of railroad lines in one part or
another of this country. These movements go on without any
interposition of public authority and little regard to any claim
of the public to be consulted or considered. Each one of them
adds strength to that corporate power whose 'malign influence'
on the National and State Legislatures was not long ago declared by a prominent United States Senator to be a 'well
grounded cause of alarm.' There was recently a report that
the New York Central and Hudson River, with the Lake Shore
and Michigan Central under its control, was about to make a
combination with the Chicago, Burlington and Quincy,
and the Atchison, Topeka and Santa Fe, which, with one more
possible connection, would bring a through line across the continent under a practically undivided management. Though
this has been denied, there have been negotiations looking in
that direction. Mr. Jay Gould has been for some time at work
making combinations in the West and South-west which evi-

dently have in view a through connection from the Mississippi River to the Pacific Ocean under one control, which is then to turn back over the Wabash system to the great lakes, thence to complete a union with some one of the trunk lines eastward to the Atlantic. Before very long there are likely to be three lines of railroad crossing the barrier of the Rocky Mountains from the Mississippi Valley to the Pacific coast, each forming, sooner or later, a union with corresponding lines from this side of the continent. The great trunk lines of the East now traverse the Northern States, but a kindred movement toward consolidation has begun in the South, conspicuously represented in the recent combinations of the Louisville and Nashville Company, while from the central ganglia on the Mississippi, lines are reaching out toward the Gulf and the Mexican border. The tendency everywhere is toward an absorption of the important short lines and a union of interests that lie in the same general line of transportation, either by actual consolidation of companies or by combinations under contracts and agreements which produce a virtual unity of control.

"Thus there is forming on the face of the territory comprised within the United States a great confederacy of railroads whose ultimate power it is not easy to forecast. However great the separate systems may be, and however far they may be rivals in the business of through transportation, they will have certain interests in common. They will have a common interest in resisting Government control, in obtaining and maintaining laws favorable to their purposes, and in strengthening and guarding their power over the business of the country. By compacts among themselves they may lay what tribute they will upon the industries and commerce of the people. They will rest like one gigantic despotism of iron upon the face of this land, and regulate the development of industrial interests, direct the currents of trade, and exercise a control over all the energies of the people which they may be powerless to resist. The business of the country is absolutely dependent upon the agencies of transportation, and any power that holds these in its grasp will have our material interests at its mercy. Of course, such a power acting without restraint would consult its own profit and safety, and aim to pursue the policy which would enable the business of the country to pay it the largest tribute. It could not injure that business as a whole without so far defeating its own purposes, but it could do great injustice to persons and places, and interfere seriously with the natural and equitable course of things, and it could lay a tax on the country for the enrichment of the plutocracy that directed it greater than that which the Government would dare to exact.

"A committee of the United States Senate reported six years ago that even at that time the men who controlled the four great trunk lines between New York and Chicago could 'by a single stroke of the pen reduce the value of property in this country by hundreds of millions of dollars.' 'An additional charge of five cents per bushel on the transportation of cereals would,' they said, 'have been equivalent to a tax of forty-five million dollars on the crop of 1873. No Congress would dare to exercise so vast a power except upon a necessity of the most imperative nature.' If this were so then, how vastly increased will this irresponsible power have become when the work of consolidation and confederation has gone on a few years more. Of the incipient strength we have had many instances already. What will be its enormous might when it has reached its full maturity? This growing corporate power has been created by the people, and we are told by high legal authority that it holds and exercises all its privileges subject to the public will. No power inherent in the States has been given up to it. The absolute right to bring it into subjection and keep it in control exists. It holds no ultimate property in the highways which it has been permitted to construct and to use, and it is exercising franchises granted by the public which give that public authority over it. But it threatens to become a question whether the master or the servant is the more powerful and which shall rule the other. The public can work only through legislation and the administration of laws, and the railroad confederacy will vie with each other in making and controlling Legislatures and Administrations. They have already entered into the contest here and there and at one time and another, and not without instances of remarkable success. The United States Senator before quoted predicted that 'a struggle is impending in the near future between this overgrown power, with its vast ramifications all over the Union and a hard grip on much of the political machinery, on the one hand, and the people in an unorganized condition on the other, for the control of the government.'

" This new and growing confederacy overlies State lines and is outgrowing local jurisdictions. Interior political boundaries can neither confine nor divide it. The Government which it will ultimately aim to control is the national Government, and the power that must bring it into subjection is the national power. The longer the struggle is put off the harder and more disturbing it will be. Shall it be postponed until the whole aroused energy of the Nation is necessary to bring the confederacy of railroads into submission to lawful authority and into a respect for the rights of the people?"

From the New York Evening Post.

" All this, we may be sure, is not a summer cloud that can overcome the community without arousing either special fear or wonder. It betokens a real, a menacing, a present danger. It implies that a time has come when the forces of public opinion must be set at work in earnest to breast and bear back a grievous calamity. Supineness will not answer; to close our eyes and stop our ears will not answer. A moment has arrived when we must change all that; a moment when legislators and those who bribe them must cry halt; " combiners" and " consolidators" and all other plotters against the common weal in the interest of corporate monopoly must be told in trumpet tones, and in something more than words if need be, ' Thus far shall ye go and no further.'"

THE COUNTRY'S DANGER.

From the New York Real Estate Chronicle.

" There is a real danger to the country in the vast expansion of power which the monopolists have secured, and by the time the people perceive the coils that are being wound around their necks there may be trouble. The safest way is to look the situation squarely in the face and to understand that the entire business of the country, linked as it is to-day to the telegraph and the Press, is virtually at the mercy of Jay Gould, Cyrus W Field and D. O. Mills. They own the cables to Europe, the entire telegraphic machinery on this Continent, and three out of the seven newspapers of the Associated Press. One paper more and the triumvirate will have the majority of that organization."

"Do the people as yet understand the importance of this? It means that this triumvirate will have the news of the markets of the world in their possession, can operate in accordance with this news long before the great public is made aware of the dealings on the London Stock Exchange, the Paris Bourse, or the Chicago grain market.   One week's operations in this manner alone will pay for the construction of more and more cables to all parts of the civilized world.

"The masses will say 'Organize an opposition Associated Press," but how can newspapers construct telegraph lines when the entire machinery is already in the hands of the monopolists?   There is only one remedy, and that is for the Government to take possession of the wires and deal on an equal and just footing with all those using the telegraphs."

From the Memphis Appeal.

"The problem is worth consideration, for monopolists and railway discriminators are certainly making matters uncomfortable.   *   *   *   It is to the interest of corporate managers so to do their business as to retain the good feeling of the people on their side, but, blinded by the desire of gain to-day, corporations do not look to to-morrow, and they are raising an indignant spirit of resistance that bodes no good."

From the Brooklyn Daily Eagle, Dec. 2, 1880.

"The New York Chamber of Commerce is to be thanked for having induced ex-Judge Black, of Pennsylvania, to write the letter which we publish to-day explaining the legal relationship of the railroads in this and other States to the public. There are few questions of more importance.   *   *   *

"While the people of the United States have been dreaming of an enlarged and perfected liberty, a tyranny with the heart and structure of a devil fish has been growing about them.

"To quote from Judge Black :

"'They express their determination to charge as much as the traffic will bear ; that is to say, they will take from the profits of every man's business as much as can be taken without compelling him to quit it.   In the aggregate this amounts to the most enormous, oppressive and unjust tax that ever was laid upon the industry of any people under the sun. The irregularity with which this tax is laid makes it still harder to bear. Men go into a business which may thrive at present rates and will find themselves crushed by the burdens unexpectedly thrown upon them after they get started. It is the habit of the railroad companies to change their rates of transportation often and suddenly and in particular to make the charges ruinously high without any notice at all. The farmers of the great West have made a large crop of grain which they may sell at fair prices if they can have it carried to Eastern ports, even at the unreasonably high rates of last summer. But just now it is said that the railway companies have agreed among themselves to raise the freight five cents per hundred weight, which is equal to an export tax upon the whole crop of probably $75,-000,000. The farmers must submit to this highway robbery or else keep the products of their land to rot on their hands.'

" Nor is this all :

"'A grain dealer of Baltimore gets a reduction or drawback which is denied to others, and he makes a fortune for himself while he ruins his competitors by underselling them. A single mill at Rochester can stop the wheels of all the rest if its flour be carried at a rate much lower. By discriminations of this kind the profits of one coal mine may be quadrupled, while another, with all its fixtures and machinery, is rendered worthless. Such wrongs as these are done not only in the few sporadic cases, but generally and habitually on a very large scale. Certain oil men, whose refinery was on Long Island, got rebates amounting to $10,000,000 in eighteen months, and seventy-nine houses (I believe that is the number) engaged in the same business were broken up. The creditors of the Reading Railroad having coal lands of their own, made discriminations between themselves and others which drove all competition out of the field, gave them the monopoly of the Philadelphia market and enabled them to charge for their coals as they charge for their freights—whatever they pleased. Thus producers, dealers and consumers all suffer together.'

" To perpetuate these abuses they seek political power. In many places elections in the face of this influence have become the emptiest of forms. The railroads send their agents to the Senates and Assemblies of the States. Laws are passed or

resisted as they dictate, and Governors approve or veto legislation at their bidding.   In the House of Representatives they
have their attorneys and in the Senate of the United States
their confidential allies.   The President cannot ignore them and
the politicians who nominate Presidents curry their favor.
They control thousands of votes in this and neighboring States,
and order them to be delivered as if the suffrage were pork or
pig iron.   *   *   *

"This, as we have said, so far from being in any sense a
wild statement, is but a partial epitome of uncontradicted evidence laid before the public as the result of official investigations.   The cheerful persons who keep on believing that things
are running beautifully, though indeed they be running with all
the feet they have in the worst possible direction, may still, as
some do, persist in believing that there is no immediate
danger, and that by and by if any evil does accrue, the people
in *some* way not specified will find a perfect·remedy ; but those
less given to consulting hope than their common sense are not
likely to remain idle much longer.   There is a pretty general
feeling that the Continent of America was not discovered by
Columbus, and civil liberty established by the Fathers of the
Republic, to the end that fifty millions of people might be
made tributary to a band of railroad magnates, or that farmers,
artisans and merchants might, by hard work and keen competition, raise up a dozen Vanderbilts, with each several hundred
millions of dollars. Those who entertain this feeling have become
persuaded that the time has arrived for the industrious masses
of this country to protect themselves, if they ever intend to do
so.   It will certainly not be easier after the adversary has
grown stronger.   In this contest every delay is to the disadvantage of the people.   Let the issue be deferred for a few
years, and nothing but a miracle or a revolution as violent as
that of France will overthrow the oppression   Of all mislead-
ing delusions, there is none more mischievous than the notion
that popular suffrage and popular power are synonymous.
Given the means of bribing multitudes, of intimidating others,
of wrecking opponents, coupled with actual possession of the
Government, and adverse sentiment must be paralyzed.   In
the face of such influences the right to vote is the veriest snare.
Will the workman vote himself into the poor house ? Will the
favored merchant vote against the capitalist to whom he owes

his fortune ? Does any one expect the average politician to be so fired with patriotism as to oppose that which gives him office ? The ballot is like a sword, utterly useless to the arm that cannot wield it. If the suffrage is to be our salvation, it must be applied sharply while there are still odds on the side of unbought and unterrorized manhood. * * * The terse and pertinent inference from this is that the public have a right to regulate the charges, and that it is their duty to do so has, we think, been abundantly shown. The right of the railroad company is to be allowed to earn a reasonable return for their money, and beyond that they have no right. What a reasonable return is there is no difficulty in determining, and what the investment is can also be ascertained with all the certainty needed for practical purposes.

" In this direction the Judge has some observations on stock watering, and the other fraudulent devices for making the public pay interest on bogus capital, which are not likely to give peace to the minds of the persons who have resorted to them or who hope to have the product accepted as genuine when the day of reckoning comes. It will be remembered that the elder Vanderbilt created $50,000,000 of such fictitious stock, and probably $40,000,000 of it went into his own safe. That stock represented no investment, nothing which gave the railroad any title to tax the public. It was a fraud in every way. It stands for simply so much spoil taken from those who use the highways.

"Into the general bearing and legal philosophy of all this it is not necessary to go further at present. The subject is now fairly before the American people, and there is every reason for believing that they will not lose sight of it until it has been settled in a proper manner. The era of sentimental politics is over. The right to earn a living and to enjoy the fruits of industry is now up. We look with reasonable confidence to a solution which will be less favorable than the existing laws are to the accumulation by railroad owners, in the course of a few years, of fortunes as large as the Rothschilds point to as the result of generations of scheming and exertion."

From the N. Y. Daily Graphic.

" If we ever have a conflict between capital and labor in this country, it will be because of the injustice done the masses by corporate monopolies. It therefore behooves all classes of citizens, and particularly those who have property, to sustain the efforts now being made by reasonable and intelligent citizens to limit the power of men who, to use the words of a committee of the United States Senate, ' recognize no principle of action but personal and corporate aggrandizement.' "

From the Anglo-American Times.

" *The tendency of all close bodies like corporations is to usurp, because they are soulless* and are therefore worked beyond any influence of sentiment. By degrees, unless checked, they will absorb all rights and privileges within their scope, till gradually the sovereignty usurped appears rightfully and by law to be exercised by them. This has always been the tendency of railroad property in such countries as the United Kingdom and the United States, because, in these, property exercises the most influence, and corporations are permitted to erect themselves into a sort of *imperium in imperio,* whereas such countries as France, Germany, Russia, assume a supreme and direct control over railways ; even so in British India. The corporation therefore, is always under the governmental check, and is not permitted to take on itself functions pertaining to government. In no other country, however, has the power of the railway corporations become so great as in the United States. * * * The ambition of the person has thus been allied with the *soulless character of the corporation ;* and as a consequence, a number of autocrats, exceeding in wealth and the control they exercise any body of nobles in any country at any period, has been created in the United States."

From the New York Times.

" Nobody questions the value of railroads to the public. But unless they are brought under the wholesome control of law, whereby the rights of individual citizens and of the community at large can be secured, sooner or later a conflict will come between their power and the might of the people which will shake the very foundation of laws and order."   .

From the New York Maritime Register.

" Much has been said about monopoly and anti-monopoly, and the latter has been condemned in influential quarters as only a spasmodic movement with politicians at its back. Time will prove the contrary. The anti-monopoly feeling is growing among the great mass of the people. They see in the gigantic monopolies which now impede healthy progress, an evil of the greatest magnitude. They see in them a power which will separate people into two great classes—those who control and belong to monopolies, and those who must submit to their mandates. Comparatively few people enter into subtle distinctions. The majority recognize two or three prominent features and are guided by them. It is this characteristic that will obtain in the monopoly fight. People recognize in a monopoly a power which closes every avenue of advancement and prosperity to all but the favored few; a power that would be master of all things, either directly or indirectly. They see that this leaves them practically at the mercy of the few. The spirit of our institutions is opposed to that. These points are all that they need to strengthen their determination not to leave the contest until a more equitable condition of affairs is established."

From the Washington Post.

" The managers of railroads in this country show less intelligence in dealing with the public than the owners of any and all other property. The patience of the people is taxed to its utmost limit year after year by railroad corporations. No obligation into which they enter with the public, or which is imposed upon them by law, is voluntarily performed. The history of their dealings with the Government is a history of evasion, deception, and stealth. They water their stock in order to absorb their earnings and make appear reasonable their otherwise extravagant dividends, the result of extortionate charges. The beneficiaries of munificent land grants disregard the conditions under which they receive these endowments and retain the benefit thereof."

From the San Francisco Chronicle.

" If the past may be accepted as a fair index of what is to come, it will be but a few years at furthest before railroad monopolists will dictate the laws and control alike the legislative, judicial, and executive departments of the Government, own the territory, and fetter the working classes with the shackles of peonage. Already some of these corporations

23

closely approximate that measure of power, and, unless their arrogance is signally rebuked, their aggressiveness checked, and they are forced to deal justly and respect the rights of the people, the existing form of government will collapse, and on its ruins will be reared an oligarchy of wealth."

From the Rochester Morning Herald.

" They have been hedged in and protected on every side by statutes in their interests, while the people who have nourished them until they have grown to the stature of giants, and in many cases the insolence and despotism of tyrants, are left almost wholly at their mercy. It is surely time that the people began to look after their own interests."

From the Cincinnati Gazette.

"Honest railroad management is what is needed in this country; and it is needed badly."

From the New York Journal of Commerce.

" Sooner or later the people will understand their rights and will maintain them, if this is their Government and not one of railroad pools and rings."

From the Boston Journal of Commerce.

" The tendency of rapid accumulation of property, or what represents property, in the hands of a few, is one of the greatest measures of subversion of sound principles of government, and has proved itself so in the history of the nations, and, as a few become richer, the masses of the people become poorer in an inverse ratio."

From the Cleveland Leader.

" A feeling prevails throughout the country that the present management of our railways is inimical to the best interests of the people. This feeling has begotten a dissatisfaction which is constantly increasing in intensity, and may eventually provoke a conflict which will end disastrously in more ways than one."

CHAPTER IV.

SICKENING CORRUPTION.

Railroad methods of controlling political action were exposed in 1873, through the agency of a railroad quarrel in the State of New York, resulting in the appointment by the Legisture of a committee to investigate the management of the Erie Railroad. The following is from the report of the Committee —testimony of Mr. Jay Gould :

I do not know how much I paid toward helping friendly men. We had four States to look after, and we had to suit our politics to circumstances. In a Democratic district I was a Democrat ; in a Republican district I was a Republican, and in a doubtful district I was doubtful ; but in every district and at all times I have always been an Erie man.'

The state of things unearthed by this investigation was officially described in the report of the Legislative Committee, as follows :

It is further in evidence that it has been the custom of the managers of the Erie Railway, from year to year, in the past, to spend large sums to control elections and to influence legislation. In the year 1868 more than one million ($1,000,-000) was disbursed from the Treasury for 'extra and legal services.' For interesting items see Mr. Watson's testimony, pages 336 and 337.

Mr. Gould, when last on the stand, and examined in relation to various vouchers shown him, admitted the payment during the three years prior to 1872, of large sums to Barber, Tweed and others, and to influence legislation or elections ; these amounts were charged in the ' India-rubber account.' The memory of this witness was very defective as to details, and he could only remember large transactions ; but could distinctly recall that he had been in the habit of sending money into the numerous districts all over the State, either to control nominations or elections for Senators and Members of Assembly. Considered that, as a rule, such investments paid better than to wait until the men got to Albany, and added the significant remark when asked a question that it would be as impossible to specify the numerous instances as it would to recall to mind the numerous freight cars sent over the Erie road from day to day.

The report of the Legislative Committee concludes with the following remarkable words :

It is not reasonable to suppose that the Erie railway has been alone in the corrupt use of money for the purposes named ; but the sudden revelation in the direction of this company has laid bare a chapter in the secret history of railroad management such as has not been permitted before. It exposes the reckless and prodigal use of money, wrung from the people to purchase the election of the people's representatives, and to bribe them when in office. According to Mr. Gould, his operations extended into four different States. It was his custom to contribute money to influence both nominations and elections.

The following testimony was taken by a committee of the last Constitutional Convention, of New York, of which the late George Opdyke was chairman :

EDWIN D. WORCESTER, SWORN :—I am treasurer of the New York Central Railroad Company, and have been for two years ; was assistant treasurer for two years previous.

Question. Do you know of the New York Central Railroad Company paying out considerable amounts of money during the sessions of legislatures ?

Answer. Yes, considerable amounts of money.

Question. I think you have succeeded in procuring legislation for two or three years past ?

Answer. Yes, we succeeded in getting the legislation.

Question. Were the expenses attending the application paid by the president of the road ?

Answer. I can state the amount of money he had; the whole amount of money paid was $205,000.

Question. Did he ever state to you any purpose for which it was to be applied?

Answer. Well, I don't remember that he did.

Question. How are the items or entries made in your books with reference to the expenditure of this $205,000?

Answer. There were no entries made with regard to those disbursements.

Question. Was the authorization given before or after the advances or disbursements were made?

Answer. It was after that the Board confirmed the advance, but did not state what should be made of the item.

Question. What is the condition of the item on your books?

Answer. It is charged to the treasurer's office and remains there. The action of the treasurer in advancing the money was confirmed by the Board.

Question. The year previous about what money was expended?

Answer. I think it was something like $60,000, that was charged to expenses pertaining to the legislature.

The railroads of New Jersey united in an effort to secure the entire water front of Jersey City under the specious guise of confirming the boundaries of a map. This infamous bill was such a flagrant disregard of public rights that the Governor, although elected by railroad votes, vetoed it. The Senate again passed it over the veto, but the Assembly hesitated and the usual monopoly weapon in such cases was resorted-to. Through the clumsiness of one of their agents they got hold of Hon. Joseph H. Shinn, a member who could not be bribed. The story is told in the following affidavit:

State of New Jersey, Mercer County, ss.: Being duly sworn, deponent saith that he is a member of the General Assembly of New Jersey from the County of Atlantic. That during Monday night, the 27th inst., he was called upon by a man

well known to him, who said he had come to talk about Senate
Bill No. 167, and during the conversation he offered the deponent
$500 to vote for Senate Bill No. 167 over the Governor's veto.
That this the deponent refused, and was then asked to call at a
certain room on Tuesday morning, the 28th inst., at 8:30
o'clock, but the deponent did not do so, and later on that day
was met by the same party, who complained because the deponent did not call at the room as agreed upon. That deponent
then stated that he would vote to sustain the Governor's veto.
In the meantime this deponent had called upon William Mc-
Adoo, from the County of Hudson, and, after informing him of
the facts above stated, it was agreed that if any more offers of
money were made to this deponent for his vote on Senate Bill
No. 167, that the money should be accepted and the whole affair exposed in the House of Assembly. That while this deponent was in his seat, he was told that a man wanted to see him,
and went out into the lobby, where he found the party first referred to in this affidavit, who said that he had a mathematical
problem to submit to this deponent, which was as follows:
"Your vote is to 167 as $500 is to your answer." That this depo-
nent stated that double the amount might make him answer, at
which the party who submitted the problem stated that the
other members who were voting for the bill only received
$500, except those who were engaged as attorneys for the bill,
but that he would see him again. That this deponent then
went to his seat and remained a short time, when he was again
called by a messenger, who informed him that a party wanted
to see him. That this deponent again went out and found the
party there who had submitted the mathematical problem, and
he submitted another in the following shape: "As your vote is
to 167 so is $1,000 to your answer." That this deponent an-
swered, all right if the money is left in my room at dinner-time;
that after this deponent returned to his seat. Again he was
told he was wanted, and on going out he was told that he would
get $500 in his room at dinner-time and $500 after the bill was
passed; that he would get it all now but the party who furnished it had used more among others than he expected. Deponent said all right, and on going to his room in his hotel
after the adjournment he sat down, when a man came there
with a package, saying he had been instructed to give it to Mr.

Shinn. That deponent then opened the envelope and found that it contained five one-hundred-dollar bills, which this deponent still has in his possession.

JOSEPH H. SHINN.

Sworn and subscribed to before me this 29th day of March, 1882.

ALLEN C. McDERMOTT,
Master in Chancery, New Jersey.

An investigation was ordered and the committee reported that the bribery was fully proven, and that John J. Cromer was the man who did it.

THE NEW YORK SENATORIAL BRIBERY.

It is only a short time since that a member of the New York Legislature rose in his seat, stated that he had been given two thousand dollars to vote for a railroad candidate for the United States Senate, and that he had given the money to the Speaker. The Speaker corroborated his statement, an investigation was ordered and a Senator and two Lobbyists were indicted for bribery, but so great was monopoly influence and so strongly did the tide of partisan passion run, that the man who exposed the bribery has been more abused than the man who did the bribing, and the case has been allowed to quietly drop out of sight, and the perpetrators of this great crime allowed to go free.

THE OHIO BRIBERY CASE.

From the New York Times, March 25th, 1882.

Lobbyists on the Witness Stand--An Editor's Corrupt Negotiations Exposed.

COLUMBUS, March 25, 1882.—The sensation of the day is the alleged attempt to bribe certain members of the Ohio Legislature with a view of gaining possession of canal property in Ohio for railroad purposes, and nothing else is thought or talked of. The committee of seven now investigating the matter has been given full power to send for persons and papers and to extend their inquiries as far as it may be deemed advisable. The testimony of members of the lobby was taken to-day, but little, if anything, could be learned from them.   It has leaked out, however, that Mr. Yates, the Democratic Representative from Pickaway County, had entered into negotiations with one of the lobby for the purchase of a farm costing about $6,ooo, and which would have been consummated as soon as the bill had been passed and the State property secured by the schemers from Cincinnati.

The sequel is told in the following press dispatch from the N. Y. *Times* of April 15th, 1882.

COLUMBUS, Ohio, April 15.—The Grand Jury of Franklin County this evening returned indictments against Representative Wm. Bloch, of Cleveland, and Representative W. A. Wright, of Hocking County, charged with accepting bribes from lobbyists interested in certain canal schemes at Cincinnati.   Two indictments were returned against J. D. Watson, of Cincinnati, who is charged with bribery or attempted bribery of members.   All three were arrested and placed in the County Jail.

THE PENNSYLVANIA BRIBERY

In 1877, the railroad riots in Pittsburgh destroyed a large amount of property.   The railroads refused to indemnify shippers, but endeavored to make the people of the State liable to the railroads.   They tried to buy a bill through the Legislature saddling several millions of dollars upon the public.   Their usual method of bribery was employed but was detected, and E. J. Petroff, a member of the Legislature, with several accomplices were tried and found guilty, *but here political influence was brought to bear, a U. S. Senator left his seat in the Senate and went home to look after things, and they were pardoned.*

THE MASSACHUSETTS BRIBERY.

From the N. Y. Times, April 15th, 1882.

BOSTON, April 14. — During a debate in the House to-day, on a motion to reconsider the reference to the next Legislature of the bill authorizing the Boston and Maine Railroad to maintain its elevated tracks between Somerville and Boston, Mr. Brown, of Boston, in advocating the reconsideration, said that he could produce witnesses to whom the attorney of the Eastern Railroad, a rival corporation, had said that he had defeated the bill in the House, and that if he had been given two days more he would have defeated it in the Senate. Mr. Allen, of Lynn, followed Mr. Brown, and said that to his personal knowledge the lobby of the Boston and the Maine Railroad interviewed a member this morning and offered that member a yearly pass if he would change his vote.

THE FREE PASS BRIBERY.

But few persons in the community realize to what an extent this form of petty bribery is carried. Immediately upon his election to office, every member of the State Government and of the Legislature, is tendered the 'courtesy' of a free pass for himself and his friends ; editors, judges, clergymen, coroners, tax assessors, aldermen, and every man who is supposed to be politically or otherwise influential in the community, has an opportunity to travel free at the expense of the rest of the community. To such an extent has this abuse proceeded that regular forms are furnished to influential men in blank, with permission to use their discretion in distributing the favors of corporations. This regular form specifies for whose account the pass is issued. On the following pages will be found (with the exception of the date and name, which we are not permitted to give), a fac-simile of a pass issued by the New York Central and Hudson River Railroad "*on account of the Supreme Court*," and fac-similes of two passes issued to a judge of a court.

THE SPECIAL RATE BRIBE.

The railroads bribe rich and influential shippers to betray the interests of all others. Whenever legislation in the public interest is proposed they mass these favored individuals at Albany and claim that they represent public opinion. This is described in the following extract from the N. Y. *Evening Post*, referring to the Hepburn bills :

"The power thus exerted upon the pending bill to prohibit unfair discriminations in freight charges may at any time be exerted upon legislation touching railroad interests. The railroads reach into every important center of population, and thousands of men may be precipitated upon the capitol at a few

Form 4. 12-1-80.

New-York Central & Hudson River R. R.

Good for one trip only, and to be used during 1881.

1881.

B   PASS

Upon the conditions endorsed hereon.

From _____ N.Y. _____ to _____ Utica

Account of _____ Suffrage Camp.

When countersigned by _____ *[signature]* Gen'l Superintendent.

COUNTERSIGNED:

[signature]

Not Transferable.

Fac-simile of Free Pass (except name) issued by D. & H. Canal R. R. Co., to a
County Judge now deceased, and forwarded to N. Y. State Anti-Monopoly League
by his executors. (The name is suppressed out of respect to his memory.)

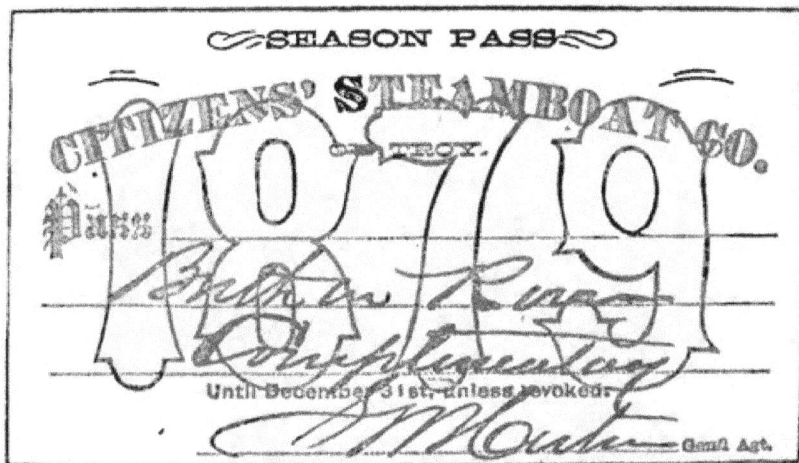

Fac-simile of Free Pass issued by Troy Steamboat Co., to the same Judge. This
only calls for "berth in room," but another specifies with meals.

hours' notice. One of the objections urged against establishing the State capital in New York city, when the subject was under discussion, was the danger of intimidation by a rabble populace. A similar means of influencing legislation is, it appears, by to-day's experience, in the hands of the railroads. Whether the pending bill be wise or not, the means taken to crush it out are reprehensible. By the admission of one of the leading opponents of the measure, the crowd around the Railroad Committee to-day was made up of men who are the recipients of favors from the railroads. They could not refuse nor neglect to obey when summoned, because the railroads, under existing laws, are their masters. If they hesitate to come to the relief of the railroads when they are wanted, they run the risk of losing the enjoyment of those favors by reason of which they fare better than their neighbors. The whole proceeding was, it is not too much to say, a species of intimidation, which, if allowed to come into practice at Albany, will be a source of great evil."

The same kind of tactics were repeated in opposition to the Railroad Commission bill. Free passes, and any "business favors" which may be asked are the reward of those who obey the railroad summons. The Assistant General Freight Agent of the N. Y. C. & H. R. R., has steadily been in attendance at Albany to see how the favored shippers do their "duty." The report of the Hepburn Committee (page 51) says :

"This power on the one hand and this fear on the other will always exist so long as the scale of freight charges is permitted to be a system of rewards and punishment. * * *

"The wrong consists in exercising a censorship over the business affairs of the community, secretly, arbitrarily and unequally varying rates, building up this, developing that, not only performing the proper functions of transportation, but taking into consideration the probable or possible profit of a shipment, and adjusting their rates accordingly. If the shipper is likely to make a large profit, they compel him to divide; if the margin is a close one, they determine whether the shipment shall be made or not, whether it shall result in a profit or loss, and the amount of profit or loss. * * * Thus, under this system of management and this method of giving rates, is every merchant, every manufacturer, every shipper, and through them every individual * * * measurably in the power of these corporations. Conciliate their good will, court their favor, and favorable rates will follow ; incur their hostility and the margin of their displeasure may be read on your freight bills."

THE LEGISLATIVE LAWYER'S BRIBE.

The legislative lawyer's bribe generally comes in the shape of a retainer before election, but instances are not wanting where it is offered and accepted after election, to influence action favorable to corporations.

THE FAVORITE BRIBE.

The latest favorite and perhaps the most dangerous form of bribery is "points" in Stock speculation. All over the country, in close proximity to our legislative halls, there will be found stock brokers' offices, and even within the halls themselves, in some instances, will be found the stock indicator ticking out the quotations which are frequently consulted by the men who make our laws. A "point" from a railroad magnate or his representative means that the legislator may be thousands of dollars richer to-morrow than he is to-day. Speculations in stocks has been considered respectable, hence the magnates or their representatives are courted by everybody. Through friendly social relations "points" are given and bribery accomplished in the most insidious manner. Speculation in stocks is also made the cover for direct bribery. The man who suddenly becomes rich through the acceptance of a bribe in money, gives out to the public that he has " *made it speculating in stocks,*" and this state of things will probably continue until public opinion looks upon stock speculation as it does upon any other form of gambling, and constituents refuse to support or have anything to do with representatives who are known to patronize Wall street.

CONTRIBUTIONS TO ELECTION EXPENSES. .

A common form of bribe is the " contribution toward election expenses." Where monopolies do not procure the nomination of their own men they go into the various districts and put their money on the candidate they select just as the gambler stakes his money on a particular card, only the stake played

for in the former case is to make LAWS in the interest of monopolies.   As a consequence the honest and independent ele-
ment in politics is so weighted in the race for political suprem-
acy that it seldom comes to the front, and the whole tone of
our legislation is debased.

BUYING VOTES ON ELECTION DAY.

In the general election in 1880, vast sums of money were
distributed for the purchase of votes.   This was notably true
in Indiana, where the result was very doubtful and where
success was considered of vital importance.   Immense bundles
of one and two dollar new treasury notes were distributed
among the workers at the various precincts, to be used with
poor men whose politics were doubtful.   One committee-man
who participated in this shameful work estimated that near *a
half million dollars* was distributed in this way.   He stated
that the one or two dollar bill was folded in the ticket in such
a way that when the end was turned down, the end of the new
treasury note was visible.   If a man seemed doubtful as to
how he would vote, the worker would turn down the end of
his ticket, and showing the money would remark, "That is the
ticket I vote; I can get you one if you want it."   In several
instances, it is positively known that these treasury notes were
sent into the state *in uncut sheets and the notes were cut apart by
the workers.*

When it becomes evident that the contest may be a close
one the votes of ignorant or venal voters are purchased under the guise, oftentimes, of hiring the voter to "work" for the
monopoly candidate.   In the recent special election in the
Eighteenth Senate district, of New York, to fill the vacancy oc-
casioned by the death of the late Senator Wagner, from three
to eight dollars per vote was paid in the interest of the
monopoly candidate.   When workingmen understand that they
are selling their birthright and that the monopoly candidates
who pay a few dollars for a vote on election day make laws
which cost the working man ten times as much in the course of
a year, there will be fewer voters for sale.

CHAPTER V.

THE HUNTINGTON LETTERS.

We now come to the famous Huntington letters. These letters were given to the public through a suit tried at Santa Rosa, California, to determine whether the widow of the late Gen. Colton was fairly dealt with in a settlement made with her by the Central Pacific managers. The italics are inserted by the publishers for the purpose of calling special attention to the questionable practices resorted to in dealing with Congressmen, Courts, Legislatures, etc. Such expressions as "caving down the bank," "convince," "fixing things," etc., show the extent to which bribery has been carried. The manner in which leading editorials in newspapers were bought, free excursions were run for the benefit of Congressmen, the extent to which the electing and defeating of Congressmen was carried, the outrageous interference in the formation of congressional committees, and the manner in which their reports were dictated, the control exercised over the Associated Press dispatches, together with the slavish subserviency of the highest government officials, should alarm every true friend of the republic.

The letters are arranged in the order of their dates :

FIXING UP OUR CONGRESSMEN.

NEW YORK, November 8, 1874.

Friend Colton : Yours of November 27th is received with inclosures. It certainly was a shabby thing in Vining to write such a letter   Towne wrote me and sent me a copy of the letter.   I saw Dillon and he seemed very much offended at V. for writing it, and said nothing of the kind should ever happen again. I think I shall show your letter to Gould, but they are not our kind of people. *I have sent out some copies of Tom Scott's bill as amended by me.* Read it carefully and let me know what you all think of it. Of course the San Diego people may not like it unless you agree to build a road from their place out to connect with our road, and you may think best to do that. It certainly is very important to San Francisco that we build the S. P. into Arizona, and it would be well for you at once to *write some letters for the influential men of San Francisco to sign, to send to all our members of Congress and Senators, to go for the bill as we want it,* and if you do not think it right as it is, fix it and send it back ; but if we can get it as it is, I would be satisfied. Storr says it will make Scott very mad and he thought it not wise to send it, and may be he is right ; but if Scott kicks at it, I propose to say to Congress, "We will build east of the Colorado to meet the Texas P. without aid," and then see how many members will dare give him aid to do what we offered to do without. My only fear then would be the cry that the C. P. and the S. P. was all one and would be a vast monopoly, etc., and that is what we must guard against, and that is one reason why you should be in Washington. I send copy of my letter to Scott on sending the bill ; he sent it for me to fix to suit me. The U. P. people are not yet ready to order steamers.   Yours truly,   C. P. HUNTINGTON.

LUTTRELL UNDER COLTON'S CARE.

NEW YORK, November 20, 1874.

Friend Colton : Yours of the 12th is received *and I am glad to learn that you have* **Luttrell** *under your charge, but you must be careful and not let* **him get** *anything to strike back with, as he is a cuss,* and I do not think it safe for Stanford to talk with him on our matters, as it would be just like him to get up in Congress and lie about what S. said to him. He must have *solid reasons* or he will go back on you.

Yours truly,   C. P. HUNTINGTON.

INTRIGUING AGAINST SCOTT.

NEW YORK, November 20, 1874.

Friend Colton : Herewith I send copy of bill that Tom Scott proposes to put through Congress this winter. Now I wish you would at once get as many of the associates together as you can and let me then know what you want. Scott sent me three copies fixed as he wants them and asked me to help him pass them through Congress, and if I would not do it, as he has fixed it, then he asked me to fix it so that I will, or in a way that I will support it. Now do attend to this at once, and in the mean time I will fix it here and see how near we are together when yours gets here. *Scott is prepared to pay, or promises to pay, a large amount of money to pass his bill, but I do not think he can pass it, although I think this coming session of Congress will be composed of the hungriest set of men that ever got together, and that the d—— only knows what they will do.* But as Scott's bill proposes to give up the A. and P. land grant (the west end of it), I am not sure that it would not be as well to let the bill stand in that way, we stopping the Texas Pacific at the Colorado river If we ask to come this side of the Colorado, it will be hard to stop the Texas P. from going west of it. I think the Texas P. or some of their friends will be likely to take the ground that the S. P. is controlled by the same parties that control the Central, and that there must be two separate corporations that run roads into San Francisco, and it will be very hard for us to make head against that argument, and I am disposed to think that Colton (?) had better come over and spend a few weeks at least in Washington. Would it not be well for you to send some party down to Arizona to get a bill passed in the Territorial Legislature granting the right to build a railroad east from the Colorado river (leaving the river near Fort Mohave), have the franchise free from taxation or its property, and so that the rates of fares and freights cannot be interfered with until the dividends on the common stock shall exceed ten per cent? I think that would be about as good as a land grant. *It would not do to have it known that we had any interest in it, for the reason that it would cost us much more money to get such a bill through if it was known that it was for us ;* and then Scott would fight it if he thought we had anything to do with it. If such a bill was passed I think there could at least be got from Congress a wide strip for right of way, machine shops, etc.

24   Yours truly.   C. P. HUNTINGTON.

MEN WHO MAY BE "CONVINCED."

NEW YORK, December 1, 1874.

Friend Colton : Your letters of the 20th, 21st, 22d are received. I agree with you as to the Stockton and Copperopolis bonds, and would give them say $500,000, 5 per cent. guaranteed by the Central for the $1,000,000 7 per cent. now out, and I would do this at once. I would like to know what is being done with the California Pacific extension bonds. *Have any of our people endeavored to do anything with Low and Frisbie? They are both men that can be convinced.* I can endorse all you say of Mt. Diablo coal, but think that I shall not do anything about the Rocky Mountain coal with Gould, but let it rest until you come over, as it is one of the many things that you understand better than I do. *I will see Luttrell when he comes over and talk with him and may be he and we can work together, but if we can brush him out it would have a good effect, and then we could, or at least would try, to get some better timber to work with.* It looks now as though I should telegraph Bradbury to close charter for two and possibly three of the White Star steamers as soon as I can get U P. R. R. Co. to sign contract for running with steamers, which contract I will send copy of to-morrow. I have thought it would be well for Captain Bradbury to go out to China in one of the steamers and fix matters there and then come to San Francisco. I see nothing else so good as to load the steamers out with coal. I am doing all I can to educate the people on the S. P. securities, and it begins to look a little as though the bonds could be sold within ten to fifteen months at prices that we can afford to take, but to do that we have got to work the Centrals up, and I am doing what I can in that way. If we can get the Centrals up to par, I hope we shall be able to start the S. P. at 90 to 95. That would be a good price. You will not sell many in California, and it is therefore very important that the few you do sell should be sold at a high price. And in this connection it would help us very much if we could fix up Cal. Pacific income and extensions on the basis that was talked of, *even if we had to pay something to convince Low and Frisbie.* As you all know the importance of getting out at the earliest day the new bonds on the S. P., I will say nothing of it here, except that I would have them like the present issue as far as the coupons and register go ; and that it will take at least two months to get them engraved and printed, so that I hope you will send them on as soon as you can, so that I can set the engraver and printer at work.

Yours truly, C. P. HUNTINGTON.

MANIPULATING SOUTHERN PAPERS.

NEW YORK, April 9, 1875.

Friend Colton : Yours of March 29th, No. 7, is received, with list of engines on the roads, drawings, etc. The engines ordered are too far advanced to make any changes, but when I come to California I will talk with Stevens and see the practical working of the machines. The 15x22 engines on the road were ordered by Mr. Crocker. The order came for fifty, and I bought and sent, I think, twenty. A few such machines are useful. As I wrote you, Bradbury cabled for 5,000 pounds sterling. I called on Dillon for their half, telling him that I thought it important that he answer such calls early. He said he thought so. I think we have called three times since and got the money to-day—a few minutes to-day before 3 p. m. It looks as though they were a little short. I have sent a cable transfer to Bradbury. I hear of Tom Scott's being at work in the Southern States on his Texas Pacific. I think he expects to make one of his greatest efforts next winter and hopes to pass his bill. *I shall send your argument before the Railroad Committee, to all the Southern papers, and also the pamphlet that I am now getting out to some of the Southern newspapers,* as it connects more with their interests than with Tom Scott's.

Yours, etc., C. P. HUNTINGTON.

AN ALLEGED WILD HOG.

NEW YORK, May 1, 1875.

Friend Colton : Yours of the 17th of April, No. 17, is received and contents carefully noted. As to the road east of Spadra, I notice there has arrived in California, out of the last eight thousand tons of fifty-six-pound iron rails bought, say forty-eight hundred tons, say twelve hundred tons more due and nearly so. So it would seem you are not to have any delay on account of rails to lay the fifty miles of the Fort Yuma line, and I think you should have the next fifty miles graded so that you can lay the track next winter ; sooner than that we will not have the rails. *I notice what you say of Luttrell; he is a wild hog; don't let him come back to Washington; but as the House is to be largely Democratic, and if he was to be defeated likely it would be charged to us, hence I think it would be well to beat him with a Democrat; but I would defeat him any way, and if he got the nomination put up another Democrat and run against him and in that way elect a Republican. Beat him.* I am glad Stubbs is coming over here. You know I do not pretend to know anything of the details of our freight business.

Yours truly,   C. P. HUNTINGTON.

A POOR OPINION OF PARK.

NEW YORK, May 21, 1875.

Friend Colton : Yours numbered 41 was received I think you and I should not disagree about Senator Jones, and as for Park, he has fooled away all the money he made in Mariposa in a little railroad in Vermont, and most that he made in the Emma mine in the N. J., Boston and Montreal road and I think his Los Angeles project is the worst of the three. *I shall do my best to cave him down the bank here.* In writing to Colonel Gray yesterday I mentioned name of new station at junction of the Mojave branch of main line. Write me what you think of the new cars for S. P. There has only two hundred tons of rails gone aboard of ship since I last wrote you about shipment of rails. They will go on board much faster after this. I have just closed for five thousand tons more fifty pound steel rails at $76, one-fourth cash, balance in nine, twelve and fifteen months.

Yours truly,   C. P. HUNTINGTON.

CAVING PICKERING AND FITCH DOWN THE BANK.

NEW YORK, September 17, 1875.

Friend Colton : Yours of the 9th inst., with inclosures, as therein stated, are received. *It looks as though you would be able to cave Fitch and Pickering down the bank.* I will do what I can to get Gould and Dillon to make the exchange of coal lands, as you desire, but I have very little hope that they will do what you want them to. I am glad to hear of your paying Reese and others, as it is well to pay, even if we have to borrow the money right over again ; and when money is due pay it or renew the note. I hope you will pay A. A. C. what we owe him. He is a good fellow, but his account has stood long enough. As we shall need a large amount of money this winter it would be well to borrow some on six to twelve months, if you could do so at fair rates. I do not expect to sell any S. P. bonds this fall. We shall need considerable gold here to pay interest on the 1st of October, but I hope to get on without calling for any from California.

Yours truly,   C. P. HUNTINGTON.

DECEIVING THE SAN DIEGANS.

NEW YORK, Sept. 27, 1875.

Friend Colton : Yours of the 18th with inclosure, as stated, is received. You must be very busy with all your associates out of the city. I notice by McCarthy's letter to Mr. Crocker that the people of San Diego will join with us if he will agree to build east from their city, and I am inclined to think we had better do that as that would strengthen Wigginton very much to have his people ask him to fight for a bill as we want it. Scott is making the strongest possible effort to pass his bill the coming session of Congress. He gets every little gathering in the South to pass resolutions favoring the Texas Pacific bill, then those that the Texas Pacific owes name is legion, and of course they are all for it ; then he is promising a connection with all the broken down roads in the South, with a promise of money to help them all if his bill passes, and by some kind of a turn he is settling up with all those that hold him personally, and that is to help him as it makes his promises worth something with the broken down fellows that he is agreeing to help. If we had a franchise to build a road or two roads through Arizona (we controlling, but having it in the name of another party) then have some party in Washington to make a local fight and asking for the guarantee of their bonds by the United States, and if that could not be obtained, offering to build the road without any aid, it could be used against Scott in such a way that I do not believe any politician would dare vote for it. *Cannot you have Safford call the Legislature together and grant such charters as we want at a cost say of $25,000 ?* If we could get such a charter as I spoke to you of it would be worth much money to us. If there is anything done it must be done quickly.

I am very sorry that Sargent is feeling so hard towards us, but I shall endeavor to see him before Congress meets. I have bought the tunnel bolts at three and a half currency instead of nine cents gold, as was being paid by Mr. Crocker when I was in California. I think money is too cheap with you all in California, and that we can be beat in building railroads by those who place more value on a dollar than we do, and I think when any one of us goes to the front in a car that weighs say twenty tons, it adds to the cost of every mile of road that we build thereafter more than $100 per mile. I wish you would let me know who ordered the officers' car that is now running on the S. P. Please let me know what the new transfer-boat cost.

Yours truly,   C. P. HUNTINGTON.

Under date of Oct. 29, 1875, is a long letter which is of but little interest to the public, except where he speaks of obtaining a certain charter. In that connection he says :

I believe the Legislature could be called together by the people for $5,000 and such a charter granted.

GWIN'S SECRET SERVICE WORK.

NEW YORK, November 10, 1875.

Friend Colton : Yours of October 23, 1875, No. 85, is before me. Dr. Gwin is also here. *I think the doctor can do us some good if he can work under cover,* but if he is to come to the surface as our man, I think it would be better that he should not come, as he is very obnoxious to very many on the Republican side of the House, and then there is so many things about our business that he does not know, and he has not the time to learn it before Congress comes and goes. It was very unfortunate that he came over in Directors' car with Mr. Crocker. I received a letter to-day from a party in Massachusetts that said that Gorham and Sargent were very much offended because Gwin was, or rather had come over to look after our interest in Washington. I am, however, disposed to think Gwin can do us some good, but not as our agent, but as an anti-subsidy Democrat, and also as a Southern man with much influence in the South in showing the Southern people that the Texas Pacific Railroad is in no way a Southern Pacific road, but a road if built by the Government would prevent the Southern

States from having a road to the Pacific for many years. But Gwin must not be known as our man. I received a letter from H. S. Brown this morning that G. was for Randall or Walker. I send copy with my reply.   Yours, etc.,   C. P. H.

GWIN'S INDISCRETION.

NEW YORK, November 11, 1875.

Friend Colton : Your letter of October 26th, 27th and 30th and November 2d, Nos. 86, 87, 88 and 89, are received. I notice what you say in No. 86 as to Gwin not connecting with us as far as the public are concerned. Of course I agree with you, and I was much surprised when I heard he was coming over in the car with Crocker. *I told the doctor to-day that he did not want to connect with us, except so far as in his argument against subsidies; he could say that the S. P. R. R. Co. was a powerful Company, and could, and no doubt would, build to El Paso without any government aid, except the land grant that had already been given.* I notice that you write in your No. 87 about the San Fernando tunnel, and I have had a talk with Mr. Crocker about it, and it would seem that that work is getting along very badly. It certainly is unless they are doing better than when I was there. I notice your remarks about the January interest and as things look now it will have to come out of the earnings of the road, for it could not be borrowed here as things now are. What thirty or forty days will bring of course I cannot say. I think you can put over current bills and take the interest out of the earnings if it should really become necessary. I notice what you say of arrival of *Northern Light*, etc. I do not think you need have any fear about getting rails as fast as needed for some months to come. By the way, I know at my breakfast of the ships that arrive at San Francisco the day preceding. I am waiting very anxiously for the decision of the Supreme Court in the U. P. interest, etc., case. I am doing considerable hard work, looking to put the South against Scott's bill, and have got them already to discussing it sharply. I wrote Crocker on the 8th of October about spikes. I wish you would answer that letter. I shall ship two thousand kegs of spikes on the next steamer, and the same on the one following, at $12 per ton.

Yours truly,   C. P. HUNTINGTON.

GWIN WORKING UP THE SOUTH.

NEW YORK, November 13, 1875.

Friend Colton : Your dispatch that you had sent two hundred thousand dollars gold is received. Dr. Gwin left for the South yesterday. *I think he can do us considerable good if he sticks for hard money and anti-subsidy schemes, but if it was understood by the public that he was here in our interest it would no doubt hurt us. When he left I told him he must not write to me,* but when he wanted I should know his whereabouts, etc., to write to R. T. Colburn, of Elizabeth, N. J. I have had several interviews with the Houston and Texas Central Railroad people. This road is built from Galveston to Austin, and is the only live road in Texas. It has a land grant to the west line of the State (Texas) of 4,769,280 acres. It is owned by William E. Dodge, Moses Taylor, W. M. Rice and other strong men of this city. I saw Dodge a few days since with the view of having them build to El Paso, and we build to that point to meet them. He said he thought they would do it. He said he was opposed to the Government granting any aid to his or any other road. D. has been sick ever since I saw him, so I went to-day and saw Moses Taylor. He said he liked the idea, and that he would talk it up with his people, etc. There will be no Government aid granted this session, and if we can get the H. and T. Central to stand in with us and offer to build a line through, we build to El Paso from the west and they from the east, I think Scott's fish will be cooked. Budd is doing good work in the Gulf States. Has the seventy shares of glass stock been got in ? How are you progressing with the machine-shop grounds? I borrowed yesterday $100,000 easy for 4, 5 and 6 months at 7 per cent. No commissions. I think I shall take up some 12 months paper at 12 per cent.

Yours truly,   C. P. HUNTINGTON.

GWIN'S LITTLE MISTAKE.

NEW YORK, December 22, 1875.

Friend Colton : Your letters of the 11th inst., Nos. 111 and 112, are received ; also your dispatch that you would send $125,000 in gold ; you need send more gold for the January interest. I notice the progress on the tunnels ; they go slow. I hope the work on that next to the longest one in the Tehachipi will be pushed. I am glad to notice that you are thinking of commencing it soon. What is the exact length of the San Fernando tunnel ? I think the Doctor will return to California in January. I have just returned from Washington. The Doctor (Gwin) was unfortunate about the Railroad Committee ; *that is, there was not a man put on the committee that was on his list, and I must say I was deceived ; and he was often with Kerr, and K. was at his rooms and spent nearly one evening.* The committee is not necessarily a Texas Pacific, but it is a commercial committee, and I have not much fear but that they can be convinced that ours is the right bill for the country. *If things could have been left as we fixed them last winter there would have been little difficulty in defeating Scott's bill*, but their only argument is it is controlled by the Central. That does not amount to much beyond this : it allows members to vote for Scott's bill for one reason and give the other—that it was to break up a great monopoly, etc. If these —— interviewers would keep out of the way it would be much easier traveling. I send a few clippings.

Yours truly,   C. P. HUNTINGTON.

HUNTINGTON IN AN ANTI-SUBSIDY ROLE.

NEW YORK, December 17, 1875.

Friend Colton : I expect to have a bill ready early next week so amending the Texas Pacific Act as to allow the S. P. to build east of the Colorado river, or rather will have some changes made in the bill you sent over. The vote in the House the other day will do much good in helping Speaker Kerr in making up the railroad and land committees in such a way that they will not be likely to report in favor of any subsidies. Of course the South were not all for Scott's bill before we commenced working there ; but we have done good work, and I am getting Southern papers every day from the line of his travels that speak right out against the Texas Pacific ; see clippings inclosed. The *Railroad Gazette*, in publishing the proceedings of the St. Louis convention, made some mistakes, which I have endeavored to correct, as you will notice by copies of letters sent to you. Nearly all the papers here have taken favorable notice of it. I send slips from *World* and *Tribune*. The editor's article in the *Railroad Gazette* I did not see until after its publication. I have looked over Governor Irwin's message ; it seems to be well enough, although not just such a one on railroad matters as I expected.

Yours truly, C. P. HUNTINGTON.

GORHAM, SARGENT AND CARR.

NEW YORK, December 23, 1875.

Friend Colton : Yours in relation to Messrs. Bird and Parrott is received. I can do nothing with the parties. The last time I saw Bird he was wildly mad. I spent an evening with Parrott : he did not show temper like Bird, but said they had been shamefully used, etc., and said that when we could satisfy Castle, he and Bird would be satisfied, etc.; *now the business must be done*, I think, on that side, but it is well to remember that *there is a limit to the value of the property*, but we all understand that *we should have it if it can be got at a fair price*, and that soon. Please let me know what arrangement we have had with Mr. Castle ; *how much we agreed to pay him for his services, and as to whether he has been paid as agreed. Mr. Parrott says he has had no pay.* Please answer at once.

Yours truly, C. P. HUNTINGTON.

NOTE.—These letters were originally published in the *San Francisco Chronicle*. After the names Bird, Parrott and Castle in the foregoing letter, names of prominent Congressmen were inserted in parentheses. Not knowing the authority upon which the *Chronicle* so printed them, we have omitted them, though it is fair to suppose the *Chronicle* was right. No denial of its correctness has ever come to our notice.

FRIENDLY BRISTOW.

NEW YORK, December 10, 1875.

Friend Colton : Yours of November 24th, 26th and 27th, Nos. 100, 101 and 102, received. I notice what you write concerning the line between San Fernando and the tunnel. I think that piece of road should have been built before the rains commenced, and so said when I was there, and it could have been run over slow without fish-plates until some arrived. I think you done well in buying Eastern exchange at the rate you did. I borrowed $50,000 to-day at 6 per cent. Some few days since the money market tightened up and looked as though there was to be a little flurry in the money market, and there was some ($50,000) twelve and fifteen months' Central Pacific paper offered at 12 per cent., and while I did not like to take it, I thought it would not do to let it be offered around at that rate, so I took it as though I wanted it. Such things do us good. The O. and O. S. S. Co. is doing well, as you say. I wish they had more money to lend. Captain Bradbury was in the office the day that he arrived, but I went to Washington, I think, the day he arrived, and only returned last night, so I have not seen him since. I think we have nothing to fear this winter from the Texas Pacific bill. *I had a talk with Bristow, Secretary of the Treasury. He will be likely to help us fix up our matters with the Government on a fair basis.*

Yours truly,   C. P. HUNTINGTON.

KEEP MUM.

NEW YORK, December 11, 1875.

Friend Colton : I have just got the new Texas Pacific bill, and will send you a copy to-day. I hope to have our S. P. bill ready to put in next week. As soon as it is ready I will send you a copy. I notice what you say of forcing Scott into an arrangement with us. Now, do we want to make any arrangement with him? I do not think it would be wise to say anything *in the bill that we are about to introduce* about the change of line via Salinas valley, as it would tend to give that break in the road more prominence than it ought to have at this time. I would like to have you place $1,000,000 here for the January interest by the 1st, if you can do so.

C. P. HUNTINGTON.

SARGENT'S NEUTRAL ATTITUDE.

NEW YORK, December 13, 1875.

Friend Colton : Your two letters of the 4th inst., Nos. 107 and 108, with inclosures, are received. The resolutions, I think, are all right. *You write you are drawing up a bill to introduce in Congress.* I am glad you are. I have been to work on one for some days, and Mr. Storrs has it in hand now. When yours comes I will use the best one, or, what is more likely, though, use the best parts of both. I hope to have it intro-

duced by Thursday, the 23d. Scott is making a terrible effort,
promising everything to everybody, and I promise nothing that I
do not expect we shall fulfill, and the Southerners being so very
poor that many of them will hold to Scott in hopes he may do
something for them. Vain hope. Sargent, as you no doubt
have seen, has gone off the Railroad Committee, *but there is a
good man in his place,* Eaton, of Connecticut. His going off
looks as though he did not care to help us or harm us much. If
he did he would have staid on the committee.   I send you to-
day Senate bills Nos. 6 and 14.   I could get control of the Atlantic and P. R. R. at very small cost, but do we want it as
a gift?   Yours truly,   C. P. HUNTINGTON.

CARR'S SALARY.

NEW YORK, January 14, 1876.
Friend Colton : Yours of December 30th and the 1st inst.,
Nos. 120 and 121, also your telegram that William B. Carr has
had for his services $60,000 S. P. bonds ; then asking how much
more I think his services are worth for the future ?   That is a
very difficult question to answer, as I do not know how many
years Mr. Carr has been in our employ, or how far in the future
we should want him.   In view of the many things we have now
before Congress and also in this sinking fund that we wish to
establish, in which we propose to put all the company's lands in
Utah and Nevada, it is very important that his friends in Washington should be with us, and if that could be brought about
by *paying* **Carr** *say $10,000 to $20,000 a year, I think we could
afford to do it, but of course not until he had controlled his friends.*
They could hurt us very much on this land matter, although I
would not propose to put the land in at any more than it is
worth, say $2.50 per acre.   I would like to have you get a
written proposition from Carr, *in which he would* **agree** *to control his friends for a fixed sum,* then send it to me.
    Between the business here and in Washington, I am worked
about up to my capacity.
           Yours truly,   C. P. HUNTINGTON, President.

HE CURSES THE INTERVIEWERS.

Friend Colton : Yours of the 7th, No. 122, is received. I
am sorry that you have to pay one per cent. for money. As I

have sold some land-grant bonds I can get on, I think, until the April interest is due ; then you will need to send again, unless we can market some of our S. P., which I do not think we shall be able to do. I received three letters from Washington this morning. They all tell me that *Scott is there in great force, and says he will pass his bill* in spite of Huntington and the Central Pacific. *He cannot do it, but it was a great mistake in not letting this matter remain as we fixed it last winter, but these damned interviewers may kill us yet.* Bond and Felsenheld answered my letter in the *Railroad Gazette.* I do not propose to answer them, but I am preparing a letter for Mr. Willcutt to answer them (I send copy of B. and H. to Hopkins), and as soon as he gets it he should telegraph me all right. I expect to go to Washington to-morrow (Sunday) night.

Yours truly,   C. P. HUNTINGTON.

ON TO WASHINGTON.

NEW YORK, January 17, 1876.

Friend Colton : Yours of the 8th and 9th inst., Nos. 123, 124 and 125, are received. The news of much rain is good, even if it does wash our roads some. I have just received an order from Mr. Towne for twenty-five 20x24 cylinder engines, which I shall buy. As I understand it, you buy this size because they will haul more cars than an 18x24, so I shall soon expect an order for a 24x30, because they will haul more than a 20x24. I wish to say for myself that while I much like Stevens' plan of arranging driving-wheels, etc., I am as much opposed to having any engines on the road with more than 18x24 cylinders, and of course other parts in proportion, and you will all come to this some time. I have received several letters and telegrams from Washington to-day, all calling me there, as Scott will certainly pass his Texas Pacific bill if I do not come over, and I shall go over to-night, but I think he could not pass his bill if I should help him ; but of course I cannot know this for certain, and just what effort to make against him is what troubles me. *It cost money to fix things* so that I would know his bill would not pass. *I believe with $200,000 I can pass our bill,* but I take it that it is not worth that much to us.

Yours truly,   C. P. HUNTINGTON.

THE MEN WHO WORE THE COLLAR.

NEW YORK, January 29, 1876.

Friend Colton : Your letters of the 19th and 20th, Nos. 128 and 129, are received. I notice and appreciate what you say about my being overworked. I am working rather hard this winter, but I think I can stand it for some time yet. Scott is making a terrible effort to pass his bill, and he has many advantages *with his railroads running out from Washington in almost every direction, on which he gives free passes to every one which he thinks can help him ever so little. The Texas Pacific seems to own almost every one in the whole country.* I hear in very many of the large towns there are parties holding stock in this construction company, and they are all in Washington working for the T. P. bill. Then on our side we have Sargent, Booth, Jones, Cole and Gorham in the Senate to help us. Sargent is very bitter, so much so that he can hurt us but little. So you can see things are very lively with me, but I shall defeat them, or I should rather say Congress will, for I doubt if he could pass his bill if I should help him, yet I am making the best fight I can, and I think I am doing very well. Scott is very able ; he has a short-hand writer, and I have not had any, but the last time I agreed to pay half and so got copy, but could not bring the marks of what you call them away with me as we did last winter. I will send you out what was said at the last meeting as soon as they are printed. The committee asked us to have them printed for their use. Much of it was printed before we went before the committee, Scott's as well as my own. I returned from Washington this morning ; shall go back next Monday night, but I dread it very much. Scott is working mostly among the commercial men. *He switched Senator Spencer of Alabama and Walker of Virginia this week, but you know they can be switched back with the proper arrangements when they are wanted ;* but Scott is asking for so much that he can promise largely to pay when he wins, and you know I keep on high grounds. *All the members in the House from California are doing first-rate except Piper, and he is a damned hog, any way you can fix him. I wish you would write a letter to Luttrell saying that I say he is doing first-rate, and is very able, etc., and send me copy.* I am working, as I have before wrote you, I think, to get up a company to build a road from Austin to El Paso. If I can get some men in it that I am working with, I will get much strength from the South for it. I have much to do to-day and will write no more this time.

Yours truly,   C. P. HUNTINGTON.

P. S.—I will get you telegraph passes.   H.

SCOTT AS A "CONVINCER."

NEW YORK, February 14, 1876.

Friend Colton : Since writing you last I have received yours of January 13th, No. 126 : 15th, No. 127 ; 21st; No. 130 ; 24th, No. 131 ; 24th, No. 132 ; 25th, No. 133 ; 27th, No. 134 ; 27th, No. 135 ; February 1st, No. — ; February 1st, No. 137 ; and February 5th, No. —. I notice what you say of your talk with Judge Parsons about A. and P. R. R. Co. Allow me to suggest to you not to touch it. If we were to agree to take that, Scott would pass his bill against all that we could do. That is his weak and our strong point with the South. I wrote Stanford that Captain Bradbury had mentioned to me that Gould had said to me that he (Gould) thought it would be well for all parties to transfer the charters of the O. & O. steamers to P. M. Co., and asked B. to speak to me about it. I answered that so far as I was concerned, that the O. and O. steamers were put on to stay ; but that if the U. P. people was in favor of stopping the line I saw no other way than for the C. P. to let go of it. Captain B. has not been well for some time ; the last time I saw him he was looking badly. Gould and Dillon was at my house yesterday for nearly three hours. We talked over P M. matters ; they thought it would be well for us to go in with them and control that line. I said I did not know about the value of the stock, etc. ; that I was disposed to work with them, etc. ; that I would write to my associates, and if they thought well of it I would look into the matter ; so you will please consider it. We talked over sinking fund matters. They have come over to my views as to putting the lands into the fund, and are very fierce for it now. Scott is developing more strength for his Texas and P. than I thought it possible for him to do. He has men all over the country to bring influence to bear on their Member of Congress. *They have considerable money, as they have convinced several parties that I thought we had sure. I am doing*

all I can, but it is the liveliest fight I was ever in. I sent a
man to Richmond, Va., on Saturday, and one to Albany to-day,
to get resolutions passed by the Legislatures against subsidies.
If I can get them I think it will control two members of the
Railroad Committee, and we want them very much. *Of course
you will see the necessity of keeping such matters to yourselves.* I
have not time to write more, as it is night, and I go to Washington at 9 p. m.

Yours truly,   C. P. HUNTINGTON.

AN EXPENSIVE FIGHT.

NEW YORK, February 26, 1876.

Friend Colton : I have been in Washington most of the time
for several weeks past, which, with my other business, has kept
me so very busy that I have neglected my correspondence with
you. Your letters have, I think, all come to hand up to No.
141, that is, by putting in some without numbers, that by their
dates have come in right to fill those missing numbers. I do
not write you much about matters in Washington, but I am having the biggest fight I ever had there, and expect to win it.
Scott is doing his best, and *has an army of men in the lobby to
help him.* He told me this week that he is sure to pass his bill.
He said he would give us enough to do to take care of what
we had without meddling with his. *I said to him, with a
smile, that I hoped that he would do nothing that would interfere
with my helping him on his Texas and Pacific.* I have sent H.
S. Brown with Judge Evans (Mr. E. is a citizen of Texas) to
Texas to set that State right on the S. P., and I sent Doc Gwin
to Mississippi, Louisiana and Alabama to set some back fires on
Scott. I expect to weaken Scott much by this move. *This
fight will cost us much money*, but I think it is worth it, as I have
written you from time to time. I have been trying to work parties up that have interests in roads in Texas outside of Scott's
interest, and they told me a few days since that if I would get
up a bill I could use their names, and I at once done so, and
they now like it very much ; and I think it makes us stronger
than we were without. I send copy of the bill with this Senate
bill No. 500. *Your letter to Luttrell was good, and I noted its
effects.* Good articles in the California papers sent to our members of Congress would do good. They get many from our

enemies which do hurt.   Wigginton gets nearly everything bad
that is said about us, I think.   I have many things that I would
like to say, but it is dark, and I quit.

Yours truly,   C. P. HUNTINGTON.

A ROUGH FIGHT.

NEW YORK, March 4, 1876.

Friend Colton : Yours of February 24th, No. 142, is received.   I have been in Washington most of the time since
Congress met, and you say truly when you write that you think
I have had a rough fight there this winter. *The Railroad Committee of the House was set up for Scott, and it has been a
very difficult matter to switch a majority of the committee away
from him, but I think it has been done*, but Scott is very able,
and then *he promises everything to everybody*, which helps him
for the day and in this fight, and just what he may yet do I
cannot say.   There is to be some legislation for the Texas and
P. or the S. P. before the Forty-fourth Congress goes out, and
as Scott promises so much and has such a fearfully long list of
creditors to help him, that I have my fears that he will be able
to pass his bill next winter, if matters are then as they are to-
day.   And I think it of so much importance that he is not allowed to build a road parallel to ours with Government aid that
I shall endeavor to get our bill passed through the Senate this
winter, if possible (and the House, too), if we only get it through
the Senate and could then get built some road in Arizona before
Congress comes together next winter, I think there would be
but little doubt we would win the fight.   What do you all
think of it ? I am doing all I can to demoralize Scott in Texas.
He has got to have legislation in that State to extend time on
his land grant, or else it is lost to him.

The Southern Pacific bonds have been admitted to the Stock
Board here.   It was a hard thing to do, as they have a rule
that no bonds shall be admitted except on completed roads.   I
think there is an even chance of selling some of the bonds this
spring.   It is such a large loan that we must be very careful in
launching it, as its final success depends very much on the way
the loan is put on to the market.

Yours truly,   C. P. HUNTINGTON.

P. S. Those memorandums giving progress of the work on
S. P. are very interesting to me.   H.

25

HE WORKS 365 DAYS IN THE YEAR.

NEW YORK, March 22, 1876.

Friend Colton: Your letters of March 3d and 8th, Nos. 143 and 144, reached me in Washington. You write me that you wish Senate bill No. 153 to pass. It gives the right of way through the military grounds at Benicia, as you no doubt understand; as amended it gives the right only to the Northern R. R. Co.

I am having a very lively fight in Washington, but things do not look bad.

Scott is making a very dirty fight, and I shall try very hard to pay him off, and if I do not live to see the grass growing over him I shall be mistaken. You know I work 365 days in a year when it is necessary.

Yours truly,   C. P. HUNTINGTON.

Indorsed on back with pencil—Do not forget to send monthly statements of progress of work on tunnels.

TROUBLESOME SETTLERS.

NEW YORK, April 18, 1876.

Friend Colton : Your letters of March 30th and April 3d, 5th and 6th, Nos. 148, 149, 150 and 151, are all before me, and I think all came to hand since I last wrote. I have been very busy of late, but if I had have had anything important to say to you, I have no doubt I should have found time to have said it.

I notice that you say that Harris tells you that he will have the San Fernando tunnel out before he does those at Tehachapi. That of course may be true, but it should not be. All the July interest will have to come from California, as things look now.

I send with this petition of settlers on S. P. lands. I called for copy of the petition with the names of those signing it, and while they gave the petition they would not give the names of the signers, but I managed to get them ; *so you need not say where you got the list of names ; the party who got the names said most of them is in one handwriting.* I think it important to find out as soon as possible whether the signatures are genuine or not, and if the parties given are occupying these lands, as stated, or on the lands as designated in the petition. If there is anything wrong in this telegraph me at once.

Yours truly,   C. P. HUNTINGTON.

UNSATISFACTORY WORK OF THE "RECORD-UNION."

NEW YORK, April 27, 1876.

Friend Colton : I returned from Washington this morning, and find yours of the 11th and 13th inst. on my desk. To day is the first time that I have been to my office here since the 19th. I returned from Washington last Saturday night, but got telegram Sunday that I must be in Washington Monday morning, so I returned there Sunday night. It seems to me well that you have arranged with the stage line via Yuma.

We are getting on with the Sinking Fund bill as well as perhaps we could expect ; not much opposition yet, and I have hopes that we can get something through that will be satisfactory to us.

Scott I think has given up all hopes of getting any subsidy this session and is asking for eight years more time, and I think he will get it against all we can do. His new bill calls for his building twenty miles each year from San Diego this way, and fifty miles west from this end of his road. Scott has several parties that I think do nothing else but write articles against the Central Pacific and its managers, and then get them published in such papers as he can get to publish them at small cost, then send the papers everywhere ; and there is no doubt but he has done much to turn public sentiment against us. If it was known that the C. P did not control the S. P. I think we could beat him all the time, although he has about the same advantage over us in Washington that we would have over him in Sacramento. *If he wants a committee-man away he gets some fellow (his next friend) to ask him to take a ride to New York, or anywhere else, of course on a free pass, and away they go together.* Then Scott has always been very liberal in such matters. *Scott got a large number of that drunken, worthless dog Piper's speeches printed, and sent them broadcast over the country. He has flooded Texas with them.* The Sacramento *Record-Union* hurts us very much by abusing our best friends. There was a number of that paper came over some little time since that abused Conkling, Stewart and some other of our friends, with Bristow's name up for President. Gorham took it around and showed it. He showed 'it to Conkling, with the remark that he did not suppose that he cared anything about it, but that he would show him what the railroad organ said about him. If I owned that paper I would control it or burn it. We had almost a panic in railroad securities in the last few days. New Jersey Central went from 110 to 94, Reading Railroad from 112 to 88, and many other roads fell off at about the same rate.

Scott is publishing much stuff about the S. P. securities which we are using as collateral, and money-lenders are timid, and we are carrying too much floating debt on a market as sensitive as this is and is likely to continue to be for some time to come. It looks now as though we should have to draw from the earnings of the road several millions of dollars in the next two months to pay bills and interest here. I wrote some days since about your doing all you could to aid in passing the Sinking Fund bill. I hope you will all continue to work on that line. I hope my next letter from you will inform me that you are quite well.   Yours truly,   C. P. HUNTINGTON.

CONTROLLING THE ASSOCIATED PRESS.

NEW YORK, May 2, 1876.

Friend Colton : Herewith I send a copy of telegraphic dispatch that came over yesterday. Who is this Webster ? *Is it not possible to control the agent of the Associated Press in San Francisco?* The matter that hurt the C. P. and S. P. most here are the dispatches that come from San Francisco. *Scott has a wonderful power over the press, which I suppose he has got by giving them free passes for many years over his roads.* I would like to hear at the earliest possible time about some questions of fact raised by S. O. Houghton as to location of road, etc.

Yours truly,   C. P. HUNTINGTON.

SARGENT'S BLUFF GAME.

NEW YORK, May 12, 1876.

Friend Colton : Your letters of April 29th and May 2d and 4th, Nos. 155, 156 and 157, are received with inclosures as therein stated. I am very glad to learn that you are able to be out again. Bad time for any of the S. P. party to be sick, as we have fight enough to go around, and give each one all he cares for ; that is if his wants in that line are any ways reasonable. I sent Hopkins an article yesterday cut from the *Commercial Advertiser ;* to-day I met one of the editors, Norcutt ; *he told me Scott paid for having it published ; that he would not have let it gone into the paper if it had been left to him, etc.* With this I send slip from to-day's *Times.* Just what is to come out of this fight I cannot say, but I expect to live to see the grass growing over these fellows ; but in the mean time we shall be hurt some. I have just learned that the slip from the *Times* (or the matter contained therein), *has gone to Europe by cable. Scott is spending money to get these things sent out, and the fight will go on for some time,* or at least so long as he thinks by so doing he can make us get out of the way of his Texas and P. swindle, which I do not propose to do. See correspondence with Judge Bell of Texas. I wish you would write on paper that would allow of my filing your letters. From the memorandum sent of the work done and to be done on the Tehachapi tunnels it would seem as though the rails ought to be laid to the summit by July 1st. This evening's papers have just come in they have a long article about the petition presented to-day by A. A. Sargent, calling for a committee to investigate C. P., C. and F., etc.   Yours truly,   C. P. HUNTINGTON.

HOUGHTON'S VICIOUS BOOK.

NEW YORK, June 1, 1876.

Friend Colton : Your letters of May 22d, Nos. 161 and 162, are received, also copies of letters from Pengra. I have had considerable correspondence with the Oregon people about a a road to connect that State with the Central Pacific, and, as far as I am concerned, shall do no better than we have offered. I notice what you say about our fight with Tom Scott and others. My idea is to fight them all until it is for our interest to make friends with them, then quit and work with them. I returned from Washington this morning. Our matters there are just so so. I am inclined to think we shall get through alive, but it is the roughest fight I was ever in. S. O. Houghton has been in Washington for several months, just what for, I did not know (but of course knowing he was not in our interest) until yesterday, when his book came out, and it is a vicious thing. I sent a copy to S. W. Sanderson yesterday. I would like Sanderson's views on it. The outlook for selling bonds on uncompleted roads was never worse than now. Sail as close to the wind as possible.

Yours truly,   C. P. HUNTINGTON.

THE CALIFORNIA DELEGATION REVIEWED.

NEW YORK, June 7, 1876.

Friend Colton : Your letters of May 29th and 30th, Nos. 163 and 164, are received. I am glad to hear that the work on the Tehachapi is moving on satisfactorily. When will the track be laid to the summit ? I notice what you say of the Lawrence bill, but it will never become a law. I went to Washington night before last and returned last night. Shall go back to-morrow so as to be at the meeting of the Judiciary Committee on Friday. I am having the hardest fight by a hundred times that I have ever had in Washington, but we shall not be eat up this time. *I hope Luttrell will be sent back to Congress. I think it would be a misfortune if he was not. Wigginton has not always been right, but he is a good fellow and is growing every day.* Page is always right, and it would be a misfortune to California to not have him in Congress. *Piper is a damned hog and should not come back.* It is shame enough for a great commercial city like San Francisco to send a scavenger like him to Congress once. I have not time to write more.

Yours truly,   C. P. HUNTINGTON.

HUNTINGTON AS A BARGAINER.

NEW YORK, June 12, 1876.

Friend Colton : Your three letters of the 26th and 27th of May, Nos. —, are received. I notice what you say of Wigginton, Luttrell and Piper. *The latter should be defeated at almost any cost.* San Francisco cannot afford to have so worthless a fellow represent them in Congress. I bought the picture and think you will like it. When I went up to buy I said to the salesman that it was a larger picture than you wanted, etc. ; he did not seem to recommend it very much, only said that $4500 gold was as low as they could sell it. I then told him I would take it. He then said there was two or three parties that wanted it at $5000, and showed me a letter that had just come in from Mr. Schaus, who is in Europe, in which he said not to sell at less than $5000 gold; that the artist was an old man and would most likely never paint so important a picture again. Yours, etc., C. P. HUNTINGTON.

SURE TO DO THEIR WORST.

NEW YORK, June 24, 1876.

Friend Colton: Yours of the 9th inst., without number, reached me in Washington, and in reply will only say the fellows are very bitter. Parrott [Gorham] is, or was, writing a brief on fares and freights *to influence, as I was told, one of the Judges of the Supreme Court.* They are sure to do their worst, but my better judgment tells me that we cannot afford to take the scamps into camp.

Yours truly, C. P. HUNTINGTON.

A BAIT FOR DEMAGOGUES TO NIBBLE.

NEW YORK, June 24, 1876.

Friend Colton: Your letters of the 14th and 16th, Nos. 168 and 169, are received. I think we shall not disagree about steamships. Only 599 feet to take out of the San Fernando tunnel. It looks as though the end would come some time. I am doing all I can to have the Government *take 6,000,000 acres of land and give the railroad company credit for $15,000,-000,* but the prospect of their doing it is not as bright as I wish it was. *I wish you would have the newspapers take the ground that this land ought to be taken by the Government and held for the people, so that when they wanted it they could have it, etc. Something that the demagogues can vote and work for.* Letting the Government take the lands now at $2.50 an acre to pay a debt due them, say in twenty years, is not more than say $1 would be put in a sinking fund at 6 per cent., interest compounded, each six months. I will see what can be done toward getting the $279 back from the Postoffice Department; but it seems to me that you should have got the postal agent in California to settle this, or at least recommend it. Seventeen cars of steel rails (sixty pounds) left Joliet Mills on the 21st, and the balance of the 1250 tons are to go forward at the rate of say sixty tons per day. I am writing a letter to answer in part Lawrence's speech against our plan of the sinking fund. I had it at my house working on it nearly all night, night before last. I rough you these letters then Colburn counter-views them. I will send you one when they are printed. I have bought five S. P. bonds that came from California at 85, and a party has just come in to find out what I would give for fifteen, also from California. I bid 85 cents. I do not like this. How can I help it?

Yours truly,   C. P. HUNTINGTON.

THE COMPLIANT ASSOCIATED PRESS.

NEW YORK, July 5, 1876.

Friend Colton : Yours of June 23d and 26th, Nos. 173 and 174, are received. I am glad to learn that the outlook for the coming year is so good, as it will help us to some of the money to do some of the many things that we ought to do. Our payments for material this month and next will be very large, and you will need to send all the money you well can.

I have received a telegram that I must come to Washington to-night. I shall go, but I dread it, as it is fearful hot. *I wish you would have it sent to the Associated Press here that the contract is let to build the S. P. R. R. bridge over the Colorado river.* Of course it should be so understood by all there that the bridge is to be built. I have had some talk with Scott about a trade. I said to him we were about closing contract for bridge, etc. Steel rails are coming along better than they did. If I had not ordered any rails until I had received orders from California, as per my letters in January to Mr. Crocker, you would have wanted them bad before you have got any. I shall come to California soon after Congress adjourns. When that will be I don't know. The d—— may.

Yours truly,   C. P. HUNTINGTON.

THE CENTRAL PACIFIC EARNINGS.

NEW YORK, July 16, 1876.

Friend Colton : Since I wrote you last I have received your letters, Nos. 175 to 182 inclusive. It would seem to me to be well to continue the survey of the line between the C. P. road and Nevada and Portland, in Oregon, for at least two reasons : one is that we want to know just how good a line can be found there, and the other is there will not be anything done on any other line so long as we are surveying on that line. The new California Pacific bonds will be ready in the first half of August. As to the parlor car, I never had any doubt about its paying if it was given any chance. It would have been as well or better to have paid Trevis in cash if he was to have the right to throw the S. P. bonds that he took on to the market. How about the five? I am glad to hear you liked the picture, although I expected you would. I have just received telegram from you and Crocker that the daylight shines through the San Fernando tunnel ; that certainly is good news. I returned from Washington last night. Our matters look better there, but we are not out of danger. It has been so very hot here for the last few weeks that it has come near using me up. You know I do not spare myself when I have anything to do. Scott is working very hard to get some bill through Congress that will prevent the earnings of the C. P. going into the S. P. How much he can do in that direction we shall know hereafter. He is very strong, *and with his many roads running out from Washington, on which he is very free with his passes to members of Congress—but we will see.* I notice the Arizona Stage Company have failed ; but I expected that, and I suppose you did.

Yours truly,   C. P. HUNTINGTON.

P. S.—On very slight provocation I get notices like the inclosed put in the papers.

A PROPOSED PICNIC PARTY.

NEW YORK, July 26, 1876.

Friend Colton ; I have been working for the last two months to get a party of say twenty-five Southern members of Congress to go out to California and over the line of the S. P. and see what we have done and our ability to do. Of course, I want no one to go except the best men of the South ; men that will go for the right as they understand it, and not as Tom Scott or somebody else understands it. *I told Senator Gordon, of Georgia, if he could get up a party of the best men of the South, we would pay all their expenses, which I suppose would not be less than $10,000, and I think it would be money well ex-*

pended. When would be the best time to come? I think it would be as well to take them over the S. P. before the connection is made between Tehachapi and Los Angeles, as they could see what we have done better than if they should go all the way by rail. Then have the rail laid as far east as it well could be, with men at work between the east end of the rail and the Colorado river. Give me your views on this.

Yours truly,   C. P. HUNTINGTON.

P. S.—I have had several talks with Gordon, and to-day I sent him a letter ; see copy. I have just received a dispatch to go to Washington to-night, and shall go.

GORDON ALL RIGHT FOR US.

NEW YORK, August 7, 1876.

Friend Colton : Your letters Nos. 190 and 191 are received. The dispatch as to suit between Central Pacific and Cohen or Robinson was published here about as you sent it. I think I wrote you some two weeks since that I was to meet Tom Scott and talk over S. P. and T. P. matters. I did not meet him. I could not get away from Washington at the time. I shall endeavor to meet him before I come to California. Scott is very ugly and very strong in Washington ; but if he keeps up this fight, we will live to see the grass growing over him. I think I am making friends in the South for the S. P. I have telegraphed to-day to have you get some of the prominent men in San Francisco to telegraph to Gordon, Senator from Georgia, with other Southern men, to go. While Gordon and some others are not afraid to go, Gordon tells me that some of his friends do not like to go on an invitation from the railroad company. If I can get the right men from the South to go to California we can capture all the Gulf States for the S. P. We must win in this fight. I was glad to learn, as I did to-day by your telegram, that you would connect with Los Angeles in thirty days.

Yours truly,   C. P. HUNTINGTON.

WORKING UP A JOB.

NEW YORK, August 14, 1876.

Friend Colton : Your two letters of the 5th, Nos. 195 and 196, are received. I am glad you are getting on so well with S. P. I will send to-day six copies each of my S. P. report for 1873 and 1874. I left Washington on Friday, the 11th. I think our matters are safe there for the session. I saw General Gordon just before I left. He had received a dispatch from some of the prominent men of San Francisco, and he said he thought they would get up a party of say thirty prominent Southern men, and visit California this fall, starting from this city about the 1st of September.

Yours truly, C. P. HUNTINGTON.

LIVELY WORK.

NEW YORK, August 25, 1876.

Friend Colton : Your letters, Nos. 197, 198 and 199, are received. You must have had a lively time in getting so many good names signed and sent on in so short a time, inviting our Southern brethren to come to California. I saw Gordon and several others just before Congress adjourned, and they said they would go, but I have some doubts about it, as most of the members of Congress are looking after their re-election. I shall get them started if I can. I notice that you write of steel rails. I hope to start for California the last of next month.

Yours truly, C. P. HUNTINGTON.

UNDER ONE AND OVER THE OTHER.

NEW YORK, November 11, 1876.

Friend Colton : Yours of the 2d inst., No. 2, is received. I am glad to learn that you will send to this office $2,000,000 by the 1st of January. About $2,000,000 on the old C. P. on October is good. *I hope Luttrell is elected and Piper defeated, as it was generally understood here that our hand was under one and over the other.* Mr. Weston has been into this office several times to get me to settle for the use of circulating plates that he says we are using on seven of our steamers and on say thirty-five of our locomotives, on which he claims a patent. He says that our people told him that by their use on the steamer *Oakland* the company had saved eighty tons of coal per month for two years, and on locomotives we had saved largely on coal as well as in protecting fire boxes. He talks largely ; says he wants $40,000 to settle for the use of it where we are now using it, and that he will sell us the right to use on all our roads, steamboats, stationary engines, etc., for $250,000. I said to him if his patent was all right and our people liked it I would give him $5,000, which he did not like. Ed. Learned has an interest in this patent, and if it is of any use, or if we use it, we shall have to pay for it, but of course no such amount as he asks. I want you to find out at once of how much value it is to us, and I will see what I can do. Weston says all his tracings were sent to our master mechanic several years ago.

Yours truly, C. P. HUNTINGTON.

SEND IT OVER THE WIRES.

NEW YORK, November 8, 1876.

Friend Colton : Yours of the 31st October is received, with copy of correspondence between you and Hopkins on the one side, and the Mayor and Common Council of Yuma on the other. If they will do what you ask, will give us what we want. I send with this a memorandum of steel rails on the way by sail and on shipboard (some few already arrived in San Francisco,) which, with the balance of the 10,000 tons (last contract with Hunt), will lay a fraction over 252 miles of track ; but I cannot see how you are to get enough in California to lay from Goshen to Los Gatos, lay the tide line to San Pablo and make necessary renewals of track, and have the necessary rails in California to lay track to Yuma before some time in March. But as soon as you can I think you should commence work on the end of track toward Yuma—as soon as you well can, with small force, *and let it come over the wires as often as you well can. It will help us in Washington.*

Yours truly, C. P. HUNTINGTON.

A FRIENDLY SECRETARY OF THE INTERIOR.

NEW YORK, January 22, 1877.

Friend Colton : Your letters of the 6th, 8th and 9th, Nos. 21, 22 and 23, are received. I have not seen Learned since I wrote you some weeks ago, hence do not know how we can settle for patent on circulating plates.

I quite agree with you that we made a point in getting Scott to agree to our coming East from the Colorado river. Horton of San Diego is in Washington working against the Texas and Pacific bill, because we will not agree to build half of the road between the S. P. and San Diego from the San Diego end.

I think it important that you get from Arizona the right for the S. P. to build on through that Territory, and also from New Mexico. I think it important that you do this.

I wish you would have it sent over the wires as often as you can that the S. P. is being rapidly built.

There has been several hitches in the Interior Department in relation to the last section completed west of Goshen. The solicitor of the Department of Interior came to the conclusion that while twenty miles was all the Act required us to build each year on the main line, we could not draw lands on a section of less than twenty-five miles, and you will notice the law is liable to that construction; *but I went to the Secretary, and he put the thing in shape, so I think we will not have any further trouble,* although Doyle has a party by the name of Johnson mousing about the departments all the time.

I go to Washington to-night. Shall do all I can to pass Sinking Fund bill (copy sent to Mr. Hopkins) unless you telegraph me that it is not satisfactory to my associates in California. It is not all I would have liked, but I think it very much better than to let matters remain as they are.

If the Texas and Pacific bill does not pass, I think we should lay at least 10,000 tons fifty-pound steel rails east of the Colorado river this year, that is, if we have a fair year in California for business.

Yours truly,   C. P. HUNTINGTON.

A SATISFACTORY COMMITTEE.

NEW YORK, March 7, 1877.

Friend Colton : Since writing you last your letters—February 10th, 16th and 23d, Nos. 28, 29 and 31—have been received. (I notice that you are looking after the State Railroad Commissioners. I think it is time.) Congress has adjourned and we have not been hurt, except by the paying out of some money in Washington for hotel bills, etc.

I am quite sure that we stand better in Washington at this time than we ever did before.

The P. M. S. S. Co. got no aid. I will tell you some things

about that some time.   The Sinking Fund bill did not pass, but it is in a much better shape to pass than it has ever been before. *I stayed in Washington two days to fix up Railroad Committee in the Senate.*   Scott was there working for the same thing ; but I beat him for once certain, as *the committee is just as we want it*, which is a very important thing for us.   You will no doubt notice before you get this that we were not able to pass the Texas Pacific bill.

I notice that you write that the reason of your sending goods via Chicago is that certain roads were exceedingly kind and afforded us facilities which we could not get over any other lines. Now as I understand it the B. and O. road came in more than once and helped us out, when the roads on the more northern lines combined against us, and it was with Garrett's roads that we broke the combination.   I am aware that the Michigan Central, at some later date, gave us a cut rate between here and Chicago, but what I want, as far as it is possible, to satisfy the whole country between here and Omaha, by sending a portion of the business via St. Louis and Cincinnati, so as to satisfy the large belt of country on that line, and why we have not done it (so that we get the same money) is one of the things I do not understand.

Yours truly,   C. P. HUNTINGTON.

NOT AFRAID OF SCOTT.

NEW YORK, March 20, 1877.

Friend Colton : Your letters of March 7th and 9th, Nos. 33 and 34, are received.   I notice what you write in your No. 33, relating to the C. P. sending goods via Chicago.   Now I have no interest as to the route over which this business travels, except it takes the route that will best advance the whole interest of the C. P., which it seemed to me would be best done by our sending a part via St. Louis and a portion via Chicago. There is considerable complaint, which shows itself in Washington, because all the business goes through Chicago and none via St. Louis and Cincinnati, and so we have the same amount for the C. P. it would seem best that we divide this business. And as to the time that is made on the northern line, I think you would have no trouble in getting the southern lines to agree to take it via New Orleans that is not taken, and they certainly would have no trouble in filling the contract as to the time.

Scott is at work, and I think is doing more than ever before, preparing to put his Texas Pacific through next winter, and possibly at the extra session, if there is one. I have little or no fears of his doing anything at the extra session, but if he can convince Congress that the S. P. is controlled by the C. P. (and I think with what aid he can get from my associates in California) I believe he can pass his bill to build on the direct line between Fort Yuma and San Diego, *and I think I know enough of Washington to know how he can do it.*

I have just received telegram from Crocker in relation to daily mails east of Yuma, but of that I will write him.

Yours truly,   C. P. HUNTINGTON.

DON'T GO ANY MONEY ON HIM.

NEW YORK, May 7, 1877.

Friend Colton: Since I last wrote you yours Nos. 41, 42 and 43 have been received.

Mr. Bryan, the Japanese Commissioner, was in our office here last week and said he had been ordered to go to Europe. How long he should remain there he could not say, but he thought not long—would see you in San Francisco on his return in relation to mails to Japan.

I am glad to get so good a report of the Ione coal. May it ever continue to burn as well.

I hope the Arizona business will meet with your expectations. We need the money that the business will bring badly.

I notice what you say of Conover, the Florida Senator. He is a clever fellow, but don't go any money on him.

I will have notice for the redemption of S. P. bonds to the amount of $200,000 published here, as you request.

I suppose you will put in the S. P. bonds that belong to the W. D. Co.; if not, I want to stand in as the others do. I would not put in any Series A.

The $70,000 that I let Jones have is tied up for ten years. I think we can make more than the interest on the amount paid for Jones' road out of our other roads by not running the Jones' road at all, and Jones is very good-natured now and we need his help in Congress very much, and I have no doubt we shall

have it. *We must have friends in Congress from the West coast,
as it is very important, I think, that we kill the open highway and
get a fair sinking fund bill,* by which we can get time beyond
the maturity of the bonds that the Government loaned us to
pay the indebtedness, and I think if any Republican is elected
in Sargent's place, he (Sargent) is worth to us, if he comes back
as our friend, as much as any six new men, and he should be
returned.

It is fearfully hard to get money here—I think never so
much so before.

Yours truly,   C. P. HUNTINGTON.

GOOD FELLOWS ALL.

NEW YORK, May 15, 1877.

Friend Colton : Yours of the 7th inst. is received. I am
glad you are paying some attention to General Taylor and Mr.
Kasson. Taylor can do us much good in the South. I think,
by the way, he would like to get some position with us in California. Mr. Kasson has always been our friend in Congress
and as he is a very able man has been able to do us much good,
and he has never lost us one dollar. I think I have written you
before about Senator Conover. He may want to borrow some
money, but we are so short this summer I do not see how we
can let him have any in California.

I have just given Senator Ingalls of Kansas a letter to you.
He is a good fellow and can do us much good and I think is
well disposed towards us.

Senator Morton is coming over; also his brother-in-law
Burbank. They are good fellows, but B. means business ; not
there, but in W.

Scott is working everywhere for his open highway, but I
think we can beat him ; *but it will cost money* and harder work
to beat him with money under the plan of some of my associates,
viz., having it understood that the C. P. and S. P. are, as it
were, one property than it would be without money if the
public could know the facts ; that is, that the S. P. is a separate
and distinct property.

Railroad credits are as badly demoralized as ever here. The
Baltimore & Ohio Railroad paper is thrown out by nearly if not
all the banks here.

I hope before this reaches you that the road will be completed to Fort Yuma and a large outlay stopped there. I would like to know what that road has cost up to this time, say from Goshen south, and have the items given.

Jay Gould told me the U. P. had contracted to have a branch built 100 miles long from their road towards the Black Hills, for which they pay for the road (no rolling stock) $9,000 per mile, iron rails. I guess he don't do as well as that.

Yours truly, C. P. HUNTINGTON.

I am disposed to think we could trade with Scott for all the T. and P. rights west of the Rio Grande for a small sum.

A COMPETING ROAD WANTED.

NEW YORK, May 17, 1877.

Friend Colton : Yours of the 9th, No. 48 is received. What you say about our stopping at Fort Yuma is well and would be almost conclusive if the S. P. was not owned and controlled by the C. P.; but when we tell Congress we are willing to build this road the answer is always the same. Of course you are to protect the Central, but what the country want is a competing road. *Now, many members of Congress believe all this stuff and others talk it for reasons that I need not mention here, but if they are not convinced, think the open highway will satisfy their constituents that they were working for the good of the whole country.* When the Texas and P. Co. were asking aid to go through the San Gorgonio pass one argument was, we have built a road there with our own money. Will Congress furnish the means for Colonel Scott to go on and destroy property that we have in good faith located ? No one would do that. But their proposition now is to build direct to San Diego under the cry of an open highway for the people. I do not believe they can get the aid from the Government necessary to do it, but they will not be prevented from doing it because the Central Pacific will do it without aid, but because the country is so generally committed against any subsidy, or because there is some interest fairly invested that would be destroyed by the building the open highway. In my opinion if we get the T. and P. land grant turned over to the S. P. it will be with such conditions that we cannot afford to build the road. Do not underrate the power of Tom Scott. He came up from a very small beginning by his own

26

force of character **to the** position **of** President **and chief mana-
ger** of one of the largest railroad organizations in the **world.**

Just what is the best course for **us to** pursue I am not certain. We certainly are not **prepared to** build east of the Colorado river this season ; if I **have a clear** view of what I think
ought to be done I will write you.

Yours truly,   C. P. HUNTINGTON.

A PERTINENT INQUIRY.

NEW YORK, May 29, 1877.

Friend Colton : Yours of the 21st, No. 50, is received ; also
your telegram that 220 S. P. bonds had been taken by the
Trustees for the $200,000 in the fund for redeeming S. P.
bonds.

I have paid Jones $100,000 on his road, as Crocker tele-
graphed me it would be safe to do so.

I notice what you write **about people telling lies about** us. **I**
am prepared **to believe** anything **in that direction.** Some **one**
in California **is continually** writing **to** parties **here** about our
matters **in** California. **I think** I wrote you that a party here
said he received a letter from some one in California that the C.
P. could not borrow any money in California unless indorsed
by the Directors. I have already said it was a mistake to use
our individual names to get money. I had the same thing told
me every day, viz., that the C. P. could not get money unless
we endorsed it, etc. By the way, is there not some reason for
these lies that the people tell about us ; or in other words, have
we not done some things it would have been better not to have
done ; as the doing of them have made our neighbors jealous
of us. A man may climb a pole in a crowd in his ordinary garb
and nothing is thought of it ; but paint him scarlet the crowd
might take it as an insult.

I find it very difficult **to** get any money here, and it seems
to grow more and more **so** every day, and just how we are to
pay our current bills in **June** and the July interest I cannot see
as clearly as I would like **to.** I have no doubt it will be done
somehow. I am very glad to hear that **you have** stopped spending money at Yuma for the present, **as that** stops a fearful
leak.

Mr. Crocker writes **me** that you will have the road between

Oakland and Banta done by October 1st, and after that is done I hope we shall be able to stop all work, unless it is east of Yuma, until we can pay off our floating debt.

Everything that I hear from California, from parties that go over the S. P., is unfavorable to the bonds. Can it not be otherwise?

Yours truly,   C. P. HUNTINGTON.

SCOTT AND THE LOBBY.

NEW YORK, October 3, 1877.

Friend Colton : Herewith I send memorandum of bills payable and transactions in September. You will notice the amount to be paid this month is very large, and just how much of it can be borrowed here is uncertain, but much of it, I hope; but a portion will have to come from the earnings of the road in California.

Your letters, Nos. 12, 13, and 14, are received. I shall go to Washington to-morrow night to see about the Colorado bridge. I think it can be fixed, but Scott is doing his very best. There has been, I think, more work done since Congress adjourned for the T. and P. than was ever done before for any interest in the whole history of this country, *but if we spend as much money in laying rails east of the Colorado as he spends on his Washington lobby, we shall, in my opinion, surely beat him.* I shall do all I can here, but I do not feel as well as I wished I did and somehow dread the coming fight.

I will endeavor to write you again to-morrow.

Yours truly,   C. P. HUNTINGTON.

TWO GOVERNORS WITH COLLARS.

NEW YORK, October 29, 1877.

Friend Colton: Yours of the 11th inst., No. 18, is received. I notice what you say of financial matters there, but there every one knows us and the vast property that we control, and, I think, rate it, too, at its full value, but here all railroad securities are distrusted ; of course the C. P. with the rest ; almost every day some of the daily papers here have articles that tend to hurt. I send one with this from to-day's *Times.;* this one though is mild ; then Scott is doing, of course, what he can to hurt us. Then our unsettled matters with the Government tend to disturb our credits, notwithstanding our credit here is good ; as proof of that, we shall borrow this month over $1,000,-000 at 7 per cent., and I think our floating debt is larger than any other road.

I think Stafford had better be in Washington at the commencement of the regular session, to get Congress to confirm the Acts of Arizona.

I saw Axtell, Governor of New Mexico, and he said he thought if we would send to him such a bill as we wanted to have passed into a law, he could get it passed with very little or no money, when if we sent a man there they would stick him for large amounts. He thought, and so do I, that a general law is what we want, giving any company the right to build railroads, they not to interfere with the rates of fares and freights until the earnings made 10 per cent. on their cost, and not to be taxed for say six years. He said if you would make such a bill and send it to him or a Mr. Waldron it could be passed. I think this should be attended to.

I think our land matters in Washington have been fixed.

Yours truly,   C. P. HUNTINGTON.

FIXING COMMITTEES.

NEW YORK, October 30, 1877.

Friend Colton : I have just been out to borrow some money ($100,000), and I found the market very nervous, although I got what I wanted on call ; very likely it will be called to-morrow. I think things will be better in a few weeks, but we must do everything in our power to pay up our floating debt. The impression has got out that we have been building a large amount of road and that our floating debt is very large. You will have to carry over all that you can of our debts in California until after January. How much do you owe the Bank of Nevada ? The committees are made up for the Forty-fifth Congress. *I think the Railroad Committee is right, but the Committee on Territories I do not like. A different one was promised me.* Sherrel has just telegraphed me to come to Washington to-night. I shall not go, as I am not well, and to always go at Sherrel's call would kill me or any one else in one session of Congress. I think there never were so many strikers in Wash-

ington before, and I think there will be more bills of an un
friendly character offered than ever before. If you can find
out from our ticket agents what Atlantic line of steamships we
are to do business with for the next thirty days, I wish you
would let me know. Maybe they won't tell, though.

Yours truly, C. P. HUNTINGTON.

THE "BULLETIN'S" CLAUSY ARTICLE.

NEW YORK, November 9, 1877.

Friend Colton : Your letters of October 29th, 30th and 31st,
Nos. 24, 25 and 26, are received. I quite agree with you that
the *Bulletin* article is not what we want. All this mixing up the
S. P. with the C. P. could and should have been different. You
write that you send copy of petition for change of S. P. to the
Salinas Valley line, which I have not received. It will no
doubt come in good time. I do not think we can get any legislation this session for extension of land grants, or for changing
line of road, *unless we pay more for it than it is worth.* Scott
seems to be very confident that he can pass his T. and P. bill.
I do not believe he can. Some parties are making great efforts
to pass a bill through Congress that will compel the U. P. and
C. P. to pay large sums into a sinking fund, and I have some
fear that such bill may pass. Jim Keene and others of Jay
Gould's enemies are in it, *and will pay money to pass.* We have
a hearing to-morrow before the Judiciary Committee. The
temper of Congress is not good and I fear we may be hurt, and
somehow I do not feel so much like doing battle with the whole
human race as I once did. I go to Washington to-night. The
petition for change of line of S. P. has just come in.

Yours truly, C. P. HUNTINGTON.

WHY MONEY MUST BE USED.

NEW YORK, November 15, 1877.

Friend Colton : Yours of the 2d, No. 27, came to hand some
days since, and would have been acknowledged before but for
the reason that I have been very busy in Washington most of
the time, and I return there again to-morrow night, as I have a
hearing before the Judiciary Committee on Saturday. You can
have no idea how I am annoyed by this Washington business,

a..d I must and will give it up after this session. *If we are not hurt this session it will be because we pay much money to prevent it. and you know how hard it is to get it to pay for such purposes, and I do not see my way clear to get through here and pay the January interest with other bills payable to January 1st with less than $2,000,000 and possibly not for that.* I hear from all directions that Scott is very sure of passing his T. and P. bill this session. I do not believe it, but he has never before, I think, made the effort that he is now making. I think Congress will try very hard to pass some kind of a bill to make us commence paying on what we owe the Government. I am striving very hard to get a bill in such a shape that we can accept it, as this Washington business will kill me yet, if I have to continue the fight from year to year, and then every year the fight grows more and more expensive, and rather than let it continue as it is from year to year, as it is, I would rather they take the road and done with it.

Yours, etc.,   C. P. Huntington.

POMEROY'S LETTER.

Personal—Copy.]

Washington, November 20, 1877.

Mr. Huntington—Dear Sir, I have noticed the movements of the Committee on Judiciary and seen the published proceedings relating thereto. Of course my advice is gratuitous, and if it is worth nothing will cost nothing, but I am not sure as you will get anything from the committee that you can accept. Indeed, I am sure you cannot accept anything they report, but can you beat it? To that question I address myself. First, I say, not by proposing to that same committee the bill of last session. They are set in another direction. Second, not by having no counter measure. How, then, can you hope to defeat them? I reply, first, by at once putting before the Committee on the Pacific Railroad such a bill as you can accept and by pressing a report from that committee. If you rely upon moving it as an amendment or substitute, you will fail, as it then has the sanction of no committee of this Congress and cannot be pushed successfully. *Second, let Mr. Mitchell of the Pacific Railroad Committee call his committee, thoroughly discuss and report such a bill as you can accept. Then antagonize the re-*

*port of the Judiciary Committee with a report from the Pacific
Railroad Committee, and our friends then can sustain the report
of the one committee against the other.* The Thurman bill will
pass if no concerted and determined effort is made to defeat it.
I live close by and see often two members of the Judiciary
Committee, and they have another measure to follow their bill
if they pass it. Their new measure is, put by law your roads
into the hands of a receiver until and while the requirements of
the law are being fulfilled, so 'that if you take the case growing
out of this new law to the Supreme Court, in the mean time
your roads and funds are controlled by a receiver. I only al-
lude to this as a plan that I have heard spoken of. These suggestions are entirely gratuitous, but as you know I am,

Yours truly,   S. C. POMEROY.

MEN WHO WORK FOR READY CASH.

NEW YORK, December 17, 1877.
Friend Colton : Yours of the 5th and 6th, Nos. 37 and 38,
are received. I notice what you say of Ione coal. "The en-
gineers and firemen are all against it. * * * less than 200
tons were used in the whole San Joaquin valley. I hope we
may bring influence enough on the employees to use more in
future." Now, in reply to the above, I have only to say that I
would give orders that no other coal should be used on locomotives between Redding and Caliente, on all the valley roads.
The piece of clay, as you call it, that I brought home (that
came from Ione) was the very best of peat. I am glad money
matters are looking better there. How are the rains and what
is the outlook for the coming year? I notice what you say of
Pengra's road. I think we should do all we can to help that
line. Oregon will have a road out before many years on some
other line than the one you speak of, via Shasta valley, but the
talking of two will not hasten the building of one, and I think
we should do all we can to help the Pengra line, which, by the
way, I think a good one. C. E. Tilton was here to night. He
is of the firm of Ladd and Tilton, Portland, Or. He is a good
man, and I told him we would like to have him and a few of his
friends in Oregon come in with us and build the Pengra road.
(I call it the P. road for short.) He may call on you on his
way to Oregon. If he does, talk with him and give him my views

of the P. line, and not yours. Now of the Salt Lake line to Oregon and other matters connected with it. The Texas and P. company have been fighting us for years, but have had but little money, *but have used passes and promises largely.* But the latter as they say, is about played out, and some little time ago they joined teams, as I have been told, with the North P. They had a little money to use, as they have no mortgage or floating debt, as I am told. They have made a little money on this end of their road and I think are using it. *Jay Gould went to Washington about two weeks since, and I know saw Mitchell, Senator from Oregon. Since which time money has been used very freely in Washington,* as some parties have been hard at work for the T. and P. N. P. with the Salt Lake branch, that never work except for ready cash, and Senator Mitchell is not for us as he was, although he says he is. But I know he is not. Gould has large amounts of cash, and he pays it without stint to carry his points. He feels that he is being menaced by the extension of the S. P. although I tell him it is in the U. P. as much as the C. P. interest that we take care of that line and that he may have half the line east of the Colorado, or ten-twenty-seconds of the whole line, etc., and he says all right; but he doesn't feel all right. There is many things I would like to say to you, but I will only say the outlook is not good.

Yours, etc.,   C. P. HUNTINGTON.

AN AGRARIAN CAMP.

NEW YORK, April 19, 1878.

Friend Colton : I returned from Washington this morning and found on my desk yours of the 10th inst., No. 74. Thurman's Funding bill has not passed the House yet, but it will, I think, although I am endeavoring to get it to the Judiciary Committee. If I can I think we can get it amended, but even that is doubtful. There were some mistakes made by us when the bill was in the Senate ; the greatest was in Gould going to Washington, but it is too long a story to write now. I will tell you when we meet, if we have nothing better to talk of. *This Congress is nothing but an agrarian camp—the worst body of men ever before got together in this country.* Scott is making a hard fight on his Texas Pacific bill. He has made a combination with the Northern Pacific, which will give him some strength;

but how much I cannot tell. The Northern Pacific are to ask for guaranty of their bonds by the United States. I shall come to California soon after Congress adjourns. Find some one to buy me out of everything there. I am tired and want to quit.

Yours as ever,   C. P. HUNTINGTON.

P. S.—We have all agreed that we will not keep Captain Bradbury any longer. He is now in Europe.   H.

HE PRICE OF A CONGRESSMAN.

NEW YORK, May 3, 1878.

Friend Colton : Herewith I hand you memorandum of bills payable and of transactions in April. I returned from Washington this morning. The President signed that Sinking Fund bill Monday, as you no doubt have learned ere this. *He was not big enough to veto it.*

The T. and P. folks are working hard on their bill and say they are sure to pass it, but I do not believe it. *They offered one member of Congress $1,000 cash down, $5,000 when the bill passed, and $10,000 of the bonds* **when they** *got them if he would* **vote** *for the bill.* *I have* **no doubt this** *offer* **was** *made and I* **have no doubt they would make this offer** *to enough* **to carry** *their* **bill if they could get parties to vote, but no one** *believes* **they** *would* **get anything more than the first sum if the bill** *should* **pass.**

Yours truly,   C. P. HUNTINGTON.

SCOTT'S LOBBY.

NEW YORK, May 9, 1878.

Friend Colton : Yours of April 29th and May 1st, Nos. 81 and 82, are received. I am very glad to learn that Mr. Crocker's health is improving.

Thurman has introduced a bill (No. 1200 S.), the object of which would seem to be to **start** another branch of the Government, whose business will be to look after the Pacific roads. You, no doubt, will receive a copy of the bill, as I gave Mr. Boyd orders to send Judge Sanderson a copy of all bills that we could possibly have any interest in.

Dillon has just left **the** office. He says he **was expecting**

Bradbury back from Europe in a few days, which was news to me, as I knew nothing of his whereabouts.

When I come to California I will bring out Western Development Co. accounts.

I was told to-day that Scott was getting up great combinations—T. and P., N. P., John Roach, the shipbuilder, who is asking subsidy for steamers to Brazil, etc., etc. I do not think he will get any aid for his T. and P., *but Washington is filled up with his lobby, and I think he has some party in three-quarters of the Congressional districts south of the Potomac and Ohio—anyway north—all working to get up petitions to members of the Senate and House, getting letters written to members and getting little meetings, then passing resolutions to send to Congress, and all these things have some effect, just how much we shall see.*

The Military Committee met Monday, I was there, as was Scott's man, Brown. Brown said it was an important matter; that they would fight, etc., but was not ready, so it went over to next Tuesday.

Yours truly, C. P. HUNTINGTON.

HUNTINGTON AS A LEGISLATOR.

NEW YORK, June 3, 1878.

Friend Colton : Yours (Nos. 89 and 90) are received. As to rails to lay twenty-two miles on west side of Sacramento river, I wrote Stanford a few days since. Could not get rails. I notice what you say about sale of land on account of Central Pacific ; also about building any more road.

I quite agree with you in the main, but all the reasons that ever existed why we should build east of Yuma now exist; only the one reason why we should not, viz., not got the money, prevents me from urging the extension of that line. *I put (something?) in the Omnibus bill to kill the T. and P. and I think it will do it.* I have received three telegrams to come to Washington to night. I go.

Yours truly, C. P. HUNTINGTON.

FIXING FREMONT.

NEW YORK, June 14, 1878.

Friend Colton : I returned from Washington last night and find on my desk your letters (Nos. 92, 93, 94 and 95) as to the

O. and O. S. S. Co. I will see Gould and Dillon when they return from the West, which I expect will be in about two weeks, and show them your letter (92) and then write you.

Mrs. Hopkins has not arrived here yet, is expected to-morrow. I will see her and talk up matters as you suggest when she comes.

I will do all I can to assist in getting Arizona freight by way of Yuma.

Fremont has been appointed Governor of Arizona. *I shall give him passes and I think it important that you see him on his arrival and see that he does not fall into the hands of bad men.* He is very friendly to us now.

Scott tried hard to defeat his being confirmed. I think it well to attend to this matter of Fremont's.

I hope to be with you early in July.

Yours truly,   C. P. HUNTINGTON.

A BAD CONGRESS.

NEW YORK, June 15, 1878.

Friend Colton : Herewith find copy of letter from Flagg in reference to Arizona freight. I have done all I can to prevent certain bills from being reached and do not think any bills can be that will hurt us, but if there are they will pass, *as this Congress is, I think, the worst set of men that have ever been collected together since man was created.*

Yours etc.,   C. P. H.

"A WILD SET OF DEMAGOGUES."

NEW YORK, June 20, 1878.

Friend Colton : Yours of June 12th, No. 98, with enclosures, is received. I think your letter to McFarland was good. I returned from Washington last night. I am almost happy to think I shall not be called there again this session, as Congress has adjourned its first session, and may the likes of it never meet again.

I think in all the world's history never before was such a wild set of demagogues honored by the name of Congress. We have been hurt some, but some of the worst bills have been defeated, but we cannot stand many such Congresses.   *   *   *

Yours truly,   C. P. HUNTINGTON.

"LET IT GO OUT."

New York, September 11, 1878.

Friend Colton : We arrived home yesterday on time—6:54 A. M. All well. Found things here about as usual.

I send with this the usual monthly memorandum.

I think as soon as you well can you had better let it go out that we are to build the S. P. to the Rio Grande, and that the work is to be commenced soon, as it will help us with Southern members in the next Congress.

Yours truly,   C. P. Huntington.

AN ARTICLE HE DID NOT LIKE.

New York, September 30, 1878.

Friend Colton : Since I wrote you last I have received from you six letters, Nos. 101 to 106 inclusive.   *   *   *

I will buy the wire for telegraph east of Yuma.

I notice the slip from the *Chronicle.* I do not know who wrote the article, but it is so like the *Chronicle* that I think they would pay for the like of it.

I think you are right about Field not sitting in the Gallatin suit.

I hope soon to be able to send say 3,000 tons of rails overland for the C. P. If so, it will enable you to lay some track this fall east of Yuma. I think it important you should do so before Congress comes together, as Scott is to make his greatest effort as soon as Congress meets. You are aware that his bill has been reported by both the House and Senate committees and will be called up and passed the first day if he has the votes. *I hear of him in almost every Congressional district, interfering in the election of members,* so I think it important you make a move east of Yuma as soon as you well can.

Yours truly,   C. P. Huntington.

www.ingramcontent.com/pod-product-compliance
Lightning Source LLC
Chambersburg PA
CBHW032316280326

41932CB00009B/836